W9-CIK-444

189

The Western European Union
at the Crossroads

The Western European Union at the Crossroads

Between Trans-Atlantic Solidarity and European Integration

G. Wyn Rees

Westview Press
A Member of the Perseus Books Group

Copyright © 1998 by Westview Press, A Member of the Perseus Books Group

Published in 1998 in the United States of America by Westview Press, 5500 Central Avenue,
Boulder, Colorado 80301-2877, and in the United Kingdom by Westview Press, 12 Hid's
Copse Road, Cumnor Hill, Oxford OX2 9JJ

A CIP catalog record for this book is available from the Library of Congress.
ISBN 0-8133-8961-5

The paper used in this publication meets the requirements of the American National Stan-
dard for Permanence of Paper for Printed Library Materials Z39.48-1984.

10   9   8   7   6   5   4   3   2

Contents

Acknowledgements

I would like to acknowledge the financial assistance of a NATO Fellowship Grant which paid for much of the research for this book and for a grant from the Faculty of Social Sciences, University of Leicester which assisted with the publication costs.

I would like to express my thanks to Paul Cornish, Stuart Croft, Ian Manners, Jörg Monar, Sally Rohan, Mathew Uttley and John Young who read parts of this manuscript and made helpful comments. I am also indebted to Thomas Thellersen and Richard Guthrie for work in preparing the manuscript.

This book is dedicated to my wife Susan with thanks for her love and patience.

G. W. R.
University of Leicester

Introduction

To publish a book in 1998 about the Western European Union (WEU) is a particularly appropriate moment for it is the fiftieth anniversary of the founding of the organisation. It is also a short time after the Amsterdam European Council (June 1997), which sought to determine the WEU's institutional position for the foreseeable future. The WEU has always been a curious structure in Europe's security architecture. On the one hand, it has represented an autonomous European defence actor, based upon a treaty guarantee amongst its members. On the other, it has acted as a grouping of European states within the North Atlantic Treaty Organisation (NATO). As a result of its dual identity, the WEU has performed a variety of roles over the years. It has assisted in preserving the security of the continent, it has helped to smooth relations between the United States and its European allies and it has resolved tensions within Europe.

Whilst the focus of this book is on the period after 1990, it is necessary in the first two chapters to elucidate the background of the WEU. Although these chapters do not seek to be historically exhaustive, they explain the genesis of its multi-functional nature and the tasks for which it was prepared. The Cold War period determined the initial development of the organisation and this was to prove highly influential on its post-Cold War character. Despite the fact that the WEU had faded into relative obscurity by the middle of the 1970s, its members chose to revitalise the organisation in 1984, demonstrating that they believed it had a useful function to perform.

In 1990, amidst a transformed security environment, the WEU was suddenly under the international spotlight. The certainties of the Cold War were over, the Soviet Union was in retreat, Germany was unified and there were doubts about the continuing presence of the United States in Europe. The WEU was at a crossroads. The organisation had to choose between two roles: its traditional function of promoting Atlantic solidarity and the new-found opportunity of becoming a key participant in the process of European integration. In the past, integration had never extended into the realm of defence but after 1990 there were ambitions to develop a meaningful defence identity in Europe and the WEU was identified as the vehicle to carry this forward.

In order to understand the development of the WEU after 1990, this book contends that two lines of enquiry must be pursued. Firstly, the WEU must be analysed in relation to its two partner and larger organisations on the continent: the European Community (later the European Union) and NATO. The extent to which the Atlantic Alliance was capable of transforming itself to the new demands of the security situation was a central issue in determining the role of the WEU. Conversely, the time was seen to be propitious to create a foreign and security policy within the European Community and grant it a competence in defence; all of which would add coherence to the European construction project. The core of the debate was about whether the WEU would develop an independent defence identity amongst the west European states that would become submerged within the EC/EU.

The second line of enquiry focuses upon the parts played in this debate by Britain, France and Germany. Although there were ten states within the WEU and a collection of other countries enjoying membership in NATO and the EC, these three were the most powerful and influential European states in foreign and defence matters. As such, they held the key to the realisation of a defence identity on the continent. Each brought different post-war experiences to the issue but unless all were united in seeking the same objective, it was doubtful whether such a goal could be achieved.

Therefore, this book seeks to trace out three interconnected strands. Firstly, what functions were historically fulfilled by the Western European Union and how important had these become by the end of the Cold War? Secondly, did the WEU as the embodiment of a European defence identity present a realistic alternative to the trans-Atlantic security framework of NATO in the post-Cold War period? Thirdly, to what extent were the three main west European states committed to realising a security and defence identity within the European Community/European Union?

1

The History of the WEU

Introduction

It can sometimes be tempting to look back on the security arrangements that were constructed in western Europe during the Cold War and imagine that they were pre-determined. Because the North Atlantic Treaty Organisation came to dominate security politics and proved to be such a durable structure, one can be forgiven for assuming that this was somehow written in stone. It may be all too easy to forget the complexity of the post-war period, the intensity of the fears for the security of the continent and the search to find frameworks that could guarantee stability.

How security was to be achieved was far from clear to decision-makers at the time. Two fundamental sets of choices were apparent. The first was the balance that was to be struck between the Europeans providing for their own defence as compared to reliance upon the United States. Although it was not clear what role the US would seek to play in the security of the continent, the Europeans had to decide how closely to align with their North American ally. The WEU came to represent an expression of a European identity in defence and whilst cooperation with the US offered to fulfil vital objectives, it was recognised that European interests could be at risk of being submerged in a trans-Atlantic structure

The other major choice in defence was over the extent of the integration that would be undertaken by the European states. Defence integration offered a means of binding the states together in the face of a common adversary. It also offered a way of overcoming the fear of nationalistic rivalries and conflicts between the leading European countries. Yet integration was a major step to take so soon after the end of World War Two and it impacted on the core issue of national sovereignty; the ability of a country to defend itself. The question of how far to pursue integration was to prove a consistent thread running through the debate on a European defence identity.

Concerting Defence Arrangements in Europe

The need to concert defensive arrangements in Europe was increasingly apparent as the 1940s progressed. There was a growing sense of threat from the Soviet Union which, although western intelligence estimates were hazy, had not demobilised the greater part of its armed forces after World War Two and there were residual fears of Germany. However, attempting to orchestrate a defence framework for the continent was beset by manifold difficulties. Firstly, the major countries were struggling under enormous economic pressures which made it imperative to minimise the weight of defence spending. Secondly, there was suspicion of the influence of communist movements in many of the countries in western Europe and particularly in France, which rendered them unpredictable partners in the eyes of their neighbours.[1] Lastly, there was uncertainty about the role that the United States wished to play in Europe and its reliability as a guarantor of security.[2]

The first step in establishing a defence framework was the signing of the Dunkirk Treaty, between Britain and France, in March 1947.[3] The Treaty was focused primarily on Germany and was designed to prevent its re-emergence as a military power. This was largely a symbolic gesture, as noted by Greenwood, because Germany was too weak to have presented an immediate danger, but could have had long term significance.[4] Nevertheless it enabled the British government to reassure its ally about its commitment to the long term security of France from a remilitarised Germany. This was recognised to be an essential prerequisite before any progress could be made on securing a broader defence arrangement for Europe.

With the Dunkirk Treaty in place, it became possible to consider the inclusion of other west European countries into a security framework. The extent to which a European security effort would have been viable has remained a contested point between historians but there was no doubting the benefits that could have been derived from greater unity. Not only was closer cooperation a way for European states to demonstrate that they could help themselves, it also increased the likelihood that the Americans would maintain and expand their contribution. The Truman Administration was more likely to be able to sell the idea of a continued American military presence in Europe to a sceptical Congress if there was evidence that the Europeans were serious about addressing their security deficiencies. The United States did not want to be the power that guaranteed security whilst its allies made no efforts of their own.[5]

Whether at this time Britain and France envisaged the creation of a European 'Third Force', sitting independently as a power base between the two superpowers, has remained open to interpretation. There would certainly appear to be corroborating evidence that British Foreign Secretary Bevin thought in terms of a strong European bloc that could talk on equal terms with the two superpowers. This would be made possible by drawing upon the strength of the overseas empires of the UK and France.[6] Leaders, such as Bidault of France and Paul Henri Spaak of Belgium, foresaw the danger that a weak Europe could come to be dominated by the United States. Hence they wanted to see the strength of the Europeans built up before entering into some sort of defensive pact with the US in case such an opportunity was foreclosed once a compact was made.[7]

Yet it did not follow that an ambitious European framework was necessarily incompatible with a major American role. Kent and Young both point out that Bevin may have seen the ultimate objective as building up a power base for Britain that could return it to the highest levels of world diplomacy.[8] Baylis also endorses this view, that US military support was perceived to be a precondition for European stability as well as for a greater British role.[9] The US was seen as a vital counter-balance to the Soviet Union and its strategic nuclear forces were the underpinning of the west's security. Furthermore, the US was needed to assist in the economic recovery of Europe, particularly through the granting of financial aid.[10] In turn, the US was supportive of plans for closer European economic and defence integration, believing that an economically strong Europe would be capable of resisting further encroachment from the Soviet bloc.

The 'Brussels Treaty of Economic, Social and Cultural Collaboration and Collective Self-Defence', signed in March 1948, provided a way for the European powers to build on the foundations of the earlier Dunkirk agreement. It created a regional defence organisation known as Western Union, whose membership comprised of five states; France, Britain, Belgium, the Netherlands and Luxembourg. In a strongly worded Treaty, the states committed themselves to assist each other with all possible means in the event of one becoming the victim of aggression (Article V). The highest authority within the Brussels Treaty became the Consultative Council which consisted of Foreign Ministers and met in the capitals in rotation. When this was not in session, authority was exercised by a Permanent Commission which met weekly in London and was supported by a small secretariat.

As the name implies, there was a broader motivation behind the Treaty than just a defensive pact. Cooperation in economic and cultural matters was seen as creating a web of relationships that would strengthen the security of Europe. Economic integration had been discussed throughout the 1940s and French Prime Minister Bidault made a speech in July 1948 which called for a customs and economic union and a European Assembly to be established between the European powers.[11] Britain was ambivalent towards these ideas, welcoming the cohesion that they might add to relations between states but wary of being drawn into European supranationalism. The sections of the Treaty that dealt with economic integration left the British feeling distinctly uncomfortable, as they had no desire to be drawn so closely into continental affairs.[12] To Britain's satisfaction, the economic dimensions of the Treaty were gradually filtered off into more specialised institutions and the cultural responsibilities were handed over to the Council of Europe.[13]

In the month after the signing of the Brussels Treaty, a Western Union Defence Organisation (WUDO) was created to enact the defence provisions. It was based upon a permanent military committee in London, a joint headquarters at Fontainebleu and three subordinate commands for land, sea and naval forces. A Western Union Chiefs of Staff Committee was formed and Field Marshal Montgomery was appointed to act as its first Chairman.[14] The Brussels Treaty also provided a framework for the standardisation of weaponry amongst the member states — a feature that was to characterise the organisation in the years ahead. Its aim was fo create a common system for developing and manufacturing weapons so that they would be shared by all the states. Countries might choose to specialise in certain types of equipment and then produce them on behalf of their allies.

The military weakness of the west Europeans was appreciated by all the countries involved. A common strategic concept was agreed which planned to defend the line of the Ijssel river in the Netherlands, down the length of the Rhine to the French Alps. Despite its questionable efficacy, it still presupposed the sacrifice of significant amounts of western territory in a conflict. In 1949 it was estimated that 34 divisions would be required within three days of hostilities commencing and then a further 22 divisions would be required within 30 days.[15] Yet by the end of the 1940s there was still only a maximum of 12 European divisions capable of being mobilised to fight in the theatre. There was a gulf between what was needed and what could actually be provided. Ranged against the west was estimated to be a massive military force. It was thought that about 40 enemy divisions might be employed in a surprise attack, increasing to around 100 divisions within the space of a month.[16]

However, there were important differences of opinion amongst the Brussels Treaty members about the most appropriate way of responding to the threat. Holland, for example, argued for emphasis on short-term planning because they feared that the danger of war breaking out was high. In contrast, Britain argued for long-term preparations that placed a premium upon the economic stability and viability of the west. They did not see that war was likely in the near term due to the US atomic monopoly and they were sceptical about the ability of the Europeans to generate a realistic defence capability.[17] In addition, Britain had wider commitments to its overseas territories that it could not ignore. To have concentrated its energies on the European theatre to the detriment of its empire was an unacceptable option. The French were known to be concerned at British unwillingness to state what level of forces they would commit to Europe in wartime and Britain did not decide to reinforce its army on the continent until March 1950.

Hence, securing an American military commitment to continental defence grew increasingly important for European states. Even after the WUDO had been established, the British Chiefs of Staff (COS) were of the opinion that the US would remain the lynchpin of the defence of Europe and recommended that an American Supreme Commander be appointed for wartime, with a British Deputy.[18] The problem in seeking an American commitment was that it was unclear what sort of military guarantees the US would be willing to undertake. In addition, there was a more covert debate about the long term reliability of the US: unease remained that a future Administration might slip back into the isolationist policies that had characterised America's post-World War One stance.

By 1949 there was growing evidence that a US–European defence pact could be secured. The Vandenberg Resolution of the previous year had prepared the way in the US Congress and events in Europe, such as the Berlin blockade, convinced the Administration that an Atlantic defence organisation was required. The result, in April 1949, was the signing of the Washington Treaty and the creation of NATO.[19] It has been argued that the securing of American assistance marked the culmination of European efforts. Indeed, Fursdon refers to the creation of the Atlantic Alliance as 'the realisation of the Bevin dream',[20] whilst Cahen notes that the Brussels and Washington Treaties stemmed from 'identical preoccupations ... and ideals'.[21] Nevertheless, the NATO Article V guarantee remained more conditional than that of the Brussels Treaty because the US was wary of foreign commitments. The Europeans were still expected to take a leading part in their own defence.[22]

Undeniably, the establishment of NATO was a milestone in European security. But even at this stage, only the institutional structure of NATO had been put in place and there was still much to be done in generating a genuine defensive capability. Field Marshal Montgomery pressed successfully for the integration of the WUDO into NATO, on the grounds of avoiding duplication between the two organisations. The defence commitments of the Brussels Treaty were henceforward operationalised through the larger and more geographically extensive NATO framework.

This inaugurated the concept of the 'European pillar' of defence within the Atlantic Alliance.

Subsequent European efforts to increase their defence capabilities have to be seen in the context of the primacy of NATO after 1950. Such efforts, even when linked to the issue of European integration, were always pursued within the trans-Atlantic relationship and were not seen as alternatives to NATO. The Europeans were searching for ways to act more effectively amongst themselves, but always in partnership with the United States. As evidence of that fact, in April of 1951, General Eisenhower was appointed as Supreme Allied Commander, Europe (SACEUR). The SACEUR was to be made responsible for establishing a strategic plan to which the Brussels Treaty powers would contribute forces.

The European Defence Community and the WEU

The sense of relief that was felt in Europe with the signing of the Washington Treaty was short-lived. The outbreak of the Korean War in 1950, coupled with the recent Soviet explosion of an atomic weapon, forced a fundamental re-think of western assumptions regarding the likelihood of conflict. The war on the Korean peninsula was interpreted by many as presaging an attack upon Europe and there was widespread agreement that the size of the continental defence effort had to be increased.[23] This raised a major dilemma for the European powers; namely the rearmament of West Germany. Only the addition of German manpower could make it possible to conduct an in-depth defence of European territory.

The French, for obvious historical reasons, were the most alarmed at the prospect of rearming Germany. They feared the return of German militarism with all the implications that this held for the security of France. The US were more pragmatic in their approach as they saw rearmament as the only way to render a defence of Europe militarily credible. There was a direct linkage between rearmament and German sovereignty and the US feared that if the former was delayed then there would be the danger that the country could slip into neutralism. This might put at risk the sacrificial path that Chancellor Adenauer had chosen for his country when he allied with the west and rejected the offer of unity on Soviet terms. As for the British, they had perceived for some time that German rearmament would be necessary.[24] Indeed, as early as 1948 Lord Tedder had stated the need for a German military contribution to the defence of Europe although he acknowledged that it was 'politically premature' to broach the idea at the time.[25] Bevin had felt that it would be wise to build up the French and Belgians before rearming Germany and the Western Union concept had been consistent with that strategy.[26]

In order to minimise the risks of a militarily strong Germany, the French Prime Minister René Pleven pushed, from October 1950, for the creation of a European Defence Community (EDC). Despite the fact that some countries were more sympathetic to seeing the German contribution controlled by NATO,[27] France argued for the EDC to become the dominant framework. In this way, it would be possible to ensure that German rearmament would be structurally controlled. There would be no German General Staff and German military units would be integrated at a low level in order to avoid the re-emergence of a national army. It was eventually agreed in the context of the negotiations that 10–12 German divisions would be raised for the EDC.[28]

The EDC or 'Pleven Plan' was designed to have a deliberately supranational character. There was to be a dedicated European Minister of Defence, answerable to a political authority of a Council of Ministers and an Assembly. They were to exercise control over a force of some 100 000 personnel, effectively a European army.[29] This was to be financed out of a common budget and the Minister would have been accorded responsibility for raising and equipping forces from the member states through a common procurement system.[30] These were indeed radical objectives so soon after World War Two as they would have eroded the sovereignty of national governments.

For countries such as France and Belgium, there was a powerful logic behind this approach. Binding the countries of Europe closely together in integrated institutions would make war impossible between them. Six states had established a supranational role model in the form of the European Coal and Steel Community (ECSC),[31] which was designed to control the war-making capacity of Germany. The EDC complemented the ECSC and closely resembled it in structure. Defence was being used as a mechanism to advance integration and there were simultaneous debates about the development of a European political community, with a parliament and a supranational executive.[32]

Britain decided not to participate in the EDC and this was confirmed by the Conservative government in 1951. Britain's continental allies were surprised as, both after the war and in August 1950, Sir Winston Churchill had called for the creation of a European Army.[33] Similarly, in his capacity within WUDO, Field Marshal Montgomery had long argued for an integrated defence effort.[34] Yet in reality, the British were proponents of defence integration between their European partners, whilst being unwilling to participate themselves. Some form of association with a European Army was considered as a possibility but the British were opposed to full membership. They perceived their own country to be a global power with a broad panoply of interests, which could not be reconciled with a narrowly focused European role.

The fifty year EDC Treaty was signed in May 1952 with the blessing of the United States who saw the project as a valuable contribution to the NATO-led defence of the continent.[35] Four of the signatories, Germany, Belgium, Holland and Luxembourg moved quickly to ratify the agreement but Italy and France lagged behind in the process. In France, there was a delay before submitting the Treaty to the Assemblée Nationale and as time dragged on, there were growing doubts as to whether it would be passed. France felt let down that the British had chosen not to participate. The US had also expressed the desire to see Britain lead the integration movement in Europe. But after 1952, when Britain made it clear it had no intention of joining the EDC, Washington did not press the matter for fear of causing further delay. The British regarded the EDC as only one element of a defence structure for the continent. Foreign Secretary Anthony Eden was later to state that the EDC was merely 'a closer union within the wider (trans-Atlantic) grouping'.[36]

Through 1953 there appeared to be a very real possibility that the EDC would collapse, which presented three sorts of problems. Firstly, there would be doubts about the political will within Europe to contribute to the common defence, which might be a source of encouragement to the Soviets. Secondly, the rearmament of Germany would be paralysed. Thirdly, European disunity might lead the United States to reduce its commitment. Indeed, Secretary of State Dulles made an explicit warning in December at the North Atlantic Council meeting that the US would have to re-appraise its own position if the EDC was not ratified. The US regarded European unity as a necessary accompaniment to the reconstruction process and were despairing at the endless prevarication.[37] According to Fursdon, the US saw 'EDC as essential to give NATO a stout and dependable heart'.[38]

The French Assemblée Nationale rejected the EDC Treaty in August 1954. There had long been doubts about the supranational elements in the agreement which limited France's sovereignty and it was feared that this might undermine the country's sense of national identity. It might also complicate its colonial commitments which was a pressing consideration for France at this time. Yet it was probably the doubts over whether France was capable of controlling Germany which weighed most heavily against ratification of the EDC. Without firm commitments for the future from either Britain or the United States, France felt that its position was too exposed. Britain had made clear its intention to keep its forces on the continent and had gone so far as to draw up a Convention of Cooperation with the EDC, to reassure France, but it was to prove insufficient.[39] It was clear that with the EDC lying in ruins, an alternative arrangement for German rearmament had to be found with the utmost speed.

It was to be a British diplomatic initiative that filled the vacuum left by the EDC.[40] In what has been described as a 'masterstoke',[41] Anthony Eden orchestrated a series of agreements that witnessed the Brussels Treaty being modified and a 'Western European Union' created from the former Western Union. This was undertaken out of necessity rather than design; the objective being to preserve an American presence. The London Nine Power Conference in September 1954, made up of the EDC 'six' plus Britain, the US and Canada, and then the Paris Agreements of October, established the appropriate framework.[42] The price Britain paid for securing the Paris Agreements was a commitment of four divisions and a Tactical Air Force to the continent for 50 years. Henceforward, the WEU was to be a symbol of Britain's pledge to be engaged in European security and represented an historic change of policy. The prize Britain won in return was the ability to present itself to the US as the saviour of European defence.[43]

The original Brussels Treaty was modified in a number of ways: most importantly, Germany and Italy were included as new members to bring the total to seven. Article 2 was modified to talk of 'encourag[ing] the progressive integration of Europe', although this was left as a general political aim amongst the participants.[44] The military activities of the WEU would continue to be delegated to NATO. In addition, a Council of WEU was created (Article IV) in which all members were given one seat and under the Council an Agency for the Control of Armaments was established. This was aimed specifically at Germany and prohibitions were placed on its development of Atomic, Biological or Chemical weapons (ABC). Further limitations were agreed on the size of its naval vessels and long-range bombing aircraft. The oversight of these limitations by the WEU facilitated German accession into NATO where all of the forces of that country were placed under the operational control of SACEUR.

The WEU was less radical than its EDC predecessor in that there was no attempt to integrate the forces of its member states. Although it contained a Standing Armaments Committee (SAC) whose task was to promote cooperation in equipment,[45] WEU remained an inter-governmental actor without any of the supranational features that had caused Britain to stand apart from the EDC. The WEU was a facilitating mechanism to enable NATO to play the leading defence role in Europe.

Therefore it was unsurprising the low-level role that the WEU was to play in European security. The WEU was not a traditional alliance, that acted to deter an external threat; rather it served as a reconciler of differences between allies. It was built around a territorial guarantee but this was operationalised through the Atlantic Alliance and it possessed no Integrated Military Structure (IMS) to direct military forces in wartime. Its role was one of reassurance and maintaining accountability over Germany. In due course, even this task came to be of limited utility as Germany proved to be a trustworthy state in its armament policies.

Whereas EDC had demonstrated an attempt to pioneer European integration through defence, its failure ensured that this area would be omitted from the integration process. The experience of the collapse of the EDC and the hastily organised creation of the WEU left a powerful legacy in Europe. According to countries such as Britain, it demonstrated the inability of European states to agree on a defence structure without the guiding hand of the United States. Economic integration was to proceed from the foundations established in the ECSC,[46] but defence matters were to remain firmly wedded to a trans-Atlantic framework. As van Staden has pointed out, it was ironical that although European integration was motivated, to a large extent, by perceptions of insecurity, the process was to develop in the economic sphere rather than in defence.[47]

The Eclipse of the WEU

After 1954, the roles directly performed by the WEU became increasingly peripheral to the management of security. Its institutional weakness was compounded by the fact that its Ambassadors met in London, whilst its Secretariat resided in Paris. One commentator has referred to the 1970s as the 'somnolent years' for the WEU until its revitalisation in the 1980s.[48] Although in the intervening period the WEU maintained a low profile, it was not completely inactive, if for no other reason than its Assembly was the sole European parliamentary forum for defence debate. The WEU remained involved in security issues in three ways: as a channel of intra-European communication and conflict resolution; as part of the debate about American leadership on the continent and as an element in the evolution of European integration. Each of these areas will now be discussed in turn.

The WEU as Forum for Dialogue

The WEU served as a channel of communication between the major west European states. This was a useful function as there remained considerable post-war tensions between the main protagonists and the WEU was able to provide a forum in which to resolve some of these difficulties. Whilst the focus for major decisions and defence planning remained NATO, the WEU offered a more informal meeting place, especially the Assembly where new ideas could be discussed amongst national parliamentarians.[49] The WEU also had the attraction of being a forum that excluded the US. This proved to be valuable in three different types of situations: Franco–German relations, Franco–European relations and Anglo–European relations.

In the case of Franco–German relations, there was the greatest degree of suspicion to be overcome. The WEU played an important role in the latter part of 1955 in resolving the impasse over the Saar territory. The Saar was originally part of the French zone of occupation after World War Two but the Paris Agreements presented the opportunity to 'Europeanise' the area and place it under the administration of the WEU.[50] In the event, a referendum provided a majority in favour of returning the territory to Germany and, after France negotiated economic concessions, this was achieved by the WEU. This removed a thorny problem in Franco–German relations.

After the case of the Saar, the WEU provided reassurance over German rearmament and enabled the bilateral relationship between France and Germany to warm considerably. As France gradually disengaged from the Atlantic Alliance, so it grew closer to the Federal Republic. Yet there was a limit to this Franco–German rapprochement as Germany was unwilling to relinquish its security dependence on the United States in order to be closer to France. This was demonstrated most explicitly in January 1963 with the signing of the Elysée Treaty. Although symbolising the reconciliation between the two countries, this also contained a French design to lure the Germans away from NATO.[51] The US emasculated the French plan by encouraging the Bundestag to attach a preamble to the Treaty which stated that nothing would be allowed to interfere with Germany's pre-existing commitment to NATO. The Germans were determined that their relationship with the US would not be endangered.

In Franco–European relations, the WEU played a useful function during a time when France was militarily detached from its allies. France's desire to play a leadership role in the security politics of the continent resulted in its separation from established defence structures. The WEU provided a forum in which France could discuss defence topics of mutual interest with other European states. This proved to have particular utility after President de Gaulle withdrew his country from the NATO IMS in 1966. The absence of the US, as well as the intergovernmental structure of the WEU, ensured that France did not feel constrained about discussing its military views in this forum.

The other use of the WEU was in sustaining an Anglo–European dialogue during a time of tension. The WEU provided a multilateral meeting place for Britain and other European states when the UK was barred from membership of the EEC. In spite of two applications to join,[52] the French veto excluded British entry into the Community until 1973, so Britain had to find other ways to maintain a constructive dialogue with its allies. Gordon notes that the WEU's chief strength was in 'the provision throughout the 1960s of an institutional framework wherein Britain could associate herself with the member states of the European Community'.[53] It accorded the opportunity for around three meetings at ministerial level per year and these were extended to two days to give the maximum opportunity for wide ranging discussions. Inevitably after Britain entered the EEC, this function of the WEU disappeared.

US Leadership in Europe

If the WEU's direct role in defence activity was marginal, nevertheless, it was involved in the burden-sharing debate about security between the two sides of the Atlantic. American leadership in NATO was an accepted fact from the 1950s onwards. In the words of Lellouche, 'European security came to be defined in terms of NATO: that is US defence policy and US foreign policy'.[54] The US was the largest military power within the Alliance, its extended nuclear deterrent was the foundation stone of military strategy and its officers held the leading military commands.[55] The Europeans recognised that there were significant benefits attendant on deferring to the US. They were able to curb their own defence expenditures and minimise intra-European frictions. This was particularly important in relation to Germany where the stationing of American troops reassured its neighbours. But the price the Europeans paid for these benefits was that their influence in Alliance decisions was reduced and this became a regular source of tension in trans-Atlantic relations.

The US was content to take the lead amongst its allies at a time when Europe was economically weak and vulnerable to Soviet intimidation. The US was supportive of European economic integration in order that the continent would prosper and be more capable of sharing the burden of defence. Thus the EEC was seen as a vital contribution to the stability of the continent. Such thinking was evident in July 1962 with President Kennedy's vision of a 'Grand Design'. This attempted to create a closer trans-Atlantic partnership[56] in which the Europeans would do more for themselves. It remains debatable, however, whether Kennedy's call for a two-pillar Alliance was ever realistic. The US expected to lead within NATO and the Europeans had grown accustomed to an attitude of dependency. It is more likely that Kennedy, for all his rhetoric, expected the partnership to remain an unequal one.

This would appear to be borne out by American security policy in the period. Here the US wanted to centralise its control over strategy and decision-making, rather than devolving responsibility to allies. Apart from the nuclear system of Britain, which was already well-developed,[57] the US discouraged the development of independent nuclear deterrents, which were described by Defence Secretary McNamara as 'lacking in credibility'.[58] The strategy of 'Flexible Response' was predicated on the US being in control of the process of nuclear escalation. An attempt was made to deflect the nuclear ambitions of some of the European powers, particularly the FRG, by offering them a system provided by the United States in order to satisfy their demands for greater influence in defence. This was to be the Multilateral Force, a fleet of ships manned with personnel from a variety of contributing European countries and armed with Polaris ballistic missiles.[59] It was clear from the manner in which the concept was pursued that the US lacked genuine commitment to the MLF project, which was never realised.

There were notable differences amongst the WEU states in their attitudes to US leadership. Britain was an enthusiastic supporter of Washington's role, believing it to be a necessary counter-balance to the power of the USSR, as well as the cement that maintained European unity. The British also benefited disproportionately due to their close bilateral relationship with the US: in terms of nuclear and intelligence cooperation and their special status as a trans-Atlantic interlocutor.[60] Germany also supported American leadership, due to its position as the most vulnerable member within the western Alliance. The FRG hoped to procure rehabilitation from its wartime past through close adherence to NATO.

However, as previously alluded to, France was critical of America's leadership position. On the one hand, this reflected France's own sense of frustration that its leadership ambitions in European and global affairs were being constrained by the dominance of the US. On the other hand, there was genuine scepticism in French circles about the reliability and depth of America's commitment to the common defence, particularly its willingness to use nuclear weapons in defence of its allies. The sense of frustration in French policy was demonstrated in September 1958 when President de Gaulle called for a Three Power Directorate of the US, Britain and France to be established. His perception was that an Anglo–American duoply was running the Alliance and he pressed for a re-balancing of NATO to reassert specifically European interests. As anticipated, the Eisenhower Administration rejected the French overture. The Americans held a low opinion of France's importance due to its failures in Indochina and the US was concerned about upsetting its other NATO allies by such a brazen demonstration of great power politics. De Gaulle used this rebuff as a pretext to distance his country from the Alliance.

France saw the Cold War system as stable and sought to maximise its own influence.[61] It grew to champion the idea of greater European independence in defence and envisioned the continent developing into a third force between the two superpowers. To realise this objective, France turned to Germany, but this was recognised in Bonn as a transparent attempt to further selfish French objectives.[62] De Gaulle did not attempt to secure further cooperation with the British as he had become disillusioned with their desire to remain wedded to the United States. Yet the French view of closer European defence cooperation sat uncomfortably alongside their own strategic military thinking, which emphasised autonomy. Although France criticised the US policy of extended deterrence as unreliable, its own adherence to national self-reliance had nothing to offer to its European allies. After breaking away from the NATO IMS in 1966,[63] there was no framework that France could advance instead of NATO. The WEU was not a realistic alternative because it lacked the resources and the commitment of its member countries to make it viable.

As the Cold War progressed and the likelihood of war appeared to recede, so the cohesion of the Atlantic Alliance became subject to increasing strain. The advent of east–west détente made the US aware of interests it shared with the USSR; whilst the Europeans saw the opportunity to conduct unilateral initiatives towards the east, which caused concern in Washington. There remained a core of shared perspectives between the two halves of the Atlantic, but there were now numerous areas of disagreement. The rise in economic prosperity in Europe led the United States to believe that it was time that their allies contributed more to the common defence. For their part, the Europeans were less willing to defer to the US which was experiencing balance of payments difficulties and was no longer the unchallenged leader of the west. They were also critical of American policies outside of Europe, particularly the disastrous war that the US was fighting in Vietnam.

By the 1970s, fissures had appeared within the Alliance over a broad range of issues, such as the modernisation of theatre nuclear forces, arms control and US policy towards the Middle East. Such was the state of trans-Alantic relations that Henry Kissinger declared 1973 to be the 'Year of Europe' in an attempt to rebuild trust and understanding between the two sides. The Americans called for a new security Charter to reaffirm common interests, but the whole initiative was viewed in Europe as a clumsy attempt to re-impose America's views on its allies and it served only to exacerbate the existing frictions. The Europeans complained of American arrogance and a failure to appreciate any perspectives other than their own, whilst the Americans viewed their allies as ungrateful and complacent in the face of growing Soviet power.

Despite the sense of crisis that pervaded intra-Alliance relations, there was no constituency for abandoning the primacy of NATO and attempting to construct a rival organisation. In 1973, in a counter-proposal to the US security Charter, French Foreign Minister Michael Jobert tried to gain agreement to revive the WEU but this failed because it was judged to be prejudicial to the Alliance. The WEU served a useful function as an airing place for European grievances — a kind of safety valve when the pressure was high — but it was never a credible alternative to NATO. The European countries established structures that were complementary, rather than antagonistic towards NATO, in order to show the United States that they were willing to respond to some of its concerns. For example, the 'Eurogroup' was created in 1968 to coordinate the European contribution to NATO and demonstrate that they were bearing their fair share of the defence burden,[64] whilst a few years later, the Independent European Programme Group (IEPG) was established in order to achieve greater standardisation in weaponry.[65] When pressure from the US was intense, therefore, the Europeans avoided the development of structures that would have increased their independence from the US.

The Influence of European Integration

Running alongside the trans-Atlantic security framework was a debate about European integration. The failure of the EDC had switched attention from defence to economic cooperation. This started with the ECSC and then gathered momentum in the Treaty of Rome. Economics had become the 'motor of friendship'[66] whilst defence and foreign policy decisions were considered taboo. The Community developed as a civilian power and security and defence were left to NATO. The trans-Atlantic relationship provided a conducive environment to cooperation, whilst the threat from the USSR provided an external source of motivation. There was a conscious decision to prevent a nascent European identity from encroaching into those areas that might bring it into conflict with the United States.

The only serious attempt to alter this division of responsibility was undertaken by France in the early 1960s. From September 1960 to 1961, France sought to create a political union amongst the EEC Six, that lay outside of the Treaty of Rome. The 'Fouchet Plan' called for a common foreign policy and defence policy between the existing members, that was separate from the Atlantic Alliance. It envisaged the formation of an intergovernmental rather than a supranational body, as France was opposed to the loss of national control over foreign and defence issues.

A second Fouchet Plan was drafted in the following year which laid additional emphasis on the intergovernmental nature of the process.[67] Boyer notes that France wanted to build a stronger European defence identity in order to counteract what it perceived as American domination of the continent's agenda.[68] Thus the Fouchet Plan, built around de Gaulle's vision of a confederation of European states, was a counter-balance to the sort of thinking that had underpinned Kennedy's Grand Design. In the event, it did not proceed due to the opposition of countries such as Holland who were worried at the damage that might be inflicted on US–European relations.[69] European countries were opposed to putting NATO at risk as well as to complicating the role of the EEC.

Nevertheless, by the late 1960s it was widely agreed that Europe needed to speak with a more unified voice if it wanted to be able to project its influence on the world stage. There was recognised to be a security dimension to a European identity, as well as foreign policy implications to EEC economic activities. This led to pressure from within the Community to coordinate the foreign policies of its members, whilst leaving aside matters with defence implications. Intergovernmentalism was judged to be the way forward as many states were wary of supranationalism. This preserved the power of member governments to make decisions based on national interests without preventing agreement on a common European perspective.[70]

Against a backcloth of improving superpower relations and the 'Ostpolitik' of West Germany, 1969 appeared to be a propitious moment for the Europeans to develop a common voice. At the Hague Summit there was support for the Community to be granted a broader range of competencies. The foreign ministers were tasked to develop options for facilitating foreign policy cooperation and this led in October 1970 to the Luxembourg, or Davignon Report.[71] The result was the birth of European Political Cooperation (EPC). It was a pale reflection of the ideas that had been embodied in the Fouchet Plan for it was a consultation process amongst national foreign policy-makers, rather than a single foreign policy. A Political Committee composed of national political directors was established with a remit to prepare an agenda for the twice yearly meetings of EEC foreign ministers. When EPC finally emerged, it was little more than an informal consultation forum under the direction of the country holding the Community Presidency. To have achieved a more ambitious policy would have required greater political will, as well as the delineation of common interests amongst the members.

By the time of the British entry into the Community, EPC had become an established feature of the European dialogue.[72] It was part of the expression of a European identity; a recognition that these countries had interests in common. Yet its effectiveness was limited, it was a reactive mechanism that made no provision for developing future policy. The experience of EC disunity in the Yom Kippur War led to expressions of dissatisfaction with the limited capabilities of EPC. This resulted in the 1973 Copenhagen Report which called for greater consultation among the member states on all important foreign policy issues. In addition, defence remained outside of EPC, a factor made more necessary by the entry into the EC of the neutral Republic of Ireland. The US also made clear its opposition to the discussion of defence issues within a Community framework, as they maintained that this would result in their own alienation.[73]

Conclusion: The WEU Fading into Obscurity?

By the end of the 1970s the WEU was fading into obscurity as an international organisation. Meetings at foreign minister level were suspended after 1973 and there was a fallow period when not even a Secretary-General was appointed. The WEU went into 'hibernation' due to the fact that NATO was fulfilling the functions for which it had originally been conceived.[74] The only part of the organisation that remained active was the WEU Assembly in Paris.[75] As the parliamentary forum, it continued a discourse on defence issues but even its own activities were hampered by the fact that the Council, to whom it reported, was not in session.

Looked at in historical overview, there appears to be an historic inevitability to the diminishing importance of the WEU. As the Western Union, it had the potential to become the vehicle for defence integration in western Europe, but this was to prove too ambitious a target as European states wanted the US to play a major role. In 1954, after the failure of the EDC, the WEU played a necessary part in German rearmament but this was only to facilitate a leading role for NATO. As Cromwell observes, the WEU was 'never regarded as an embryo of an ... alternative to NATO'.[76] Rather than a collective defence organisation, the WEU became a political organisation that dealt with security issues. Trans-Atlanticism became the overarching framework for defence and European integration was channelled into the economic sphere.

This reflected the priorities of the leading states in Europe. Britain was closely aligned to the US and regarded a European defence system as unworkable, due to the continent's lack of power. Germany was not in a position to assert its own views to any great extent, its emphasis was upon its own rehabilitation. Only France attempted to advance a rival concept of security that extolled the unique interests of the European states and down-played the role of the US. However, France alone lacked the strength to realise its aims and it was condemned to a sense of frustration with its allies.

After the signing of the Paris Agreements, the role of the WEU became one of secondary importance, acting as a means of communication for European states.[77] Because of the importance attached to the American defence guarantee, no action was taken within Europe that could be construed as prejudicial to US interests. Yet the concept of a European defence identity never completely disappeared from the agenda. There remained tensions in the US–European relationship which led to the interests of the two sides diverging as the Cold War declined. Additionally, the spill-over effect from economic integration encouraged the European countries to coordinate their foreign policies more closely. Against this backcloth, it becomes possible to see why the WEU, although quiescent, did not die. It also contributes to an understanding of the complex range of forces that combined to promote the revitalisation of the WEU in the 1980s.

References and Notes

1. Deighton, A. *The Impossible Peace. Britain, the Division of Germany and the Origins of the Cold War*, Clarendon Press, Oxford, 1993, p. 163.

2. For a broader perspective on this period see Gaddis, J. *The Long Peace: Inquiries into the History of the Cold War*, Oxford University Press, 1987.

3. See Zeeman, B. 'Britain and the Cold War: An alternative approach. The Treaty of Dunkirk example', *European History Quarterly*, Vol. 16, No. 3, July 1986.

4. Greenwood, S. *The Alternative Alliance: Anglo–French Relations Before the Coming of NATO, 1944-48*, Minerva Press, Montreux, 1996, p. 283.

5. As Lord Tedder stated in 1948, 'It had always been the American view that Western Union must show how far it could go in planning and preparing its own defence ... [w]hen that had been done to the satisfaction of the Americans it might be possible for them to convince Congress that closer cooperation was desirable'. Public Records Office (PRO), DG 1/6/36, Western Union Chiefs of Staff Committee — FC (48) 2nd Meeting, 8/10/1948, 'Western Union Defence Policy'.

6. See Kent, J. and Young, J. 'British policy overseas: The "Third Force" and the origins of NATO — in search of a new perspective', in Heuser, B. and O'Neill, R. (eds) *Securing Peace in Europe 1945-62: Thoughts for the Post-Cold War Era*, Macmillan in association with St. Anthony's College, Basingstoke, 1992.

7. PRO, DG 1/1, Records of Sessions of the Consultative Council, 2nd Meeting, The Hague, 20/7/1948.

8. Kent, J. and Young, J. op. cit. p. 48.

9. Baylis, J. *The Diplomacy of Pragmatism: Britain and the Formation of NATO, 1942-1949*, Kent State University Press, Ohio, 1993, p. 75.

10. Secretary of State George Marshall delivered his famous Marshall Aid speech at Harvard University in June 1947 which marked the beginning of US economic assistance for European recovery.

11. PRO, DG 1/3/13, M Bidault Speech at the Second Session of the Consultative Council, 'Federation of Europe', The Hague, 20/7/1948.

12. Barker, E. *The British Between the Superpowers, 1945-50*, Macmillan, London, 1983, p. 114.

13. The idea for the Council of Europe arose within discussions conducted under the aegis of the Brussels Treaty.

14. United States and Canadian representatives attended meetings as full participants. See PRO, DG 1/1, Records of Sessions of the Consultative Council, 2nd Meeting, The Hague, 20/7/1948.

15. PRO, DG 1/5/32, MD (49) 7, 28/3/1949.

16. This led the British Chiefs of Staff to conclude as late 1957 that 'it will always be impossible militarily, and economically, for NATO to resist a Russian conventional attack using conventional weapons only'. PRO, DEFE 4/96 JP (57) 28 (Final), 22 March 1957, Brief for Chairman, Chiefs of Staff Committee.

17. PRO, DG 1/11/56, Western Union Defence Organisation Military Committee — MD (50) 12, 5/7/1950, 'Measures to Improve Our Defence Preparedness'.

18. PRO, DG 1/5/30, Meeting of Ministers of Defence at the Ministry of War, Paris, 27-28/9/1948.

19. See Henderson, N. *The Birth of NATO*, Weidenfeld & Nicholson, London, 1982.

20. Fursdon, E. *The European Defence Community: A History*, Macmillan, Basingstoke, 1980, p. 40.

21. Cahen, A. *The Western Union and NATO: Building a European Defence Identity Within the Context of Atlantic Solidarity*, Brassey's Atlantic Commentaries No. 2, London, 1989, p. 17.

22. PRO, Records of 5th Meeting of the Consultative Council, London, 14-15/3/1949.

23. DePorte, A. W. *Europe Between the Superpowers: The Enduring Balance*, Yale University Press, New Haven, 1979, pp. 156-7.

24. See Dockrill, S. *Britain's Policy for West German Rearmament 1950-1955*, Cambridge University Press, 1991.

25. PRO, DG 1/6/36, op. cit.

26. PRO, DG 1/11/56, op. cit.

27. Mager, O. 'Anthony Eden and the framework of security: Britain's alternatives to the European Defence Community, 1951-54', in Heuser, B. and O'Neill, R. (eds) op. cit. p. 131.

28. Fursdon, E, op. cit. p. 78.

29. Dockrill, S. op. cit. pp. 42-44.

30. Mathews, R. *European Armaments Collaboration: Policy, Problems and Prospects*, Harwood Academic Publishers, Reading, 1992, p. 30.

31. Otherwise known as the 'Schuman Plan' after its architect Robert Schuman.

32. For a more detailed discussion of this issue see Vanhoonacker, S. 'A critical issue: From European Political Cooperation to a Common Foreign and Security Policy', in Laursen, F and Vanhoonacker, S. (eds) *The Intergovernmental Conference on Political Union: Institutional Reforms, New Policies and International Identity of the European Community*, European Institute of Public Administration, Martin Nijhoff Publishers, Maastricht, 1992.

33. Eden, A. *Full Circle*, Cassell, London, 1960, p. 30.

34. Montgomery stated, 'The nations of the west can hope to make their defence a reality only if it is integrated'. PRO, DG 1/11/56, op. cit.

35. Ullman, R. *Securing Europe*, Adamamtine Press Ltd, Twickenham, 1991, p. 49.

36. Eden, A. op. cit. p. 36.

37. Winand, P. *Eisenhower, Kennedy, and the United States of Europe*, St Martin's Press, New York, 1993, pp. 30-54.

38. Fursdon, E. op. cit. p. 210.

39. Young, J. (ed) *The Foreign Policy of Churchill's Peacetime Administration 1951-1955*, Leicester University Press, 1988.

40. Duke makes the point that this is ironic in the light of Britain's subsequent ambivalence about the WEU thirty years later. See Duke, S. *The New European Security Disorder*, Macmillan, London, 1994.

41. Eekelen, W. van,'WEU and the Gulf Crisis', *Survival*, Vol. 32, No. 6, November-December 1990, p. 519.

42. 'Brussels Pact changes', *The Times*, 25/10/1954, Box 538, Colindale Press Library, London.

43. Deighton, A. 'Britain and the creation of Western European Union, 1954', in Deighton, A. (ed) *Western European Union 1954-1997: Defence, Security, Integration*, European Interdependence Research Unit, St Antony's College, Oxford, 1997, p. 23.

44. Brussels Treaty, as amended by the Protocol modifying and completing the Brussels Treaty, signed at Paris October 23, 1954, WEU Information Service, Brussels.

45. The French had tried but failed to obtain agreement on the setting up of a European Armaments Agency. For details on the arms procurement aspects of the WEU see Politi, A. 'Western European Union and Europe's defence industry', in Deighton, A. (ed) op. cit. pp. 135-137.

46. Winand, P. op. cit. p. 70.

47. Staden, A. van, 'After Maastricht: Explaining the movement towards a common defence policy', in Carlsnaes, W. and Smith, S. (eds) *European Foreign Policy: The EC and Changing Perspectives in Europe*, Sage, London, 1994, p. 140.

48. Cahen, A. op. cit. p. 5.

49. For details on the functioning of the Assembly see WEU Assembly Report, Rapporteurs Mr Henares and Mr Tummers, WEU Information Report, February 1993, Parts 1-3.

50. Cahen, A. 'The emergence and role of the Western European Union', in Clarke, M. and Hague, R. (ed) *European Defence Cooperation: America, Britain and NATO*, Manchester University Press, 1990, p. 56.

51. Haglund, D. *An Alliance Within the Alliance? Franco–German Military Cooperation and the European Pillar of Defense*, Westview Press, Boulder, 1991, p. 85.

52. The 1967 application to enter the EC was actually made at a WEU meeting by British Foreign Secretary George Brown.

53. Gordon, C. 'The WEU and European defense cooperation', *Orbis*, Vol. 17, No. 1, Spring 1973, p. 253.

54. Lellouche, P. 'Thinking about the unthinkable: Guidelines for a Euro-defence concept', in Alford, J. and Hunt, K. (eds) *Europe in the Western Alliance: Towards a European Defence Entity?* Macmillan, Basingstoke, 1988. p. 63.

55. See Osgood, R. *NATO: The Entangling Alliance*, University of Chicago Press, 1962.

56. Winand, P. op. cit. p. 190.

57. See, for example, Navias, M. *Nuclear Weapons and British Strategic Planning 1955-1958*, Clarendon Press, Oxford, 1991.

58. Cromwell, W. *The United States and the European Pillar: The Strained Alliance*, Macmillan Press, London 1992, p. 25.

59. See Clark, I. *Nuclear Diplomacy and the Special Relationship: Britain's Deterrent and America, 1957-1962*, Clarendon Press, Oxford, 1994.

60. Baylis, J. *Anglo–American Defence Relations 1939-1984*, Macmillan, London, 1984.

61. Gordon puts forward a slightly different interpretation that de Gaulle did not believe the Cold War was durable and was acting accordingly. See Gordon, P.

H. *A Certain Idea of France: French Security Policy and the Gaullist Legacy*, Princeton University Press, 1993, p. 187.

62. Germany had not been included in the plan for a Three Power Directorate and McCarthy describes this as an example of France offering Germany 'legitimacy but not equality', McCarthy, P. (ed) *France-Germany 1983-1993: The Struggle to Cooperate*, Macmillan, Basingstoke, 1993, p. 12.

63. Under the secret Lemnitzer-Ailleret Accords, the French declared their intention to participate in a general defence of western Europe in the event of a Warsaw Pact attack.

64. The Eurogroup met at the level of Defence Ministers and included France as an Observer.

65. As Schmidt points out, the IEPG was designed to build upon the work in arms collaboration that had been the responsibility of the WEU. Schmidt, P. 'The WEU — a Union without a perspective?' *Aussenpolitik*, Vol. 6, 1986, p. 396.

66. McCarthy, P. op. cit. p. 9.

67. Cromwell, W. op. cit. p. 31.

68. Boyer, Y. 'France and the security order in a new Europe' in Schmidt, P. (ed) *In the Midst of Change: On the Development of West European Security and Defence Cooperation*, Nomos Verlagsgesellschaft, Baden-Baden,1992, p. 15.

69. Nuttall, S. *European Political Cooperation*, Clarendon Press, Oxford, 1992, p. 44.

70. See Hill, C. (ed) 'National Foreign Policies and European Political Cooperation', Royal Institute for International Affairs by Allen and Unwin, London, 1983.

71. For details of the Davignon Report see Ifestos, P. 'European political cooperation (EPC): Its evolution from 1970 to 1986, and the Single European Act', *Journal Of European Integration*, Vol. 11, No. 1, Fall 1987, p. 49.

72. Nuttall, S. op. cit. pp. 93-110.

73. Wallace, W. 'European defence cooperation: The reopening debate', *Survival*, Vol. 26, No. 6, November/December 1984, p. 255.

74. Cahen, A. 'Western European Union: Birth, development and reactivation', *The Army Quarterly And Defence Journal*, October 1987, p. 393

75. Gordon, C. op. cit. p. 249.

76. Cromwell, W. op. cit. p. 45.

77. Rummel, R. 'West European cooperation in foreign and security policy', in Laurent, P-H. (ed) *The European Community: To Maastricht and Beyond*, The Annals of the American Academy of Political and Social Science, No. 531, January 1994, Special Edition.

2

Revitalisation in the 1980s

Introduction

Based upon a cursory examination, it appears paradoxical that west European countries should choose to revitalise the WEU in the 1980s. This was a period in which tensions between east and west increased to the extent of precipitating a 'Second Cold War'.[1] The paradox would seem to lie in the west Europeans breathing new life into a moribund organisation when the Warsaw Pact threat was at its highest. By revitalising the WEU, the European states appeared to be investing faith in a small and unproven organisation whilst signalling a lack of confidence in the Atlantic Alliance. Traditional notions of alliance theory would suggest that the Europeans should have remained wedded to the existing NATO structure, under American leadership, in such a time of external danger, rather than experimenting with alternatives.[2]

Yet there were a complex array of factors which led to the revitalisation of the WEU. Tensions in US–European relations and the progress in European integration provided the necessary motivation. But it would be erroneous to think that the aim of the Europeans was the replacement of the Alliance. Rather, the reinvigoration of the WEU was an attempt to address the concerns over trans-Atlantic burden-sharing. With countries such as the UK and Germany within the WEU, any policy that threatened to harm the linkage with the United States was inconceivable.

US–European Relations

The early 1980s witnessed growing tensions in US–European relations, particularly over the question of appropriate policies to pursue towards the USSR. The United States had emerged disillusioned from the period of détente, unable to secure the expected moderation in Soviet foreign policy. The invasion of Afghanistan and the unabated progress in Soviet military modernisation had left the US feeling it had been deceived. Hence, the Reagan administration entered office in January 1981 with a determination to reassert American power and to confront the Soviet Union around the globe in order to constrain its expansionist tendencies.[3] The experience of subsequent crises, such as the declaration of martial law in Poland in 1981 and the shooting down of Korean Air Lines flight 007 over Sakhalin in 1983,[4] reinforced the US view that it was engaged in a righteous crusade.

In contrast, the west Europeans were reluctant to sacrifice the benefits that they had derived from the détente process.[5] As a region, Europe had enjoyed a decrease in tension and had witnessed the signing of the Helsinki Final Act, in 1975, which formalised the status quo. Individual countries had also experienced important improvements in their contacts with the east: Germany, for instance, had transformed its relationship with the German Democratic Republic and had established a prosperous trading relationship with Moscow. Such factors made west European states cautious about following the US anti-Soviet lead. They were all too aware that renewed Cold War hostility would focus once again upon Europe and increase the risk of it becoming a battleground between the superpowers.

Differences in trans-Atlantic attitudes towards the USSR resulted in tensions within NATO.[6] The US tended to view the European approach as deriving either from 'military timidity'[7] or selfish economic interest. Washington also complained about the unwillingness of their allies to bear a larger share of the defence burden. With sharp increases in American military spending[8] and with a ballooning budget deficit, Washington criticised the Europeans for failing to do more. In particular, this focused on the failure to implement the NATO target of a three per cent real increase in defence spending that had been agreed in 1979. The Nunn Amendment of 1984, emanating from a Senator who was an acknowledged expert on defence matters, pressed for cuts in the size of US forces on the continent unless the Europeans met their annual target.[9] Americans looked across the Atlantic and detected a lack of resolve amongst their allies to stand-up to Soviet intimidation.

From the European perspective there were a host of concerns about 'he direction in which US policy was moving. At core was the age-old European dilemma about the trustworthiness of the US security guarantee during a period of renewed East–West hostility. The Europeans were anxious about the reliability of the US nuclear guarantee and the deployment of new Intermediate-range Nuclear Forces (INF) became a test of America's good faith. However, at the same time, the Europeans were fearful about being dragged into a conflict by an overly bellicose administration. European leaders were alarmed by the evidence of US unilateralism and its reluctance to consult, even on arms control

negotiations which were of vital interest to them.[10] They detected an
arrogance of power and, in the words of British Foreign Secretary Geoffrey
Howe, 'More and more Europeans were coming to feel that ... the
governments had no real influence on America's strategic thinking and that
established NATO mechanisms for consultation risked becoming
uni-directional'.[11]

European countries responded to these trans-Atlantic tensions in
different ways. To a large extent, the British and French responses were
predictable. The Thatcher government remained committed to preserving
a close relationship with Washington.[12] In contrast, France regarded the
Atlantic relationship as in need of an overhaul. It was suspicious of the
American policy of confrontation and held the view that the US was
exaggerating the Soviet threat in order to reassert its hegemonic control
over its European allies. The Mitterand government wanted to lessen
American influence, although not to the point that the US security
guarantee was withdrawn. France was not seeking to bring down the
Alliance but to supplement it with a stronger European dimension.[13]

The West German response to trans-Atlantic strains was not the most
strident but it was nevertheless the most significant. Throughout the Cold
War, the FRG had been the staunchest supporter of American security
policy, regarding it as vital to its own security interests. But the early 1980s
witnessed the first signs of open discord in US–German security relations.[14]
The hard-line American stance towards the USSR was perceived to damage
the cooperation that Germany had carefully cultivated with the east and
re-emphasised its vulnerability as NATO's front-line. Conventional
American military strategies such as Follow-on-Forces Attack (FOFA) and
Airland Battle 2000 proved to be unsettling for the Germans for they
smacked of a more aggressive stance.[15] The FRG was finding itself
diverging with its superpower patron over the sorts of issues that had
hitherto proved to be the bedrock of their relationship.[16]

A mechanism had to be found, therefore, both to heal the divisions in
trans-Atlantic relations and to give the Europeans more influence in
security policy. If disagreements were left to fester, they might have
escalated into public recrimination. The Europeans required a forum to
help them concert their views before addressing them to the US.

Intra–European Relations

A second strand contributing to the revitalisation of the WEU was the
quickening pace of European integration. The trans-Atlantic security
framework had been important in providing a favourable environment in
which integration had been able to flourish.[17] Furthermore, the need to
compete economically with the US acted as a stimulus to bring the

Europeans together. Wallace, for example, notes that the sense of unease amongst European governments, over US policies, was an important factor in closer cooperation.[18]

However, it would be misguided to portray the emerging European identity only as a rejection of American dominance.[19] It was also something positive, a recognition that continental interests were converging. There were those who felt that Europe needed to be capable of charting a course for itself, rather than standing in the shadow of the superpowers. The motives of these advocates varied but the prescription usually concentrated on renewing the impetus of economic integration within the European Community and enlarging its range of activities.[20] Through the 1970s Europe had been successful in learning to speak with once voice, distinct from the US, over issues such as the Middle East.[21] Yet EPC had also been shown to be liable to periods of inertia, such as the latter part of the 1970s, when none of the major European countries were eager to enhance its development. Domestic political problems could lead to EPC falling into neglect and only the impact of major international crises re-focused the minds of European leaders on the need to coordinate a response.

Proponents of the EC argued that it would remain a one dimensional actor until it gained foreign and defence responsibilities.[22] No serious attempt since the Fouchet Plan had been undertaken to move the EC into the sphere of security policy cooperation, despite official reports that had advocated such a development.[23] EPC, as a loose coordinating instrument of foreign policy, had provided a means to obtain a common European viewpoint on such issues as arms control but not on defence. This approach was endorsed in the London Report of 1981 which acknowledged the full association of the Commission in EPC affairs and proposed a skeletal secretariat that would afford greater assistance to the country holding the Presidency.[24]

In November 1981 German Foreign Minister Hans Dietrich Genscher and his Italian counterpart Colombo, proposed that EPC should be extended to include security and defence issues. The German initiative aimed to construct the rudiments of a common foreign policy amongst the Ten, as opposed to just the coordination of national foreign policies. Although the European Council was to ensure intergovernmental oversight, the Parliament and the Commission were both accorded functions.[25] The Genscher–Colombo plan failed to attract sufficient support from other Community members and was stillborn. The fact that France and Britain refused to support it ensured its demise. In addition, Ireland was determined not to see its neutrality compromised and Denmark opposed breaking the civil power taboo of the EC.[26] Expanding the competencies of the EC into defence raised the sensitive issue for many European countries of a potential rival military organisation to NATO.[27]

A face-saving compromise was agreed subsequently in the 'Solemn Declaration' of Stuttgart in June 1983.[28] Here it was concluded that EPC, whilst outside the Community, could also cover the economic and political aspects of security. This decision was of marginal significance as this had already been accepted in the London Report. Its only importance was that it acknowledged security as a legitimate area for EC interest, even if it failed to provide the mechanisms for action. Arguably, it established a precedent that could be exploited.

Hence, there were competing pressures within Europe over a security and defence identity. Although it was recognised to be timely to assert a European voice, there was no unanimity about the vehicle by which this could be accomplished. Several countries were wary of enlarging the competencies of the EC, either for fear of encouraging supranationalism or for undermining the traditional strengths of the organisation. Consequently, there was pressure to find a body that could represent a reinvigoration of European defence activities without alarming the US or transforming the EC. Such an opportunity existed within the WEU.

The Revitalisation of the WEU

Appreciating the background issues assists in understanding both the reasons for the WEU's revitalisation as well as the form that it took. The nature of the organisation meant that it had a number of potential benefits to offer. Firstly, it was a long standing institution that already possessed legitimacy in the sphere of defence, based upon the modified Brussels Treaty. Secondly, its intergovernmental character reassured states that it would not undermine their sovereignty and made it more acceptable than the EC. Thirdly, smaller countries hoped for greater influence within this intimate forum. In short, the advantage of the WEU was that it was institutionally separate from the EC yet represented the interests of many of the same European states.

However, the factors that contributed to the reactivation of the WEU also established the parameters of its re-birth. Since 1954 the WEU's role had been a modest one and therefore even after its revitalisation, it did not present a challenge to the primacy of NATO. Its members accorded the WEU the mission of rectifying the weaknesses in the existing security order, such as assuaging US demands for Europe to contribute more, rather than creating a new order. It had a dual role: to improve US–European relations by addressing the issue of burden-sharing and to act as a clearer expression of a European security identity, that did not trespass on NATO's defence role.[29]

This is not to suggest that the revitalisation of the WEU was free from difficulty. After all, this was an organisation that was emerging from a period of suspended animation and it had no clearly defined role. Furthermore, Germany was ambivalent about the prospect of raising the organisation's profile considering its chief purpose during the Cold War had been to oversee limitations upon its military capabilities. It was quickly agreed that these restrictions would be lifted and this was formally announced in the Rome Declaration of 1984.[30]

The year 1984 represented the 30th anniversary of the founding of the WEU and some commentators noted the parallels with the circumstances of 1954, such as US–European tensions and the burden-sharing debate.[31] The preparations for its revitalisation were agreed at the Paris meeting in June 1984 and were announced at Rome in October.[32] Henceforth, European defence ministers would be able to convene under the aegis of the WEU. German Foreign Minister Hans Dietrich Genscher, acting as Chairman of the Rome meeting stated that European action in security policy 'would contribute to strengthening the European pillar of NATO'.[33] The prime motivation for the reinvigoration of the WEU was to remedy the weakness of the European countries within the Atlantic Alliance.

French Foreign Minister Claude Cheysson played an active part in laying the groundwork for the WEU's reactivation and the same enthusiasm was demonstrated during the period of the French Presidency.[34] France had long called for the reinvigoration of the organisation, seeing it as a way to concert European views on defence and to develop a limited defence capability outside of NATO. Paris was also desirous of projecting its priorities into the debate about continental defence.[35] In turn, other countries recognised that the WEU offered a vehicle for drawing France into a tighter web of security cooperation.

In the words of Foreign Secretary Geoffrey Howe, Britain approached the reactivation of the WEU with 'caution'.[36] Successive British governments had been sceptical about what a European defence grouping could achieve. They were particularly concerned that the Europeans might coalesce around positions that could cause friction with Washington. Critics contended that the British were being characteristically deferential to the United States. The UK approved a modest renaissance of the WEU, on the grounds that it might convince American policy-makers that the Europeans were taking their complaints seriously.[37] There were those within the Conservative government, such as Defence Secretary Michael Heseltine and the Foreign Secretary, who were eager to demonstrate that Britain was committed to cooperation with its European partners. Heseltine[38] perceived that the WEU could offer significant benefits in the field of greater European armaments collaboration, where the struggle was to keep up with the technological strides of the superpowers.[39]

Once agreement had been reached, steps were taken to enhance the WEU's structures. In the Rome Declaration, the workings of the Council and the Council Presidency were refined, new working groups were established and a Secretary-General, Alfred Cahen, was appointed. Three broad areas of responsibility were chosen for the WEU, with due consideration paid to its past activities. The first was general security and defence matters where there was an implicit desire for the WEU members to move towards common views. The second area was weapons development where the WEU was made responsible for increasing the extent of collaboration. The Standing Armaments Committee (SAC) was to develop activities in this area, in cooperation with NATO's Committee of National Armaments Directors (CNAD) and the IEPG.[40] The third area was arms control, which had grown into a source of friction between the US and its continental allies.

The US reacted to this emerging European defence identity with unease. In principal, the Americans welcomed any effort by their allies to take more responsibility for their defence and in this respect the WEU appeared to represent a step in the right direction. Yet officials in the State Department and the Pentagon were unconvinced that revitalising an aged institution would make a significant difference. There was a suspicion that the WEU was being used by the Europeans to raise their profile in defence but without contributing a larger share of the resources.[41]

Viewed from a different perspective, the US was uncomfortable about its allies investing political effort in a singularly European forum in which America was without a voice. A debate about the primacy of the Atlantic security framework, which had been put to sleep with the failure of the EDC, was being shaken from its slumber. The American government was unhappy with the prospect of being faced with privately agreed European negotiating positions. This distaste for anything that resembled a European caucus was deeply ingrained as it threatened to call into question America's leadership. There was undeniably an element of hypocrisy in the American attitude because the US had hitherto shown itself to be prepared to undertake unilateral demarches, if it thought its interests would be furthered, but was unwilling to see its allies do the same.

A potentially cohesive European position was in prospect at the end of 1985 over the issue of the Strategic Defence Initiative (SDI). The SDI had been announced by President Reagan in March 1983 as a revolutionary contribution to western defence, but it aroused considerable disquiet in Europe because it threatened to start a de-stabilising avenue of the arms race and because it threw into question the long term viability of the British and French nuclear deterrents. Even British Foreign Secretary Geoffrey Howe had been critical of what he described as 'Maginot Line' thinking in the project.[42] Other countries such as France refused to participate in the research project that America opened to allied participation. France replied by initiating the European Research and Coordination Agency

(EUREKA), which was aimed at strengthening Europe's civil, rather than military, technology base. The US was sufficiently worried about the European response to SDI to prompt Assistant Secretary of State for European Affairs, Richard Burt, to write to allied capitals warning against the discussion of arms control positions without reference to the US.[43]

Discussions on the European response to SDI were concentrated in the WEU forum and a meeting in Bonn in late April 1985 was dedicated exclusively to the issue,[44] but failed to agree upon a common line of action. This was due to the fact that countries such as Britain believed it to be in their own interests to participate in the research programme. They believed that such action would ensure their influence in Washington as well as grant UK researchers access to lucrative contracts. Eventually, in December of that year, the GermanGermany, Federal Republic of;SDI and government decided to allow its own companies to take part in the research on the grounds of Alliance solidarity and economic gain.

In retrospect it was therefore overly pessimistic of American officials to fear that the Europeans would use the WEU to assert a unified set of views in opposition to their own. No such common European perspective had existed historically, nor was it present in the 1980s. Rather, there were a multiplicity of views from the various national capitals which were liable to be exploited and played off against each other by skilful American diplomacy. If concerting west European views had been so straightforward, then there would not have been the post-war tradition of relying on the US to provide leadership.

The Hague Platform

Although the Rome Declaration of 1984 emphasised that the reactivation of the WEU was designed to strengthen US–European relations, it was deemed to be necessary to reaffirm the compatibility of the security interests of the two sides. This was prompted by two factors: a desire to reassure the United States and a response to the step forward in European integration that had been secured by the passing of the Single European Act (SEA).

The SEA had been agreed at the Luxembourg meeting of the European Council in December 1985 and its principal purpose was to create a single market by 1992. Under Title III, it granted a legal base to EPC which had hitherto rested upon informal agreements and understandings.[45] Title III had the effect of ending the sharp separation between the EC and the EPC.[46] The political and economic dimensions of security continued to be the limits of EPC and defence remained outside the reach of the EC, thereby preserving a role for the WEU.[47]

In order to balance progress in integration with Atlantic solidarity, it was decided to draw up a document within the WEU that re-emphasised the centrality of US–European security relations. This took the form of a security charter that was discussed at the WEU Council of Ministers meeting in Luxembourg in April 1987. The charter was designed to demonstrate Europe's commitment to burden-sharing and define a common set of security principles for the continent. It also attempted to obtain a common European position on how to respond to conflicts outside of the region. In the following September, the President of the European Commission Jacques Delors made a speech in which he echoed the aims of the charter by stressing the role of the WEU as the interface between the EC and NATO.[48]

The British supported the creation of a security charter as a way of enshrining the WEU as the 'European pillar' within the Atlantic framework. The long-standing fear of the British government was that France would seek to hijack the revitalisation of the WEU by trying to develop it as a rival structure to NATO. This was seen to be the underlying aim of France in securing for itself a leadership role in Europe. The French Prime Minister, Jacques Chirac, had indeed played a major part in calling for the WEU to assert a clearer European identity, most pointedly in a speech in December 1986 to the WEU Assembly.[49] The fact that a form of words was found in the charter to which the French were prepared to subscribe, was a major source of satisfaction to the British.

The 'Platform on European Security Interests', was adopted in the Hague in October 1987. It declared the aim of constructing a more integrated Europe with an identity that would be incomplete without security and defence aspects. Of equal importance, the Platform stated that closer European cooperation was designed to support NATO and that security could only be ensured 'in close association with our North American allies'.[50] As Luxembourg Foreign Minister Jacques Poos remarked, the WEU must not duplicate the work of the 'military organs of the Atlantic Alliance'.[51] In essence, the British vision of the role of the WEU was adopted.

The Hague Platform clarified the fundamental tenets of Europe's security policy. In particular, it reasserted the need for nuclear deterrence, following the superpower meeting at Reykjavik in October 1986. Here, Reagan and Gorbachev had discussed the potential abolition of ballistic missiles and nuclear weapons within a ten year time period.[52] This raised in stark relief the fear of a superpower deal executed over the heads of the Europeans. It questioned not only the independent deterrents of Britain and France, but also the entire basis of western security strategy that was founded on the US extended nuclear guarantee. British Prime Minister Margaret Thatcher subsequently visited the US to express concern at what had been discussed at Reykjavik and used the conclusions from a WEU discussion as evidence of European unity on the subject.[53] As a result, the Hague Platform restated the need for an 'appropriate mix of nuclear and conventional forces' for the defence of Europe.

Franco–German Relations

The revitalisation of the WEU advanced the cause of a European defence identity within a multilateral forum that was compatible with US leadership. Nevertheless, it camouflaged the fact that the driving force underlying this progress came from the relationship between two countries; France and West Germany. It was their bilateral cooperation that served as the engine for the WEU. It was no coincidence that a French initiative had sparked the reactivation process and that German thinking had lain behind the attempt to give the EC a security dimension.

The motivation behind the Franco–German partnership was two-fold. On the one hand, it reflected a sense of shared opportunity. Both countries regarded closer European cooperation as a way to advance their interests: to France it offered the prospect of leadership,[54] whilst to Germany it offered influence that would not be perceived as threatening by its allies. From their own perspective, integration offered a means to overcome the historical antagonisms between the two countries and enable them to harness their combined strength.[55] On the other hand, there was a recognition of shared danger. US–German security tensions in the early part of the 1980s had caused Bonn to feel isolated and led France to fear that its security buffer to the east was in danger of crumbling. This resulted in France relinquishing its traditionally autonomous posture and drawing closer to Germany. This it did through bilateral mechanisms and through the WEU.[56]

Defence cooperation between the two countries took many different forms, institutional as well as practical. In 1982, a symbolically important decision was taken to operationalise the defence clauses of the Elysée Treaty, which resulted in the establishment of a Franco–German Commission on Defence.[57] This initiative was developed further in 1988 with the creation of a Franco–German Defence Council, whose particular focus was in weapons procurement. As part of France's policy of extending reassurance to its neighbour, exercise 'Bold Sparrow' in 1987, witnessed the deployment of elements from the 'Force d'Action Rapide' (FAR) to the inner-German border. This reinforcement of the Bundeswehr was something that had never been attempted before.[58] Furthermore, the two countries established a joint military brigade, which although militarily insignificant, was a powerful political signal of their commitment to cooperative military structures. France also made efforts to calm German fears about the use of short-range, 'pre-strategic' nuclear weapons, such as Pluton missiles, that would be fired from French territory.[59]

Predictably, other states in Europe were suspicious of the exclusivity of Franco–German relations. The government in Britain was especially irked by the warmth between Paris and Bonn, not least because it seemed to challenge Anglo–American primacy in security matters. Prime Minister Thatcher expressed her opposition to the establishment of bilateral defence structures within Europe, such as the joint brigade, which she was worried might antagonise the Americans and lead them to reduce their presence. Hence, part of the British strategy of supporting the WEU was a tactical measure designed to water down the relationship between France and Germany and ensure that a UK voice was present in influencing the future direction of European cooperation.

Nevertheless, the fact that two erstwhile enemies had taken such strides in joint decision making structures and even infant multilateral formations, gave heart to advocates of a more ambitious future role for the WEU. The organisation provided a forum in which to harness the energies of these two states and enabled other European countries to be associated. Franco–German efforts demonstrated that the rudimentary foundations for European defence cooperation were present, ready to be enlarged upon when the circumstances were more favourable. This bilateral relationship was destined to have an important role to play in the post-Cold War period.

'Operation Cleansweep' and the Persian Gulf Conflict

The first occasion when the WEU experienced an operational mission was in 1987 during the Iran–Iraq war.[60] This was viewed as a real opportunity for the organisation because it occurred in a region outside of, but in close proximity to, Europe. It also sprang from an American request for assistance which enabled Europe to appear as a full burden-sharing partner.

The objective of the intervention was to preserve the freedom of navigation for ships of all nations from the threat of mines in the Persian Gulf, which was being used by each protagonist to disrupt the oil exports of the other side. A shipping lane, some 300 miles in length, needed to be swept for mines whilst at the same time tankers were escorted and protected from air and naval attack. Many of the European navies possessed dedicated mine counter measures (MCM) vessels, a capability which the US had largely neglected during the Cold War. Some countries already had naval assets in the Gulf, such as the British 'Armilla Patrol', but these were bolstered until eventually forces from five out of the seven WEU members were involved in 'Operation Cleansweep' (Belgium, France, Italy, Netherlands and the UK). The Federal Republic, constrained by its Constitution from participation, sent naval forces to the Mediterranean to substitute for the withdrawal of allied vessels and Luxembourg demonstrated its solidarity by a financial contribution.

The Dutch Presidency of the WEU took the lead in galvanising the participants into action and enjoyed strong support from the British government.[61] The WEU coordinated the naval forces of the five members but did not attempt to provide a unified command. The WEU had the benefit of being able to draw together the foreign and the defence ministers of the participating powers, thereby making it possible to deal simultaneously with the military and the political aspects of the crisis. It also lent a political legitimacy to the operation without which many of the European countries would not have become involved.

However, the significance of the WEU's role should not be exaggerated as Operation Cleansweep was a limited operation and the organisation acted merely as a coordinating agency. It was from within national defence ministries that the operation was planned and executed. Indeed, the WEU possessed no planning capabilities of its own — in contrast to the large planning staff that resided within NATO. Despite the symbolic importance of the WEU's role in such an 'out-of-area' mission, its actual involvement was modest.

The Gulf operation was therefore a fitting conclusion to the revitalisation process of the WEU. It remained essentially a consultative body of limited operational capability, overshadowed in Europe by NATO. British Foreign Secretary Geoffrey Howe had put the organisation into perspective when he described its utility as that of a 'ginger group', in which European ministers could discuss their particular concerns.[62] This was echoed in the writing of its Secretary-General, Alfred Cahen in 1987, who stated that the 'WEU is not a decision-taking or operational forum, but one in which greater harmony of views can be achieved'.[63]

As well as its limited remit, the WEU continued to face several difficult problems. In the first place, there was an intense wrangle over the choice of a permanent location. A majority of the members wanted it moved to Brussels where it would work alongside NATO. But France was opposed to this development for fear of losing some of the WEU's agencies that were based in Paris and because it suspected that the organisation's distinctive identity would be diluted if it was brought too close to the Alliance.[64] In addition, there were criticisms of the WEU's size and inadequate resourcing. Its bureaucracy was pitifully small, which limited its speed of decision making.[65] Its financing was also a source of concern: for example, at the time of its reactivation in 1984, the budget of the WEU was only £3 million.

By the end of the 1980s, much of the optimism that had surrounded the re-birth of the WEU had evaporated. The tension in US–European relations, that had helped to stimulate its revival, had now subsided in the light of Soviet 'new thinking'. There was a danger that the WEU would grind to a halt due to the lack of political impetus to move it forward. The organisation faced an uncertain future. On the one hand, it had to trace out a working relationship with NATO, that avoided the alienation of the US. On the other, it needed to ensure for itself an identity that distinguished it from the European Community.[66] Steering the WEU through these waters was likely to prove a difficult task in the ensuing decade.

Conclusion

The WEU found itself at the confluence of a series of debates at the time of its revitalisation. One was about the trans-Atlantic relationship during a period of turmoil, whilst another was the progress in economic integration and the emergence of a European defence identity. The WEU was able to play a part in calming fears on both sides of the Atlantic and preserve the status quo. It did not represent an attempt to build up a separate defence capability to supplant NATO. In the absence of agreement on bringing defence within the purview of the EC, the WEU became the early expression of a west European security and defence identity that was dedicated to propping up Atlanticism.

However, even after taking into account the WEU's revitalisation, its role in the management of European security remained modest. It played only a marginal role in the major issues that characterised east-west tension,[67] such as nuclear force modernisation and the west's relationship with the USSR. It was within NATO that the focus of effort continued and the WEU was employed only as a forum for resolving intra-Alliance problems.

The west European countries had to acknowledge that they still possessed different interests and there was no consensus amongst them on defence issues. Such a multitude of views made a defence identity an inherently complex task and encouraged continued reliance on the leadership function of the United States. But the 1990s was to raise a new and unexpected challenge for the continent. The threat, which had for so long bound them to the US, was to disappear and the role that their superpower ally would play on the continent was to be thrown into doubt.

References and Notes

1. See Halliday, F. *The Making of the Second Cold War*, Verso, London, 1983.
2. For investigation of the theory of alliances, see Walt, S. *The Origins of Alliances*, Cornell University Press, Ithaca, 1987.
3. Weinberger, C. *Fighting for Peace*, Michael Joseph, London, 1990, pp. 20-25.
4. Newhouse, J. *The Nuclear Age: From Hiroshima to Star Wars*, Michael Joseph, London, 1989, pp. 365-368.

5. See Davy, R. (ed) *European Detente: A Reappraisal*, Royal Institute for International Affairs, London, 1992.

6. See Hillenbrand, M. 'American foreign policy and the Atlantic Alliance', in Goldstein, W. (ed) *Reagan's Leadership and the Atlantic Alliance: Views from Europe and America*, Pergamon-Brassey's, London, 1986, pp. 40-54, and Calleo, D. *Beyond American Hegemony. The Future of the Western Alliance*, Basic Books, New York, 1987.

7. Nunn, S. 'NATO: Saving the Alliance', *The Washington Quarterly*, Vol.5, No. 3, Summer 1982, p. 20.

8. Cordesman, A. 'The Reagan Administration: Its past, and future impact on the Western Alliance', *Royal United Services Institute Journal*, Vol. 31, No. 1, 1986, p. 36.

9. The Nunn Amendment of June 1984 called for a reduction of 30 000 troops over 3 years and was only defeated in the Senate by 3 votes.

10. Roberts, F.'Continuity and change in American foreign policy' in Goldstein, W. (ed) op. cit. p. 9.

11. Howe, G. *Conflict of Loyalty*, Macmillan, London, 1994, p. 393.

12. See White , B. 'Britain and East-West relations' in Smith, M., Smith, S. & White, B. (eds) *British Foreign Policy: Tradition, Change and Transformation*, Unwin Hyman, London, 1988.

13. Menon, A.'France' in Moens, A. and Anstis, C. (eds) *Disconcerted Europe: The Search for a New Security Architecture*, Westview Press, Boulder, 1994, p. 201.

14. See, for example, Moreton, E. (ed) *Germany Between East and West*, Cambridge University Press, 1987.

15. Schwarz, W. 'Genscher calls for the revival of WEU' *The Guardian*, 21 June 1984.

16. Hoppe, U. 'The Western European Union', in Jopp, M., Rummel, R. & Schmidt, P. (eds) *Integration and Security in Western Europe: Inside the European Pillar*, Westview Press, Boulder, 1991, p. 273.

17. Staden, A. van, 'After Maastricht: Explaining the movement towards a common European defence policy', in Carlsnaes, W. & Smith, S. (eds) *European Foreign Policy: The EC and Changing Perspectives in Europe*, Sage, London, 1994, p. 147.

18. Wallace, W. 'Introduction' in Hill, C. (ed) *National Foreign Policies and European Political Cooperation*, Royal Institute for International Affairs by Allen and Unwin, London, 1983, p. 8.

19. See Calleo, D. op. cit.

20. Lellouche, P. 'Thinking about the unthinkable: Guidelines for a Euro-defence concept', in Alford, J. and Hunt, K. (eds) *Europe in the Western Alliance: Towards a European Defence Entity*, Macmillan in association with the IISS, Basingstoke, 1988, p. 62.

21. See Nuttall, S. *European Political Cooperation*, Clarendon Press, Oxford, 1992.

22. Halstead, J. G. 'The security aspects of European integration', *Journal Of Economic Integration*, Vol. 9, No. 2-3, Winter/Spring 1986, p. 183.

23. For example, the Tindermans Report of December 1975.

24. Serre, F. de la, 'The impact of Francois Mitterand' in Hill (ed) op. cit. p. 21.

25. Nuttall, S. op. cit. pp. 183-188.

26. Cromwell, W. C. *The United States and the European Pillar: The Strained Alliance*, Macmillan Press, London, 1992, pp. 171-172.

27. Forster, A. 'The European Community and WEU' in Moens, A. and Anstis, C. (eds) op. cit. p. 56.

28. For details see Neville-Jones, P. 'The Genscher-Colombo proposals on European union', *Common Market Law Review*, Vol. 20, 1983.

29. Edwards, G. and Nuttall, S.'Common Foreign and Security Policy' in Duff, A., Pinder, J. and Pryce, R. *Maastricht and Beyond: Building the European Union*, For the Federal Trust, Routledge, London, 1994, p. 86.

30. Reuters, 'WEU lifts Bonn arms ban', *The Financial Times*, 28 June 1984.

31. Davidson, I. '1954 comes around again', *The Financial Times*, 16 April 1984.

32. For details of the revitalisation process see WEU Assembly Report, Rapporteurs Mr Henares and Mr Tummers, WEU Information Report, February 1993, Parts 1-3.

33. Transcript of speech by Hans Dietrich Genscher, 'Strengthening WEU', Press Department, Embassy of the Federal Republic of Germany, London, 12, September 1984.

34. Wyles, J. 'European Foreign Ministers will discuss closer defence cooperation', *The Financial Times*, 9 April 1984.

35. Yet Schmidt contends that the French interest in WEU was tactical and that it was one amongst a variety of organisations for advancing its interests. See Schmidt, P. 'The WEU — A Union without a perspective?' *Aussenpolitik*, Vol. 6, 1986, p. 393.

36. Howe, G.*Conflict of Loyalty*, Macmillan, London, 1994, p. 386.

37. Bloom, B. 'Europe may breathe new life into WEU', *The Financial Times*, 12 June 1984.

38. Heseltine later resigned from the Cabinet over a weapons procurement issue that centred on a choice between European or American collaboration. See Freedman, L. 'The case of Westland and the bias to Europe', *International Affairs*, Vol. 63, No. 1, Winter 1986-87.

39. Siccama, J. G. 'Towards a European Defence Entity?' in Alford, J. and Hunt, K. (ed) op. cit. p. 36.

40. For the work of the IEPG in the latter part of the 1980s see Moravcsik, A. 'The European armaments industry at the crossroads', *Survival*, January/February 1990, pp. 70-71.

41. Schmidt, P. op. cit. p. 398.

42. Speech of Foreign Secretary Geoffrey Howe, quoted in Newhouse, J. op. cit. p. 383.

43. Schmidt, P. op. cit. p. 398.

44. Mauthner, R. 'Star Wars to dominate Bonn talks', *The Financial Times*, 22 April 1985.

45. Rummel, R. 'West European cooperation in foreign and security policy', in Laurent, P-H. (ed) *The European Community: To Maastricht and Beyond*, The Annals of the American Academy of Political and Social Science, No. 531, January 1994, Special Edition, p. 116.

46. The Court of Justice continued to be denied jurisdiction over foreign policy matters, whilst the Parliament could only debate and the Commission seek to implement what had been agreed.

47. Kirchner, E. 'Has the Single European Act opened the door for a European security policy?' *Journal Of European Integration*, Vol. 13, No. 1, 1989, p. 13.

48. Cahen, A. *The Western Union and NATO: Building a European Defence Identity Within the Context of Atlantic Solidarity*, Brassey's Atlantic Commentaries No. 2, London, 1989, p. 15.

49. Morrison, J. 'Chirac calls for Western Europe to draw up its own security charter', *The International Herald Tribune*, 3 December 1986.

50. 'The Platform on European Security Interests', The Hague, 27 October 1987, in Cahen, A. op. cit. p. 92.

51. Poos, J. 'Prospects for the WEU', *NATO Review*, Vol.35, No.4, August 1987, p. 18.

52. See Perle, R. 'Reykjavik as a watershed in US–Soviet arms control', *International Security*, Vol. 12, No. 1, Summer 1987, pp. 175-178.

53. Cahen, A. 'The emergence and role of the Western European Union' in Clarke, M and Hague, R. (ed) *European Defence Cooperation: America, Britain and NATO*, Manchester University Press, 1990, p. 61.

54. Lellouche, P. 'Does NATO have a future? A European view', *The Washington Quarterly*, Vol.5, No. 3, Summer 1982, p. 43.

55. See Feld, W. J. 'Franco–German military cooperation and European unification', *Journal of European Integration*, Vol. 12, No. 2-3, 1989.

56. See Yost, D, 'France, West Germany and European Security Cooperation', *International Affairs*, Vol. 64, No. 1, 1988 and Haglund, D. *Alliance Within the Alliance? Franco–German Military Cooperation and the European Pillar of Defense*, Westview Press, Boulder, 1991.

57. Gordon, P. 'The Franco–German security partnership' in McCarthy, P. (ed) *France-Germany 1983-1993. The Struggle to Cooperate*, Macmillan, Basingstoke, 1993, p. 143.

58. The FAR had been set up in 1983 as an overseas interventionary force of some 47 000 troops.

59. Yost, D. op. cit. p. 97.

60. The WEU was used under the terms of Article VII of the modified Brussels Treaty. Hoppe, U. 'The Western European Union', in Jopp, M., Rummel, R. & Schmidt, P. (eds) op. cit. p. 276.

61. Dutch stewardship led to the first ever meeting between the Chiefs of Staff of the WEU nations. The WEU's role in the crisis has usually been interpreted as a success but some analysts have questioned the effectiveness of the organisation's coordination. Interview conducted at the Instituto Affari Internationali, Rome, October 1996.

62. Howe, G. 'The WEU: the way ahead', *NATO Review*, June 1989, p. 13.

63. Cahen, A. 'Western European Union: Birth, development and reactivation', *The Army Quarterly And Defence Journal*, October 1987, p. 394.

64. Gambles, I. *Prospects for West European Security Co-operation*, Adelphi Paper 244, Brassey's for the IISS, August 1989, p. 32.

65. Hintermann, E. 'European defence: A role for the Western European Union', *European Affairs*, Vol. 2, No. 3, Autumn 1988, p. 32.

66. Jopp, M. and Wessels, W. 'Institutional Frameworks for Security Cooperation in Western Europe: Developments and Options', in Jopp, M., Rummel, R. & Schmidt, P. (eds) op. cit. p. 33.

67. Cromwell, W. op. cit. p. 196.

3

Post Cold War to Maastricht

Introduction

The end of the Cold War presented an unprecedented opportunity for the development of a European Security and Defence Identity (ESDI). With a transformed external environment, the US preoccupied with reassessing its post-Cold War role and pressure in Europe for deeper integration, the moment appeared propitious for an ESDI to 'come of age'. The WEU would be the most likely vehicle chosen to advance this identity. Yet the enhancement of the WEU could only be achieved at the cost of encroaching upon NATO's position of primacy.

In order to develop the WEU, it had to be perceived to be capable of meeting the new demands of states. If it failed to achieve this, then there would be little point in endowing it with additional resources. In the first place, the WEU needed to develop a relationship with the European Community to complement the progress that had been achieved in economic integration. Secondly, the WEU would be required to contribute more effectively to the territorial defence of Europe. Lastly, the organisation had to be made capable of responding to crises outside of Europe. The likelihood of the WEU fulfilling these aims depended on the determination and unity of France, Germany and Britain. There was no single European country that was capable of taking a leadership role in the WEU, as the US had in NATO, and all three countries were required to be committed to the objectives. It was far from clear, however, that these aims were universally shared by the three powers and there was evidence that differences of perspective would be likely to undermine their unity of purpose.

A Changed Environment

It is beyond the remit of this book to assess the implications of the ending of the Cold War,[1] but its significance for this study lies in appreciating the depth of the transformation that took place. The foremost change was that the prospect of major inter-state war, which had dominated the European mindset for the previous four decades, was removed. No longer did the Warsaw Pact present a threat that structured the western defence debate.[2] Although a residual threat from the USSR remained, by virtue of its military power and its uncertain political orientation, a de-militarisation of west European and American policy was rendered possible. This led to growing differentiation in the way states in Europe viewed their security and to a question mark arising over the continuation of a US military presence on the continent.

Although the threat to the territorial integrity of western Europe had declined, it was recognised that a broader range of multi-directional 'risks' had taken its place; namely, conflicts that could occur in, or emanate from, neighbouring regions.[3] The end of the Cold War had heralded the emergence of a variety of weak and unstable countries in central and eastern Europe that had detached themselves from the Soviet empire.[4] The tensions were predominantly intra-state economic, ethnic and nationalist issues. They were located in countries that suffered from inadequate democratic structures and poor economic growth rates. Such tensions had often been held in abeyance by the Cold War but were liable to bubble to the surface now that superpower control was removed. This situation was further exacerbated after the breakup of the USSR in November 1991, when a large group of newly independent republics emerged, such as Ukraine, Kazakhstan, Belarus and the three Baltic states, some of whom had inherited nuclear weapons.

Not only were the security risks to the continent derived from a greater range of directions, they were also more diverse in nature. Issues such as internal security, ethnic unrest and secession, refugee movements and environmental hazards had to be included as part of the new agenda. These now stood alongside more traditional concerns, such as nuclear proliferation, the spread of ballistic missile technology and the fear of 'rogue' states gaining access to chemical and biological weapons. The inclusion of new issues reflected the fact that military matters were perceived to have decreased in salience with the end of the Cold War whilst non-military matters were now of higher prominence.[5]

The Insecurities of Britain, France and Germany

Western Europe emerged from the Cold War as a Deutschian 'security community'[6] in which the threat of war had been removed from the relationships between the member states. However, the external threat, that had encouraged defence cooperation between the west European countries and imbued them with a common purpose, had now disappeared. A variety of challenges were evident. One was to project the political stability that was enjoyed in western Europe into central and eastern Europe. Another, was to reconfigure western military forces so as to be capable of intervening in humanitarian and peacekeeping operations in regions outside of Europe. Nevertheless, in the midst of such a benign security environment, the major west European countries could be forgiven for believing that their security problems, and therefore their need to cooperate, were things of the past.

However, the hesitant and uncertain manner in which Britain, France and Germany approached the new security environment belied any sense of optimism. This was due to the fact that although the external perceptions of threat had declined, the relationship between the three powers had changed fundamentally, due to German unification. Germany had become a *status quo* power now that its enforced division was at an end but its unity reawakened many historical fears. The speed with which doubts about German dependability reemerged suggested that mistrust still lurked beneath the surface.[7] Despite having paid lip-service to the goal of unification for several decades, its sudden realisation caused allies such as France and Britain to reflect on its desirability.

The Kohl government was sensitive to the concerns of its allies. Germany was eager to have its voice heard on the international stage, but at the same time it was determined to reassure friend and former adversary alike that a united Germany was a trustworthy power. Although Kohl had chosen to abandon the caution of his Ten Point Plan and proceeded to a rapid unification of the two German states, in spite of the concerns of some neighbours, he nevertheless chose to attain his objective under the 'Two plus Four' formula.[8] In addition, he took steps to address the concerns of the Soviet Union and central European states by restating Germany's acceptance of her borders in the east and by reducing the size of the Bundeswehr to a figure of 370 000 troops.[9]

As far as Germany's European allies were concerned, the optimum strategy for reassuring them was determined to be integration.[10] Tying Germany into existing multilateral structures would ensure its self-containment and would serve to defuse tensions. It was made clear that Bonn foresaw remaining a part of NATO, whereby the military forces of its partners would remain on German territory. The European Community was also perceived to have an important role in relation to German economic power and providing a platform from which it could develop trading relationships with CEE states.

France, under President Mitterand, was an enthusiastic supporter of this policy, seeing integration to be the most appropriate way of assuaging its own concerns regarding excessive German power.[11] France was determined to preserve a balance in the relationship between the two countries and was aware that the influence it had hitherto derived from its possession of nuclear weapons was no longer of such significance now that German insecurity was at an end. Both countries agreed that through the process of integration, the strengths of Germany could be directed towards commonly acceptable objectives. It was therefore a mixture of fear and common interest which provided the momentum for post-Cold War Franco–German cooperation. 'Europeanising' the fears offered a way to overcome the bilateral tensions.

For its part, Britain shared France's concerns about the disproportionate influence that Germany could wield in Europe and expressed reservations about the path of unification.[12] Yet it parted company with both of its partners in its prescriptions for resolving this matter. The Thatcher government endorsed the prospect of Germany remaining within a variety of multilateral institutions, such as the EC, NATO, the CSCE and WEU, but it opposed the speeding up of European integration as the main instrument for constraining Germany. Any plan that moved beyond the goal of a Single Market, towards the creation of a federal European structure with competencies over all areas of national policy, was anathema to British thinking.

The WEU as the Future Defence Framework for Europe?

What was apparent at the end of the Cold War was that amidst the turbulence of events there was no consensus, or 'vision' amongst the west European states about the most appropriate security framework.[13] As a result, policy developments tended to emerge either from bargaining between the leading players or resulted from the influence of external events.[14]

Considerable initial interest was invested in the Conference on Security and Cooperation in Europe (CSCE — later renamed the OSCE), particularly by Germany and the central European countries. Its obvious attractions were its pan-European membership, its potential as a collective security rather than collective defence organisation and the breadth of issues over which it ranged.[15] With great fanfare at the Paris Summit in November 1990 an ambitious Charter ('The Charter of Paris for a New Europe') was announced that seemed to place the CSCE at the heart of Europe's security nexus, establishing institutions to deal with security problems and setting a seal of approval upon both the Conventional Armed Forces in Europe (CFE) agreement and German unification. Yet the CSCE was ill equipped to serve as the continent's principal security framework, not least because it did not enjoy the unqualified support of the major western powers, including the United States and Britain.[16] They were sceptical of its diverse membership and its consensual decision-making. It also lacked any means of enforcement and was reduced to paralysis when one of its leading powers, the Soviet Union, used force on the territories of the Baltic states in January 1991.

If the CSCE lacked the wherewithal to meet the demands of the post-Cold War environment, there were also doubts as to the suitability of NATO. By the end of the Cold War, NATO had evolved into an organisation that fulfilled a number of functions: it deterred aggression against its signatories, it legitimised the US presence on the continent and it helped to resolve numerous tensions between the member countries, such as the long-standing conflict between Greece and Turkey. There was no denying the historical contribution of the Alliance to assuring stability on the continent but, with East–West tension at an end, there was a risk of NATO becoming a victim of its own success.[17] There was now a question mark over the future relevance of the Alliance and it faced the choice of either adapting or facing redundancy. To choose to adapt would require substantial political investment from its members which could no longer be taken for granted.

Alongside the continuing utility of NATO had to be assessed the opportunity for the WEU to assume the mantle of the premier defence organisation. Despite the fact that it was starting from a modest base, writers such as Ullman[18] foresaw the potential, over a period of time, for the WEU to assume responsibility for European defence. This would have to be achieved at the expense of supplanting NATO. The extent to which this was possible depended on the WEU being capable of fulfilling key functions for the west European states. These revolved around the issues of European integration and enlargement to states in central and eastern Europe; territorial defence and extra-European intervention.

European Integration

Although the European Community had previously remained a limited foreign policy actor through the mechanism of EPC, with the demise of the Cold War many assumed that it would develop a truly common foreign policy. Such a foreign policy would then be under-girded by a defence dimension; both of which would be necessary for it to extend stability into central and eastern Europe.[19] The assumption was that European integration needed to be extended to include foreign policy and defence which had hitherto been regarded as the preserve of nation states.[20] The WEU, whose Hague Platform committed it to the goal of European unity, would provide a means of achieving a common defence within the EC. This would require European states to develop a common appreciation of their interests, to determine military responses by shared analysis and planning, to have agreed decision-making mechanisms and then be capable of drawing upon a pool of forces.

France was a particularly vigorous proponent of this viewpoint as it expected to be the major beneficiary if an ESDI was fully realised. It accorded with France's historical aspirations for Europe to be the master of its own destiny. This would only be possible with a defence structure that was separate from the US. This was sharpened by a belief that the US would eventually disengage from the continent following increasing differences of perspective in trans-Atlantic relations. France saw no reason for disproportionate US influence in the management of security issues to continue. According to the French government it was time to work towards an integrated Europe with its own defence policy, capable of drawing on forces outside the Atlantic Alliance. It was appreciated in Paris that this would demand a substantial change in France's policy of military independence but it was considered a price worth paying as it would serve two goals. Firstly, it would advance the goal of European construction, whilst secondly, it would contribute to the constraint of German power.

The Germans shared the French aim of creating a foreign, security and defence dimension within the EC.[21] The government in Bonn regarded the Community as a vital actor in projecting stability into central and eastern Europe, which was a particular priority in the German calculus. It was also deemed important in addressing the broader agenda of post-Cold War security issues.[22] In addition, there was a more self-interested German consideration. They recognised that the key to the effective exercise of their power was through the EC and that this vision could only be operationalised in conjunction with France.[23] Therefore Germany was determined to respond to some of France's priority aims regarding Europe, especially defence. Franco–German leadership was to be the hallmark of the drive for integration in Europe.

The Germans were not so naive as to fail to see that their French colleagues pursued a different agenda, one in which the expansion in the competencies of the EC would be achieved at the expense of NATO. The Kohl government rejected such an approach and remained eager to see both the EC and NATO evolve in tandem. The Germans believed that a plurality of institutions was in the interests of their country in order to minimise the risk of a renationalisation of defence policy.[24] Furthermore, there was a lingering German suspicion of French reliability in the light of the traditional emphasis of Paris upon preserving a measure of national autonomy. This rendered a narrow Paris–Bonn axis in security matters an unattractive basis for German policy.

Both Margaret Thatcher and her successor John Major, opposed an EC defence identity and argued for the WEU to be strengthened within the framework of NATO. The British viewed the EC as an inappropriate forum for defence matters, due to its lack of experience and the diversity of cultural attitudes amongst its members. The British were adamant that defence cooperation had to remain intergovernmental and its compatibility ensured with the Alliance. Britain was therefore a powerful obstacle in the way of Franco–German ambitions as they opposed both the goal of closer European integration and the use of the WEU to achieve political, rather than security, objectives.[25]

Territorial Defence

A second function that the WEU would have to be capable of contributing to was west European defence. This had traditionally been the sole preserve of NATO, under the guardianship of the United States. It was apparent that the WEU could not supplant NATO's position in the short term as its member countries lacked the requisite operational structures. The WEU, for example, was without a military command structure, a planning organisation and dedicated forces in peacetime. Furthermore, western European states had grown accustomed to relying on America for the defence of their territories and it would require a considerable change in the mindset to assume that responsibility for themselves.

That NATO would continue to fulfil a residual task of collective defence, was consequently agreed by all the allies. Even France endorsed the preservation of NATO for Article V purposes and supported continued German membership, in order to assure the greatest possible degree of stability. Paris 'was not against Atlantic solidarity, only [it] distinguished it from European continental interests'[26] and envisaged an ESDI gradually expanding its areas of responsibility. Yet there was widespread appreciation that to consign NATO to its Article V mission would be to relegate it to second class status. With the former threat having disappeared, the collective defence role was no longer a sufficient basis to justify the continuation of the Alliance. As van Eekelen noted in 1993, 'collective defence is no longer the main factor cementing Euro–US relations'.[27] The desire of countries such as France and Spain to circumscribe NATO's field of responsibility was tantamount to its marginalisation. Unless the Alliance adapted to new tasks, an alternative defence framework was likely to take its place.

The attitude of Germany towards the issue was ambivalent. The demise of the Soviet threat had enabled Bonn to undertake a reassessment of its security relationship with the US — something that had been considered sacrosanct during the Cold War.[28] Security was no longer the all-pervasive consideration it had once been in German policy and a re-balancing of its priorities led to greater emphasis on its goal of European integration. Yet it would be wrong to underestimate the continuing importance Bonn attached to the Atlantic Alliance. It was considered to remain essential for the provision of residual defence, particularly nuclear, guarantees.[29] In the eyes of the Defence Ministry, the US needed to be encouraged to stay as a central decision maker in all the security questions of the continent. In 1993 German Defence Minister Rühe declared that 'The presence of US armed forces in Europe ... remains an indispensable source of stability'.[30]

The British represented the most staunchly 'Atlanticist' position of all. They still believed that NATO, led by the US, was necessary both for defence and for providing the glue that kept the west Europeans together.[31] Without it, they anticipated a fracturing of western unity and the inability to respond to crises. The UK government was afraid that the US could be alienated by the debate over ESDI. From a selfish perspective they were concerned that the special relationship that Britain had cultivated with Washington, over issues such as nuclear sharing, intelligence information and US–European relations, would be placed in jeopardy.

Out of Area Tasks

The Out of Area mission appeared to provide a ready justification for the development of a non-NATO organisation. With conflicts more likely to occur in neighbouring regions to Europe, there was a need to be able to respond to such challenges speedily and flexibly. NATO's capacity to respond was limited because its Treaty was specific to the territories of its members.[32] It was recognised that it would be difficult to mobilise action from amongst its signatories on actions outside of Europe. In addition, the US was unlikely to share the same sense of urgency as west European states about such conflicts. This strengthened the argument for a dedicated European defence actor.

In contrast, Article VIII of the WEU's modified Brussels Treaty enabled members to consult over issues outside their territory, thereby circumventing any geographical limitations. It was declared that the organisation did not experience, 'the traditional obstacles' to a NATO extra-European role.[33] One of the arguments that was advanced for a European defence identity was the contribution it could make to extra-European operations, facilitating a greater degree of burden-sharing within the trans-Atlantic relationship.[34]

This drew widespread support, led by France who was eager to see a role for the WEU expand from this starting point. Even some countries that were hesitant about a stronger European defence role could accept an out of area mission for the WEU. Britain, for example, was willing to endorse WEU missions outside of Europe, as it accepted the need for continental states to contribute more to their security. To this end the British government was prepared to countenance the creation of a Rapid Reaction Force that would be at the disposal of both the WEU and NATO, for overseas interventionary operations.[35] The British saw this as a way of ensuring French participation in future crises. Germany was also sympathetic to an extra-European mission for the WEU. In spite of its status as the most powerful country in Europe, Germany's past had resulted in constitutional limitations on its ability to deploy military forces to overseas crises. Therefore, the prospect of developing a European multinational framework offered Germany the opportunity to be able to participate in foreign operations.[36]

However, there was to prove to be a tension between the theory and the reality. In the first military crisis to follow the end of the Cold War, a western-led coalition found itself ranged against a formidable Iraqi military machine in 1990–91.[37] Not only were forces of the adversary large, they were also experienced in battle and armed with a mixture of Soviet and French military equipment. Although the EC was able to implement sanctions against Iraq and the WEU served in a coordinating role over European naval forces,[38] the overall European contribution in the Gulf War was limited. France was embarrassed by the limited capabilities of the force it sent,[39] whilst Britain had to cannibalise their entire armoured formation in Germany in order to deploy a division in Saudi Arabia. The conflict demonstrated that post-Cold War confrontations could be sizeable affairs and in such circumstances the participation of the US would be vital. America provided much of the diplomatic expertise that sustained the coalition; the leadership on the battlefield and the greater part of the offensive military power.

Furthermore, there were other important lessons to be drawn from the crisis which illuminated the debate about the European defence identity. The conflict showed that the Europeans lacked the capabilities to project military power over long distances. They were also unable to present a unified front in the crisis, which highlighted the gap between their peacetime aspirations and what was possible during a conflict. Corbett refers to them 'scattering in all directions' once military action began.[40] Germany, for example, was constrained from participating in the coalition and had to content itself with the provision of aircraft to protect Turkish airspace.[41] At the time preoccupied with unification, Germany's major contribution took a financial form, which led to criticism of 'chequebook' support.[42] There were tensions between Britain and Belgium over the latter's unwillingness to furnish artillery ammunition[43] and France chose to pursue an independent diplomatic initiative from its allies before the war began, demonstrating a tendency for national strategies to prevail in times of tension. After the crisis was over, the British felt that the experience had injected more realism into the European debate about defence. France and Germany drew different lessons from the crisis. It confirmed their view that Europe had to be a more capable actor with a broader range of instruments at its disposal.

The Inter-governmental Conference on Political Union

The idea of an Inter-governmental Conference (IGC) on Political Union, to complement the established proposal for Economic and Monetary Union (EMU), was launched by a Franco–German letter to the President of the European Council in April 1990. It was endorsed at the EC Summit in Dublin in June 1990. The debate about foreign policy, security and defence needs to be seen as one set of issues amongst others in the lead up to the Maastricht summit. The positions adopted by the major European states on these issues were complex but reflected their appreciation of their respective post-Cold War interests. Consistent with tradition, the British were cautious and sceptical of change, whilst the French and German governments were in the vanguard of those calling for a new approach. Germany, in particular, looked upon political union, which included security and defence issues, as a way to increase its influence in Europe as well as to develop a genuine community of nations.[44]

The period leading up to the negotiation of the Treaty at Maastricht was characterised by numerous political initiatives.[45] The IGC on Political Union opened at the end of 1990 with the European Council meeting in Rome in which the French and the Germans called for the creation of a common foreign and security policy.[46] In addition, debate focused on whether the EC should seek to move towards a common defence policy which would represent a radical move forward.

In February 1991, Germany and France advanced a series of proposals in the context of the Luxembourg EC Presidency and at an Extraordinary Meeting of the WEU Council. Both countries made it clear that they envisaged the WEU becoming the defence expression of the Community until a time when the modified Brussels Treaty could be merged into the Rome Treaty. France saw this as a long term goal and, in the meantime, it wanted to see the WEU subordinated to the European Council.[47] This was nearly agreed in the WEU when it was proposed that the European Council should lay down guidelines for the organisation.[48] However, the Dutch government opposed this move on the grounds that it prejudged the decisions of the IGC and ruled out a Community dimension in foreign and security policy.[49] Nevertheless, the principle of including defence as an aim in the EC had been established and was endorsed at the Vianden meeting of the WEU in June 1991.

Under the leadership of its President Jacques Delors, the Commission injected its own views into the debate. In a lecture at the International

Institute for Strategic Studies in London,[50] Delors argued that the Gulf War had demonstrated the need for a common security policy to be constructed within the EC, but this faced strong resistance from Britain. Although acknowledging that defence and security could only be separated artificially, Delors argued that it would take some time for defence to be brought within the competence of the EC. In the interim, the WEU would serve as the EC's defence identity.

By the end of the Luxembourg Presidency of the EC in June 1991 a draft treaty was presented to the other eleven states. It was widely judged to represent a thoughtful document and was well received. It proposed the creation of a European Union which would be based upon a three pillar structure: one would be the existing EC, whilst the other two would deal with foreign policy and justice and home affairs. The pillar structure was only designed to be a temporary measure but facilitated an inter-governmental approach on foreign and defence issues, and limited the role of institutions such as the Commission and Parliament. This proposal strongly reflected the wishes of France and Britain who wished to preserve their national powers over these matters. They still considered themselves to be countries of global stature and responsibility in light of their overseas dependencies, their seats on the UN Security Council and their possession of independent nuclear deterrents.[51] This approach disappointed Germany, as well as other countries such as Belgium and Spain, who feared that the cohesion of the EC would be put at risk. Bonn argued, unsuccess-fully, for greater powers of initiative to be invested in the Commission as a form of compensation.

Holland took over the EC Presidency and presented a new draft of the Treaty in September 1991. The Dutch were unusual in that they were Atlanticist in defence terms but committed to the principle of supranational integration in other areas of policy.[52] Thus, with the support of the Commission, they attempted to revert to a single pillar structure, in order to restore the maximum degree of coherence. The Dutch argued that only an institution with a broad range of competencies could act with influence on the international stage. Yet the Dutch had succeeded in alienating all the other governments, due to their lack of consultations and their draft was rejected.[53] This was a humiliating set-back for the Hague and resulted in a return to the earlier Luxembourg draft as the basis for negotiation. With time running out, there was now a scramble to refine the details of the Treaty before it was submitted for signing by the heads of state.

Into this rather frantic series of negotiations a surprising Anglo–Italian letter was submitted in October 1991, even though these two powers had hitherto adopted different stances.[54] The British saw an opportunity to seize the initiative, whilst Italy was desirous of playing the role of arbiter between the UK, France and Germany.[55] The letter signalled that the

British were prepared to envisage a link between the WEU and the forthcoming EU, but they foresaw the former continuing as an autonomous defence actor.[56] Furthermore, a European defence policy could be considered but only on the preconditions that it be treated as a long term idea and that it should not detract from NATO. The British raised the idea of a European reaction force that would be made available to both the WEU and NATO. The force would have its own planning structures but it would detach its forces from NATO responsibilities in the event that NATO did not want to be involved in an operation. WEU Secretary-General Willem van Eekelen, had called for such a force after the experience of the 1990-91 Gulf War[57] and the Anglo–Italian letter now resurrected the idea as a way to give the WEU operational strength.

Germany and France, with Spanish support, replied with their own joint letter in mid-October. It contained three main aspects. In the first place, both countries called for the creation of a strong foreign and security policy within a newly created European Union. This policy was to be under the direction of the European Council and decisions would be made through qualified majority voting (QMV). Secondly, they pressed for a commitment to work towards a common defence policy and ultimately a common defence.[58] The WEU was to be made an integral part of the Union, and guidelines were to be laid down by the European Council. Finally, the Franco–German letter envisioned the building up of a European Armaments Agency which would be responsible for the purchase of weapons amongst the member states of the EU.

The overall effect of this document would have been to accord the WEU only a tangential relationship with NATO and place the EU on a competitive course with the Atlantic Alliance. The WEU would have lost its separate identity and would have become absorbed under the umbrella of the EU. As such, it would have been the repository for a European defence policy and, ultimately, a common defence with the involvement of supranational structures. In order to give this some operational strength, the letter proposed that the Franco–German brigade, that had been established in 1987 as a symbolic force, should be enlarged into a Corps. This was a powerful vision of the future security arrangements for the continent but it extended far beyond what Britain was prepared to accept.

Right up until the end there remained fundamental differences of viewpoint between the three major European states. The countries that lined up in support of the Franco–German approach included Spain, Belgium and Luxembourg, whilst those that were sympathetic to the British approach were the Netherlands, Portugal and Denmark. Italy attempted to reconcile the contrasting positions. As van Eekelen has noted, the Maastricht agreement owed much to the convergence facilitated by the

Anglo–Italian and Franco–German letters of October. These two proposals represented 'the two poles of the current negotiations concerning the precise arrangements for WEU's relations with the European institutions and the Atlantic Alliance'.[59] The final document reflected the bargaining that took place between principally the British and French governments.

The Maastricht Endgame

At Maastricht, the three pillar structure, which had been envisaged in the Luxembourg draft, was accepted as the architecture for the newly created European Union.[60] The second pillar was dedicated to a 'Common Foreign and Security Policy' which succeeded EPC. A distinction was drawn between security and defence issues: defence was understood to include matters related to the planning and use of military power, whilst security was to cover softer issues, such as arms procurement and disarmament. Security was considered to be a legitimate topic in the second pillar whilst defence was kept, for the time being, within the purview of the WEU.

As Ginsberg has pointed out, the agreement on CFSP represented a choice between two traditions. The first was the integrationist approach based on the 'acquis communautaire' and derived from the supranationalism of the Treaty of Rome. The other was the intergovernmental approach based on twenty years of experience of EPC.[61] The unwillingness of countries such as Britain to modify their positions ensured that the CFSP avoided 'communautarisation': rather, the European Council was given the responsibility for defining its guidelines. The EC's external trade relations were confined to the first pillar, where the powers of the Commission and the Parliament were important. The CFSP was to draw for its finances from the EC budget or, based on unanimity, from its member states.

Within the Treaty on European Union, the CFSP was framed only in the most general terms to safeguard the interests of the members, increase security, preserve peace and promote democracy (Title V, Article J.1.2). No attempt was made to define the interests of the member states more specifically.[62] Two instruments were fashioned to carry out the CFSP; Common Positions and Joint Actions. Common Positions, effectively a continuation of the practice of EPC, laid on members the obligation to consult and were designed to enable the EU to speak with a single voice, although they were not legally binding. The more ambitious instruments, Joint Actions, lay at the behest of the Council (Title V, Article J.3.1) and sought to develop the EU as a single, purposive actor. Joint Actions were to be the instruments by which policy would be implemented and could be executed by Qualified Majority Voting, once unanimous approval had been secured in the Council (Title V, Article J.3.2).[63] The results of the Treaty were criticised on the grounds that the distinction between Common Positions and Joint Actions was left vague whilst the entire edifice of the CFSP rested on the principle of unanimity.

A further issue of contention was the range of topics that lay within the authority of the CFSP and might become subject to Joint Actions. In a Declaration by the European Council it was agreed that four areas of security policy were to be included; namely, arms control, arms exports, nuclear non-proliferation and the CSCE. Once again, this demonstrated the compromise between the views of the member states and the potential for tension between institutions. Firstly, these subjects were in no way a radical departure from those that had been addressed in EPC: for example, EPC had been involved with the CSCE since the early 1970s. Secondly, these subjects stood at the interface between the Community and the WEU and risked causing overlap between the organisations.

On the subject of defence, the British government and its supporters were successful in preventing the EU becoming a defence actor because it was unable to draw directly upon military capabilities to underwrite its Joint Actions. Nevertheless, the EU was provided with a defence dimension and thereby Franco–German aspirations were addressed. This took the form of subcontracting defence issues to the WEU, which was given the task of 'elaborat[ing] and implement[ing]' actions on the Union's behalf (Title V, Article J.4.2). Where the French had wanted the European Council to have the ability to 'instruct' the WEU, all that could be agreed was for it to have the power to make 'request(s)' (Title V, Article J.4.2). Britain was to set great store, in the future, by this agreement to maintain the legal separation of the WEU from the EU.

Thus, considerable ambiguity was left over the precise form of relationship between the WEU and the European Union. The French interpreted the phrase that the WEU was to be 'an integral part of the development of the Union' (Title V, Article J.4.2) as denoting a tight linkage, which presaged the eventual absorption of the WEU into the Union. In contrast, the British viewed the relationship between the organisations in much looser terms. A further lack of clarity remained about how the WEU could seek to 'elaborate' issues for the EU that had defence implications. There was to be considerable debate in the post-Maastricht period about the correct interpretation.

Article J.4 of the Treaty stated that the CFSP would include 'the eventual framing of a common defence policy, which might in time lead to a common defence' (Title V, Article J.4.1).[64] This originated from the French letter to the Italian Presidency in December 1990,[65] and albeit vague, was highly symbolic. The British had succeeded in keeping defence separate from the CFSP in the present, but had left open the possibility for the future.

Admittedly no time scale had been agreed, but defence was now within the construct of European integration and advocates envisaged the progression from intergovernmentalism to a supranational common defence. Henceforward, it would be legitimate for countries such as France to seek to advance their agenda through a 'process involving successive phases' (Declaration on Western European Union, TEU, paragraph 1).

Whilst Britain and its supporters had compromised in accepting the WEU as an integral part of the Union, they insisted in return that the organisation should represent the 'European pillar of the Atlantic Alliance' (Declaration on WEU, Section B, paragraph 4). There were strong echoes here of British Foreign Secretary Geoffrey Howe's call, in 1987, for the WEU to become 'The arch between NATO's two pillars'.[66] The key objective became to ensure complementarity between the developing European defence identity and NATO. This was to be achieved through consultations, the synchronisation of meetings and close cooperation between the Secretariats-General of WEU and the Alliance.

The WEU emerged from the TEU, therefore, as part of the European integration process but also the embodiment of the European identity within the Alliance. Whereas the French had wanted a more distinct European structure, anchored within the EU, what resulted was an organisation straddling both approaches. This was a characteristic reflection of the WEU's experience since its revitalisation in the early 1980s. In the eyes of some it was the hoped-for kernel of an ESDI, whilst for others it was the means for the Europeans to prove their commitment to burden-sharing with the United States.

Conclusion

There were grounds for feeling both gratified and disappointed with the results of the Treaty on European Union. On one level, the Treaty had confounded those sceptics who argued that with the Cold War over, European integration would grind to a halt and would be susceptible to unravelling.[67] Even with no obvious external stimulus, the west European states had demonstrated their determination to create a Union with an unparalleled breadth of competencies. On the other hand, disappointment was also an appropriate reaction as the tortuous progress of negotiating the TEU had exposed the manifold differences of view amongst the Twelve about the Union's future as an international actor. Although the post-Cold War situation had presented an opportunity to develop a truly common foreign policy and employ the WEU as an instrument of defence integration, the chance had not been seized. Many were left with the impression that the theology of integration had outstripped the political will of the members to see it realised.

The TEU was a series of elaborate compromises, as illustrated by its ambiguous language. It succeeded in taking two important steps as far as a European defence identity was concerned. Firstly, with the creation of the European Union, the taboo over discussing defence matters, which had existed since the time of the EDC, was brought to an end. Henceforth, security and defence were treated as legitimate issues in the debate about European integration. Secondly, an expectation was raised that the EU would move towards a common defence policy and, ultimately, a common defence, even though the implications of these objectives were only poorly understood.

Beyond these two aspects, the TEU left open a debate about the evolution of the WEU, both for the ensuing period after Maastricht and for the review conference that was planned for 1996. The WEU had emerged Janus-faced from Maastricht, linked formally to the EU but simultaneously representing the European pillar within NATO. This left a fundamental question over its future development, whether it would cleave primarily to one institution or the other. The extent to which the WEU would develop in relation to the EU would be influenced by the sorts of capabilities that its members would be willing to invest in the organisation as well as the political energy devoted to the CFSP. As for its relationship with NATO, much depended on the roles that the WEU sought to fulfil. Maastricht had only set the stage for these issues to be played out and as far as the leading European countries were concerned, the prize remained to be won.

References and Notes

1. For such a study see Hyde-Price, A. *European Security Beyond the Cold War: Four Scenarios for the Year 2010*, Sage, London, 1991.

2. Buzan, B., Kelstrup, M., Lemaitre, P., Tromer, E. and Wæver, O. *The European Security Order Recast. Scenarios for the Post-Cold War Era*, Pinter, London, 1990.

3. Ifestos refers to this as a 'fluctuating aggregation of risks'. See Ifestos, P. 'The North Atlantic Alliance politics in a European context: Problems, prospects and the question of a European Political Union', in Trifunovska, S. (ed) *The Transatlantic Alliance on the Eve of the New Millenium*, Kluwer Law International, The Hague, 1996, p. 201.

4. Miall, H. (ed) *Redefining Europe: New Patterns of Conflict and Cooperation*, Pinter, London, 1994.

5. Wæver, O., Buzan, B., Kelstrup, M. and Lemaitre, P. *Identity, Migration and the New Security Agenda in Europe*, Pinter, London, 1993.

6. Deutsch, K. (et al) *Political Community and the North Atlantic Area: International Organisation in the Light of Historical Experience*, Princeton University Press, New Jersey, 1957.

7. See Stares, P. (ed) *The New Germany and the New Europe*, The Brookings Institution, Washington, 1992.

8. This ensured that the Four Occupation Powers of the United States, Russia, France and Britain played a leading role in the process.

9. See Gutjahr, L. *German Foreign and Defence Policy After Unification*, Pinter, London, 1994.

10. See Gordon, P. H. *France, Germany, and the Western Alliance*, Westview Press, Boulder, 1995.

11. Menon, A. 'Defence policy and integration in Western Europe', *Contemporary Security Policy*, Vol. 17, No. 2, August 1996, p. 267.

12. Note the infamous Thatcher seminar at Chequers which had discussed the German national character.

13. Mahncke, D. *Parameters of European Security*, Chaillot Papers 10, Institute for Security Studies of the Western European Union, Paris, September 1993, p. 10.

14. For a more detailed analysis of the interplay of external events and neo-functionalist dynamic on the defence integration process see Staden, A. van, 'After Maastricht: Explaining the movement towards a common European defence policy', in Carlsnaes, W. & Smith, S. (eds) *European Foreign Policy: The EC and Changing Perspectives in Europe*, Sage, London, 1994.

15. See, for example, Mastny, V *The Helsinki Process and the Redefining of Europe 1986-1991: Analysis and Documentation*, Pinter, London, 1992, and Cuthbertson, I. (ed) *Redefining the CSCE: Challenges and Opportunities in the New Europe*, Westview Press, Boulder, 1992.

16. See Duke, S. *The New European Security Disorder*, Macmillan, London, 1994.

17. On this theme see Sloan, S. 'NATO's future in a new Europe', *International Affairs*, Vol. 66, No. 3, July 1990.

18. Ullman, R. *Securing Europe*, Adamantine Press Limited, Twickenham, 1991.

19. Jopp, M. *The Strategic Implications of European Integration*, Adelphi Paper 290, Brassey's for the IISS, London, July 1994, p. 5.

20. This thinking derived from the concept of 'spillover' in integration from the work of Haas, E. *The Uniting of Europe: Political, Social and Economic Forces 1950-57*, Stanford, Stanford University Press, 1958. For a fuller discussion see Laursen, F. 'Explaining the Intergovernmental Conference on Political Union' in Laursen, F. & Vanhoonacker, S. (eds) *The Intergovernmental Conference on Political Union: Institutional Reforms, New Policies and International Identity of the European Community*, European Institute of Public Administration, Martin Nijhoff Publishers, Maastricht, 1992.

21. See Jopp, M., Rummel, R. and Schmidt, P. (eds) *Integration and Security in Western Europe: Inside the European Pillar*, Westview Press, Boulder, 1991.

22. Eekelen, W. van, 'Building a new European security order: WEU's contribution', *NATO Review*, Vol. 38, No. 4, August 1990, p. 19.

23. See Pond, E. 'Germany in the New Europe', *Foreign Affairs*, Vol. 71, No. 2, Spring 1992.

24. Gordon, P. H. *France, Germany, and the Western Alliance*, Westview Press, Boulder, 1995,p. 90.

25. Brenner, M. 'Multilateralism and European security', *Survival*, Vol. 35, No. 2, Summer 1993, p. 144.

26. Jones, E. 'Small countries and the Franco–German relationship' in McCarthy, P. (ed) *France-Germany 1983-1993. The Struggle to Cooperate*, Macmillan, Basingstoke, 1993. p. 116.

27. Eekelen, W. van, 'Western European Union — The European security nucleus', *NATO's Sixteen Nations*, No.3, March 1993, p. 13.

28. See, for example, Smyser, W. *Germany and America: New Identities, Fateful Rift?*, Westview Press, Boulder, 1993.

29. Kaiser, K. 'Reforming NATO', *Foreign Policy*, No. 103, Summer 1996.

30. Rühe, V. 'Shaping Euro–Atlantic policies: A grand strategy for a new era', *Survival*, Vol. 35, No. 2, Summer 1993, p. 131.

31. Bellamy, C. 'Soldier of fortune: Britain's new military role', *International Affairs*, Vol. 68, No. 3, July 1992, p. 454.

32. The North Atlantic Treaty, Washington DC, 4 April 1949, Article VI.

33. Eekelen, W. van, 'WEU and the Gulf Crisis', *Survival*, Vol. 32, No. 6, November-December 1990, p. 519.

34. Sauerwein, B. 'WEU closing in on NATO: Room for two?' *International Defence Digest*, March 1993, p. 187.

35. Birch, T. and Crotts, J. 'European defense integration: National interests, national sensitivities' in Cafruny, A. and Rosenthal, G. (eds) *The State of the European Community, Volume 2: The Maastricht Debates and Beyond*, Longman, London, 1992, p. 271.

36. Jopp, M. July 1994, op. cit. p. 9.

37. See, for example, Mathews, K. *The Gulf Conflict and International Relations*, Routledge, London, 1993.

38. The French Presidency called an extraordinary meeting of the WEU on 21 August 1990 to coordinate the response to the Iraqi invasion.

39. Heisbourg, F. 'France and the Gulf Crisis' in Gnesotto, N. & Roper, J. (eds) *Western Europe and the Gulf*, Institute for Security Studies, Western European Union, Paris, 1992, p. 17.

40. Corbett, R. 'The Intergovernmental Conference on Political Union', *Journal Of Common Market Studies*, Vol. 30, No. 3, September 1992, p. 282.

41. Salmon, T. 'Testing times for European political cooperation: The Gulf and Yugoslavia, 1990-1992', *International Affairs*, Vol. 68, No. 2, April 1992, p. 228.

42. Janning, J. 'A German Europe — a European Germany? On the debate over Germany's foreign policy', *International Affairs*, Vol. 72, No. 1, January 1996, p. 38.

43. *The Economist*, 'Europe's foreign policy: The 15 at sixes and sevens',18 May 1996, p. 47.

44. A further motivation of the German government was to convince its own people that the country had obtained a just recompense for relinquishing its strong currency, the Deutsche Mark, in return for a European common currency.

45. For details see Duff, A., Pinder, J. and Pryce, R. *Maastricht and Beyond: Building the European Union*, For the Federal Trust, Routledge, London, 1994.

46. It had been agreed that this would be a common rather than a single policy. De Schoutheete de Tervarent, P. 'The Creation of the Common Foreign and Security Policy' in Regelsberger, E., de Schoutheete de Tervarent, P. & Wessels, W. (eds) *Foreign Policy of the European Union: From EPC to CFSP and Beyond*, Lynne Reiner, London, 1997, p. 47.

47. Jopp, M. July 1994, op. cit. p. 7.

48. Bloed, A. & Wessel, R. A. (eds) *The Changing Functions of the Western European Union: Introduction and Basic Documents*, Matinus Nijhoff Publishers, Dordrecht,

1994, p. 107. I am indebted to an official in the Secretariat of the WEU Assembly for drawing this to my attention.

49.   Interviews conducted in the Dutch Ministry of Foreign Affairs, The Hague, August 1995.

50.   See Delors, J. 'European Integration and Security', *Survival*, Vol. 22, No. 2, March-April 1992.

51.   Hurd, D. 'Developing the Common Foreign and Security Policy', *International Affairs*, Vol. 70, No. 3, July 1994, p. 423.

52.   Interviews conducted in the Dutch Defence Ministry, The Hague, August 1995.

53.   Corbett, R. op. cit. p. 277.

54.   'An Anglo–Italian Declaration on European Security and Defence', 5 October 1991, reproduced in Laursen, F. & Vanhoonacker, S. (eds) op. cit. Annex, p. 414.

55.   There was also a perception in Rome that its influence in European affairs was being sidelined by the Franco–German relationship. Interviews conducted at the Institute for International Affairs, Rome, October 1996.

56.   Menon, A., Forster, A. & Wallace, W. 'A common European defence?' *Survival*, Vol. 34, No. 3, Autumn 1992, p. 109.

57.   Eekelen, W. van, November-December 1990, op. cit. p. 530.

58.   Menon, A., Forster, A. & Wallace, W. op. cit. p. 110.

59.   Eekelen, W. van, 'WEU's post-Maastricht agenda', *NATO Review*, Vol. 40, No. 2, April 1992, p. 14.

60.   The alternative that had been discussed was for a tree structure under which various subjects would be dealt with in particular 'branches'.

61.   Ginsberg, R. 'The EU's CFSP: the politics of procedure' in Holland, M. (ed) *Common Foreign and Security Policy: The Record and Reforms*, Pinter, London, 1997, p. 15.

62.   This was the subject of subsequent criticism due to its imprecision. See Federal Trust, *Security of the Union: The Intergovernmental Conference of the European Union*, Federal Trust Papers 4, London, October 1995, p. 6.

63.   For details of the voting procedures see Edwards, G. and Nuttall, S. 'Common Foreign and Security Policy' in Duff, A., Pinder, J. and Pryce, R. Duff (eds) op. cit. pp. 95-96.

64.   There was still no definition of either a 'common defence policy' or a 'common defence'. See Roper, J. 'Defining a common defence policy and common defence' in Martin, L. and Roper, J. (eds) *Towards a Common Defence Policy*, Institute for Security Studies of the Western European Union, Paris, 1995.

65.   Serre, F. de la,'The impact of Francois Mitterand' in Hill, C. (ed) *The Actors in Europe's Foreign Policy*, Routledge, London, 1996, p. 33.

66.   Quoted in Cahen, A. *The Western Union and NATO: Building a European Defence Identity Within the Context of Atlantic Solidarity*, Brassey's Atlantic Commentaries No. 2, London, 1989, p. 64.

67.   See, for example, Mearsheimer, J. 'Back to the future: Instability in Europe after the Cold War', *International Security*, Vol. 15, No. 1, Summer 1990.

4

Relations Between the WEU and the European Union

Introduction

In the spheres of foreign, security and defence policy, the TEU laid out little more than a framework for their possible development within the European Union. If the EU was to become a serious actor in these spheres then it needed to develop the relevant instruments. In order to make the Common Foreign and Security Policy workable, it required the EU members to agree upon a set of common interests that would underpin their policies. This was problematic due to the conflicting historical priorities of the leading member states. Blending these divergent interests was likely to be difficult and would be influenced by external events in the period following the signing of the TEU.

For the EU to become more than a 'civilian power' demanded the fulfilment of the common defence policy aspirations of the Treaty. This would result in the European states being less dependent on trans-Atlantic arrangements for their security and defence policies. Yet to bring a common defence policy, and eventually a common defence, to fruition required substantial new military capabilities and a more collaborative European procurement system. These would demand additional spending and considerable political will, at a time when domestic audiences were expecting a post-Cold War 'peace dividend'. Until such a policy could be realised, the WEU would serve as the defence arm of the EU. The extent to which its members were willing to invest in the WEU and build up its linkages with the EU, would act as a gauge of the seriousness of their intent.

The attainment of such goals required that Germany, France and Britain be fully committed to these objectives. The Franco–German relationship would be expected to provide the driving force towards these goals. As far as Germany was concerned, a meaningful foreign and defence identity within the EU was a necessary corollary to its political and economic goals. For France, these objectives appeared to be consistent with its long term ambitions for its role in Europe. The British attitude was less certain but would prove vital in determining the viability of the overall project.

The Development of the CFSP and a Common Defence

The most immediate task after the signing of the TEU was to develop a working relationship between the WEU and the EC. This took longer to achieve than was expected and augured badly for the more ambitious plans for cooperation. The delay reflected a number of factors. Partly it was that the roles of the two institutions were not easily disentangled: security matters lay within the remit of CFSP but defence issues were the responsibility of the WEU.[1] Partly, there was a cultural and institutional tension between them as the WEU faced the future possibility of being subsumed within the EU. For example, efforts by the European Parliament to become involved in defence issues were perceived as a threat to the autonomy of the WEU Assembly, which refused to cooperate with the Parliament.

As a result, the development of a smooth interface between the two organisations proved difficult to achieve. Despite the transfer of the WEU Council and its Secretariat from London to new offices on the Rue de la Régence in Brussels, it took time for working practices to be made compatible. The Secretary-General of the WEU was only rarely invited to the highest level meetings of the EU General Affairs Council and this tension percolated down throughout the two organisational structures. Not until 1993 was it agreed that officials from each institution could attend meetings of the other and documentation could be exchanged.

Apart from these incompatibilities, further problems were encountered in the attitude of member states towards the development of the EU's second pillar. At its most fundamental level, EU states have struggled to define foreign policy interests that they have in common. There has been an unwillingness on the part of some to transcend the intergovernmental form of cooperation that was the hallmark of EPC. The result has left the CFSP unable to fulfil expectations because states have continued to view problems through the lenses of their separate national interests, rather than developing common perspectives. This has led the CFSP to be described as a 'toothless amalgam'.[2] The CFSP units within each of the respective foreign ministries have been rendered little more than coordinators of national foreign policies.

Although the mechanisms for developing the CFSP have existed in the form of Joint Actions and Common Positions, the political will to use them has been absent.[3] Common positions have been reached on subjects such as former-Yugoslavia, and, under Article J.3, Joint Actions have been undertaken by sending election observers to Russia and South Africa and on the renewal of the nuclear Non-Proliferation Treaty (NPT). Yet these initiatives have tended to be cautious in nature, whilst other Joint Actions prepared by the European Commission have not been taken up by the Council. Sceptical states have proved unwilling to extend the coverage of majority voting beyond existing areas and the power of national vetoes has been preserved. The TEU gave the WEU authority to carry out Joint Actions but this has not been used, resulting in the absence of meaningful EU-WEU cooperative action.

The minimal progress achieved in CFSP has rendered it all the more difficult to move towards a common defence policy. According to Jopp, the identification of shared security interests could only take place over a long period of time and would require governments to regard Europe as 'an entity, whether individual interests always coincide or not'[4]. Yet there has been resistance to all but the most elementary progress in this area.[5] The UK, in particular, was hostile to the very concept of a common defence and used the vagueness of the Treaty language to obstruct any advance. The British were determined to retain sovereignty over defence matters and were unconvinced by the argument that a common policy would draw together Europe's separate national capabilities. They contended that without the US providing leadership, Europe would be condemned to inertia in a crisis. In addition, they feared that if momentum built up behind a European defence policy, it would eventually encroach on NATO's Article V responsibilities . This was confirmed by van Eekelen's admission in June 1992, that he did not want the WEU to be 'relegated to an Out of Area role only'.[6] Britain was resolutely opposed to WEU seeking to fulfil a territorial defence role.

As a result, there was little progress in defining an EU common defence policy. Not until the WEU Noordwijk meeting was a conceptual document on a common defence policy submitted for discussion.[7] Such a policy was only deemed to be possible 'in the years to come'[8] Nevertheless, agreement was reached on establishing a 'Common Reflection' group which would explore the sense of shared objectives amongst the European states and their perceptions of threat. This was designed to mirror the work of the EU's Westendorp Reflection Group for the 1996 Intergovernmental Conference. The first report sought to set out the common interests on which such a defence policy could be based, whilst the second was tasked to recommend a course of action.[9] Progress was very slow and proceeded right up until the 1995 Madrid meeting of the WEU Council of Ministers.

It was evident that fundamental disagreements remained over security and defence issues, frustrating the desire of the French to move to the publication of a European Defence White Paper. The problem was expressed lucidly by a former French Defence Minister, Francois Leotard: 'The common European vision of defence matters is slow to take shape. The only missing ingredient is the commitment at the highest political level that alone can give the desired impetus to the wish for a European defence identity'.[10]

The absence of agreement over the building blocks of a European defence policy meant that debate never reached more complex issues. Yet lurking in the background was the issue of nuclear deterrence, for if Europe had made progress towards a common defence policy, then it would have raised the question of a nuclear guarantee. Ostensibly, such an issue would have concerned only the two nuclear powers of France and the UK, but in reality the matter was pertinent to all continental states. Britain and France might have been expected to serve as the nuclear custodians for their allies, which, in the light of the paucity of post-Cold War threats was arguably more credible than ever before.

There had been a long standing French interest in the concept of a European nuclear force as they perceived correctly that this would present the ultimate challenge for a common European defence. Although Paris had seen it as premature to conduct nuclear consultations within a multilateral forum such as the WEU, numerous leaders had made reference to the desirability of an intra-European dialogue on the role of nuclear forces.[11] The French also instituted regular meetings with their British counterparts[12] and in 1990 Prime Minister Beregovoy suggested that Britain and France might move towards a common nuclear concept which could be offered to their European partners.[13] In 1993, the two countries chose to formalise their dialogue by establishing an 'Anglo–French Joint Commission on Nuclear Policy and Doctrine'.

Yet there were formidable obstacles to be overcome if a European nuclear policy was to be anything more than rhetoric. Just as European countries disagreed about their security interests, so there were differences of view between the nuclear and non-nuclear states. France would have had to reverse its cherished attitude that nuclear weapons could only be used for national deterrent purposes, whilst Britain would have been forced to reassess its special bilateral relationship with the US. As for the non-nuclear states, Germany would have been reluctant to sacrifice a trusted guarantee provided by the United States for a much smaller one provided by France and Britain. Although Germany had agreed at the Nuremberg Summit to conduct with France a 'dialogue on the role of nuclear deterrence in the framework of the European defence policy', this was a long way from relinquishing US protection.[14] In addition, adding a nuclear dimension to a European defence policy would be likely to increase the discomfort of neutral members within the EU. Hence, all these factors militated against the possibility of a common defence policy being agreed.[15]

Enhancing the Military Capabilities of the WEU

It was unrealistic to expect that a meaningful European defence capability could be created without building up the military resources of the WEU. At the time of Maastricht, the WEU was still largely a paper organisation. It lacked military forces that it could call upon in a crisis, its military doctrine was that of NATO, it was without the infrastructure to enable it to project power overseas and it was without a command and planning organisation. Britain, France and Germany endorsed the idea of enhancing the capabilities of the WEU in order to make it more operationally capable. France saw this as an opportunity to place real defence choices at the disposal of the European Union. Even the British government was supportive of a task-based approach as it shifted attention away from theological debates about competing security architectures.[16] The British were willing to increase the operational effectiveness of the WEU as long as this did not conflict with NATO.

The first practical step was the creation of a Planning Cell in Brussels, which was made operational in April 1993 under the directorship of an Italian Major General. This was an important development as it gave the organisation its own planning capability for the first time, able to synthesise the profusion of national ideas. France and Britain had differed over the Planning Cell, France had wanted a larger structure whilst Britain wanted it closely linked to NATO. Under parameters laid down by the Council, its task was to prepare for a wide variety of situations. In the event of an actual crisis, it would be necessary to appoint a Force Commander from one of the troop contributing countries to develop a plan to suit the specific needs of the situation.[17] Plans laid down within the Cell were therefore generic in nature, in order to avoid the danger of upsetting national sensitivities. Subsequently, the Planning Cell was complemented by the creation of a Situation Centre,[18] that provided a twenty-four hour monitoring facility for regional crises; an Intelligence Section and a Military Committee, that represented the Chiefs of Staff and improved the military decision-making within the WEU.[19]

However, the command capabilities of the WEU remained weak in spite of the improvements that were made. It still lacked the Integrated Military Structure of NATO and its Planning Cell was pitifully small, comprising less than 50 people. With such a limited staff, WEU remained heavily dependent upon inputs from its member governments, which circumscribed its autonomy of action. It was envisaged that in certain types of operations individual states would be accorded responsibility for managing a task and the WEU would act only in a coordination capacity. In the absence of an agreed European defence policy, the WEU was consigned to operate within a political vacuum, unsure of the types of activities in which the member states would participate.

The Europeans were reluctant to create new forces for their infant defence structure. Due to pressure for post-Cold War defence savings, there was little prospect of additional resources being forthcoming. British forces, for example, suffered large reductions in personnel after 1990 and the strength of the Army fell from 150 000 to 111 000.[20] The British were prepared only to 'dual-hat' existing forces: they would remain integral to the Alliance but be detachable for WEU purposes. This contrasted with the views of France who wanted WEU-specific forces to be assigned. In June 1992, the concept of 'Forces Answerable to WEU' (FAWEU) was launched by which states declared those units that they would make available to the organisation in a crisis. Britain declared the UK/Netherlands Amphibious Force and elements within the NATO Multinational Division (Central) as available for WEU tasking. It supported giving the WEU Planning Cell the responsibility for assembling packages of forces for specific types of operations.

Fiscal and personnel constraints were also in evidence in the armed services of Germany. The Kohl government faced both external and domestic political pressure to reduce the size of the Bundeswehr, as part of the unification process. Reductions in its military establishment led to the creation of new multinational formations, such as the German-Dutch Combined Corps.[21] But the Germans drew back from the widely pursued policy on the continent of ending conscription and moving to smaller, professional armed forces. This reflected their attachment to the legitimising concept of a citizens army.[22]

However, where the Germans were willing to act, in contrast to the British, was in the setting up of a new structure for European defence with France. In May 1992, at their summit meeting at La Rochelle, President Mitterand and Chancellor Kohl announced the establishment of the Franco–German Corps that was later retitled the 'EuroCorps'. This was to comprise a force of about 50 000 troops, based in Strasbourg. At the outset, it was seen as having a European, rather than a trans-Atlantic, vocation which resonated with the French vision of assembling alternative defence and command structures to NATO. With a multinational headquarters, it offered a military capability to the WEU for operations both in and outside of Europe. German Defence Minister Volker Rühe said it represented, 'The first elements of a future European armed force'.[23] Although created as part of a bilateral initiative, it was subsequently opened to Belgium, Spain and Luxembourg.

Yet the genesis of the EuroCorps was more complicated than just an attempt to set up a symbolic European Army. Germany argued that the EuroCorps offered a means to tie France into collaborative defence arrangements and away from its long-held position of independence. After President Mitterand had threatened in September 1990 to remove the entire French Second Army from German soil within four years, the EuroCorps ensured a continuing French presence and in turn facilitated a token German force on French territory.[24] Germany was insistent that its role in EuroCorps should not be interpreted by its allies as a radical policy change away from NATO. It claimed to see no incompatibility between preserving the Atlantic Alliance and strengthening the WEU. However, the German government could not fail to be aware that other allies, such as Britain and the United States, feared that the establishment of a separate European defence structure was inherently threatening to trans-Atlantic stability.[25] It confirmed their suspicions that France was seeking to lure Germany into rival structures that were designed to undermine NATO.

Such reactions exaggerated the significance of the EuroCorps but they resulted in stern rebukes from London and Washington.[26] These were focused particularly upon Bonn, and warned of the likely damage to US-European relations. Frictions were also evident in relation to other European countries, even those sympathetic to a stronger European defence identity. Italy, for example, was displeased at what it perceived as a Franco–German bid for leadership in Europe and was wary at the prospect of its own exclusion.[27] Germany had demonstrably failed to convince its allies of the wisdom of the EuroCorps idea. An agreement was duly negotiated in January 1993 between France, Germany and the NATO SACEUR, General Shalikashvili that reconciled the key area of tension. It made it possible, in a time of emergency, for the EuroCorps to be tasked by the Supreme Commander, as well as being available for independent operations under the WEU. This reassured Germany's allies of the compatibility of Bonn's Euro–Atlantic policies. Ironically, the EuroCorps initiative had the effect of bringing the French closer to NATO as there was now a recognised mechanism by which SACEUR could request the use of French troops in a crisis.

France was the only country out of the three that was willing to make available extra defence resources for the WEU and the European Union. After the end of the Cold War, France rejected the opportunity to reduce its defence spending and actually achieved small annual increases. It strove to generate the sorts of defence capabilities that would enhance European independence.[28] In cooperation with Italy and Spain, the French government prioritised the provision of the Helios I optical satellite intelligence system. It proceeded to press the German government to join successor programmes, such as the Helios II and Horus radar observation satellite programmes, but Bonn continued to express reservations.[29] Not until their 'Common Strategic Concept' was signed at Nuremberg did both France and Germany acknowledge that an independent strategic intelligence capability would be required by their countries.[30] France was also a leading supporter of the establishment of the WEU's own satellite interpretation centre at Torrejon in Spain which draws on commercially available data from SPOT, LANDSAT and ERS systems.

As well as its founding role in the EuroCorps, France participated in specifically European military initiatives that were focused upon the Mediterranean region. In May 1995, France, Spain, Portugal and Italy signed documents that created EUROFOR, a land force comprised of several earmarked brigades. The headquarters of EUROFOR was established in Florence, and the force was designed to provide a rapid reaction capability in the northern Mediterranean, that was at the disposal of the WEU.[31] A complementary naval force, EUROMARFOR, with dedicated amphibious capabilities and air support was also created by these states at the same time. Like its ground-based equivalent, the EUROMARFOR was set up with the emphasis on the rapid projection of military force.

Yet even France had to come to accept that its ambitions for a European defence were not going to be fulfilled. With only the contingent support of Germany, and in the face of the direct opposition of Britain, the French came to accept that their vision could not be realised. Even a Franco–German axis would have been insufficient, principally because Germany continued to reside under self-imposed limitations on its capacity for overseas military involvement, as exemplified during the Gulf War. Germany remained the most reluctant state to resort to the use of force in crisis management and Gordon has drawn attention to the different strategic cultures between the two countries, one built on parochialism whilst the other under-girded by a global approach.[32] Despite the evidence that German attitudes were changing[33] and the willingness of leading political figures, such as Defence Minister Rühe and Foreign Minister Kinkel, to call for Germany to play a role more commensurate with its power;[34] this would be an insufficient basis for a European defence. In recognition of the inevitable, France announced major cuts in the size and the expenditure of its military forces in 1996 and a switch to a professional army.

Operational Tasks

The unwillingness of European states to invest greater military capabilities in the WEU helped to determine the type of operational roles that it could undertake. Without large forces at its disposal and in the absence of aerial[35] and sea-based heavy lift capabilities and logistical support, there was little point in the WEU planning to conduct high-intensity warfare overseas. The Gulf War had provided hard lessons about the future of warfare: that battlefields could be in distant theatres, that expensive precision-guided weapons would offer a qualitative edge and that victory was likely to go to the side with the superior observation and intelligence systems.[36] This accorded with early British thinking that future WEU operations would be relatively small in scale. One UK Ministry of Defence official estimated that the WEU could run no more than a brigade sized operation by 1996.[37] As a result, the emphasis was placed upon low-intensity, out of area crises. In so doing, the WEU moved away from the kinds of roles for which it was envisaged in the 1950s, showing how far its operational context had changed.

In the Petersberg Declaration of June 1992, the WEU laid out three categories of tasks, in addition to its historical Article V mission. These were humanitarian operations, peacekeeping and the employment of combat forces in crisis management, including peacemaking.[38] These tasks could either be undertaken at the request of the EU or by a unanimous decision of the member states. The WEU would be likely to need a broader mandate if an operation involved the deployment of its members' forces outside their territories and it offered to act on behalf of the CSCE and the United Nations.

The vagueness of some of these tasks meant that there would be practical problems in defining their limits. For example, at one end of the spectrum, humanitarian assistance could involve the evacuation of European nationals, by a small covering force, from a civil war situation; or assistance to a country suffering from a natural disaster. Yet at the other end of the spectrum, it could amount to the distribution of essential supplies by a heavily armed WEU force in the midst a large-scale conflict. Domestic public pressure could lead European governments to become embroiled in conflicts even when their militaries might be counselling caution. There was a danger that the WEU's desire to secure a role for itself alongside established institutions like NATO could result in it becoming a dustbin for those missions that other organisations wished to avoid.

It was decided that the WEU would begin by planning for humanitarian missions on the grounds that these were the most likely operations to occur and that they lay within the capabilities of the European states to undertake. The first WEU exercise, code named 'Ardente', took place in October 1993 and was focused on a humanitarian scenario in which nationals were evacuated and a corridor for relief supplies was established.[39] At the Lisbon meeting of the WEU in May 1995, the parameters for this type of operation were laid out in a document entitled 'Emergency Responses to Humanitarian Crises: a Role for a WEU

Humanitarian Task Force'.[40] The Italians and the British then undertook much of the detailed work on the concept, determining the circumstances in which the WEU would get involved and the likely interfaces with relevant civil agencies.

Peacekeeping was seen as a more ambitious task for the WEU, one that could demand the investment of considerable military resources. The theory of peacekeeping presumes a policing function, with the approval of both combatants, at a time when they have either decided to stop fighting or have reached a state of exhaustion.[41] Yet with the kinds of crises that could occur in the world, lines of distinction could become blurred and the inter-positioning force could become drawn into the conflict. In the face of this possibility, it might be necessary for the WEU to maintain heavy forces in the theatre in case the peace breaks down and the forces need to fight their way out of the situation.

In a speech on peacekeeping to the Belgian Institute of International Relations, van Eekelen floated four different ways in which the WEU could become involved. In its most direct form, the WEU could act either alone or in concert with another organisation. A third permutation might be for the WEU to serve as a command centre for members operating as an informal coalition, perhaps in conjunction with non-members. The last option would be to coordinate members acting in a UN-mandated operation. Peacekeeping tasks had traditionally been carried out by the UN, but the profusion of post-Cold War crises has increased the likelihood of the UN or OSCE requesting a security organisation to act on their behalf. If a task required peacekeeping duties to be conducted on the territory of a former Soviet republic, it is possible that a WEU force might be perceived as less sensitive by Russia than a NATO-led operation.[42]

The last of the categories that were laid down at Petersberg were crisis management tasks that could be linked to peacemaking. These were the least easily definable of the military tasks. However, it represented an important signal by the WEU as it acknowledged its aspiration to act in situations that could demand the controlled use of force. In a potential scenario, the WEU could be called upon to impose peace upon warring factions. This reinforces the need for the WEU to be able to call upon highly trained, professional armed forces from amongst its members that could operate in politically and militarily demanding environments. At the Birmingham Council meeting in May 1996, the French Defence Minister Charles Millon discussed two ways in which the WEU could be mobilised for a crisis management task: either the members acting independently under the banner of the WEU or acting with material support from the Atlantic Alliance.[43]

In attempting to create planning structures, delineate forces and define likely missions, the WEU was experiencing its early operational development. This was a European actor that was attempting to carve out a role for itself, albeit in the face of disagreements amongst its leading members. Had the security environment of Europe been more benign, then there might have been a chance for the WEU to have developed its limited roles to a fuller extent. However, this was not to be the case. Instead, the west European states found themselves facing a security crisis in former-Yugoslavia that was to rob the WEU of its nascent credibility.

The WEU and the Yugoslavia Crisis

The conflict in former-Yugoslavia served to highlight the inability of western Europe to manage a crisis in a neighbouring region. It dealt a severe blow to the development of a security and defence identity because it belied the ambitious rhetoric of the CFSP and exposed the hollowness of European military capabilities. Furthermore, it demonstrated their lack of unity in the absence of American leadership.

The conflict, which came to focus on the ethnically complex region of Bosnia-Hercegovina, became a vicious civil war in which external parties, such as the Serbs, provided military support to their brethren in Bosnia.[44] Although the west Europeans were engrossed in their own institutional wrangles over the IGC, there was a body of elite opinion which regarded the crisis as an opportunity to demonstrate their new-found unity. As a result, the European Community, despite the fact that the CFSP was not yet ratified, took upon itself responsibility for trying to resolve the crisis. When it became apparent that the use of economic instruments would be insufficient to halt the fighting, the member states fell back upon the exercise of diplomatic influence and mediation. The EC chose to sponsor a Peace Conference in the Hague and appointed a British former Foreign Secretary and Secretary-General of NATO, Peter Carrington, to broker a series of cease-fires that were broken almost as soon as they were made. The inherent weakness of the Community's position began to emerge as member states differed in their prescriptions for resolving the crisis and over their willingness to use force.

An early argument for European military intervention was championed by France's Foreign Minister, Roland Dumas, in August 1991, before the conflict had spread to Bosnia. He called for a WEU inter-position force, of about 30 000 troops, to be sent to eastern Croatia to police a cease-fire, provided that one could be made to hold. This was clearly an attempt to place the WEU at the forefront of the crisis. The WEU met in London in the first week of August to discuss the idea and support was forthcoming from Italy and Germany. Britain, on the other hand, was opposed to intervention because it feared being dragged into a complex conflict from which it would become progressively more difficult to extricate itself.[45]

The British were also reluctant to see the WEU execute a mission that might increase its prestige at the expense of NATO — particularly in the sensitive period leading up to the Maastricht Summit.

The debate about intervention was reopened in September after President Mitterand had met with Chancellor Kohl in Berlin.[46] France and Germany jointly requested a reappraisal of the situation and the EC Foreign Ministers asked the WEU to assess the feasibility of sending a military force to support the role of EC monitors on the ground. At a WEU meeting at the end of September a series of proposals that had been made by the WEU were considered. These ranged from the provision of logistic support to the EC monitors, right up to a large-scale peacekeeping force.[47] France, Italy, Belgium and the Netherlands argued for a more capable military force to be despatched to the region but there was an absence of consensus amongst the other members. The issue was confined to political discussion as there never proved to be a peace to implement, but if a cease-fire had been accepted, then there was some support for a WEU policing force. Shortly afterwards, the focus of activity moved to the United Nations and France and Britain provided their contributions to humanitarian assistance under its mandate.[48]

The argument about a WEU peacekeeping force and the subsequent controversy regarding the European provision of humanitarian relief, highlighted the different governmental approaches to the crisis. The core of the problem was that European countries still perceived themselves to possess differing interests and the CFSP was incapable of concerting attitudes. Germany, for example, was willing to press for the recognition of states in the region even though its allies and the US were opposed. This created an impression of weakness: the EU was unable to speak with one voice and it lacked the political will to task the WEU.

Britain remained the state most wary of embroiling itself in the conflict in Bosnia, even though, along with France, it was the largest contributor of troops to the UN humanitarian operation. Neither Britain nor France foresaw a military solution to the crisis and were afraid of their personnel becoming combatants in the conflict. Other countries, such as the Netherlands and Germany, periodically expressed disappointment with the British approach as they felt outraged by the 'ethnic cleansing' policies of the Bosnian Serbs. Yet the British were aware that a more confrontational policy would result in the onus of effort being placed on the French and themselves. Although Germany accepted a disproportionately high number of refugees, its historical linkage with the region precluded it from military participation. With the benefit of hindsight it would appear that the decision to act only with the consent of the warring factions was the correct one. Until a major change in the balance of the war had occurred, a more forceful western intervention would have led to the termination of its humanitarian mission and lay beyond the military capabilities of the Europeans to undertake.

In the event the WEU was accorded only minor tasks during the crisis. Although there were calls for its role to be expanded,[49] its lack of military strength, operational experience and absence of detailed plans, made it incapable of acting even if the political will had been forthcoming. The WEU undertook only two missions: the enforcement of the UN-mandated embargo on economic goods and arms (Security Council resolutions 713 and 757) and assistance to the EU in the administration of a Bosnian city.

The embargo mission was divided into two parts, an Adriatic task force and a presence on the River Danube. In the former case, in July 1992 under Italian direction, the WEU began its monitoring of compliance with UN resolutions. In November the WEU expanded its operation, under the title 'Sharp Fence', to enforce the embargo. This was conducted in parallel with a NATO force and the absurdity of two naval forces from many of the same nations acting in competition undermined the rhetoric that they were 'interlocking institutions'. In July of the following year a joint session of the WEU Council and the NATO North Atlantic Council (NAC) agreed to a combined enforcement that became known as 'Operation Sharp Guard'. To facilitate this a WEU contingent was placed inside NATO's Southern Command in Naples.[50] This enforcement operation continued throughout the rest of the conflict until October 1996.

The Danube operation was exclusively the responsibility of the WEU. It was a police and customs support operation, aimed to assist the efforts of Bulgaria, Hungary and Romania to implement the UN embargo. The WEU assisted in establishing two control centres in Mohacs, Hungary and in Ruse, Bulgaria and then contributed 250 personnel and a force of seven patrol vessels.[51] The detailed negotiations on the Memorandums of Understanding were effected under the Italian Presidency of the WEU[52] and were signed in Rome at the meeting of WEU Foreign and Defence Ministers in May 1993.[53]

In the case of the EU's activities in Bosnia, a request for assistance was made, under Article J.4.2, to the WEU over the divided city of Mostar. This involved the provision of a police contingent to train the Croat and Muslim populations in the principles of joint policing. Seven out of the nine WEU states (plus a further 5 other countries) contributed a total force of 181 police officers who then operated in the city under the authority of its EU appointed Administrator. The exercise was of limited value due to the intense animosities that persisted between the two communities, something that the WEU force proved to be incapable of overcoming. It was mooted that a larger WEU police contingent should be despatched to Bosnia as part of the Dayton Accords but this proposal never materialised.

From a positive perspective, these operations demonstrated the flexibility of the WEU and its capacity to adapt to unconventional missions. In the case of Mostar, for instance, the mission was of a hybrid nature, lying at the interface between civilian and military tasks. However, from a negative perspective, these missions demonstrated the organisation's limited role. After the end of 1993, beyond its existing tasks, the WEU played no part in resolving the conflict. When the western countries intervened decisively in Bosnia in the summer of 1995, using aerial bombardment to compel the Bosnian Serbs to the negotiating table, the WEU was not involved. This action had been preceded by the despatch of a European Rapid Reaction Force (RRF) to Bosnia, consisting of two brigades of French, British and Dutch troops, but the WEU was involved neither in the assembling nor the oversight of the force.[54] The RRF was treated as a contribution to a NATO operation and the Western Alliance was accorded sole responsibility for prosecuting the military effort against the Bosnian Serbs.

To some analysts, the experience of Bosnia appeared to prove that any European initiative was doomed to failure. The Europeans did indeed lack resolve during the conflict[55] but this alone does not account for the inability to end the war. From 1991 to the end of 1994 it was apparent that no country, or group of countries, possessed the political will to intervene with decisive levels of force. Both the Bush and Clinton Administrations had made clear their desire to stand apart from the conflict, fearing that they could be drawn in to a Balkan quagmire, and were unable to identify either clear objectives or a rapid means of escape. It would therefore be overly simplistic to conclude that Europe's failure in Bosnia negated the argument for an ESDI based around the WEU. Nevertheless, Bosnia demonstrated that such a capability was still in its infancy.

A European Armaments Agency

Whilst the areas of operational capabilities and missions have often enjoyed high salience in the European defence debate, the issue of armaments cooperation has tended to be accorded a Cinderella status. This is ironic for two reasons. Firstly, the modified Brussels Treaty, from the outset, affirmed its objective as developing collaboration and standardisation in military production.[56] Secondly, it has been appreciated that weapons collaboration could provide a useful motivator of closer European integration. The idea of using a common armaments policy as the driving force behind ESDI was explicitly raised by EU Commissioner Hans van den Broek in October 1996.[57]

Apart from monitoring German military production, the WEU never developed a role as a promoter of defence industrial cooperation during the Cold War. Neither was this seen as a legitimate task for the European Community which was excluded from the arms market by Article 223 of the Treaty of Rome, which protected domestic arms industries. In the event, arms collaboration was channelled through the IEPG (see Chapters One and Two) and the Committee of National Armaments Directors (CNAD) in NATO. Past emphasis was upon making European cooperation compatible with a trans-Atlantic 'Two-Way Street' in defence goods.[58]

However, following the end of the Cold War, the attractions of improving armaments collaboration were considerable. In the first place, industrial cooperation promised to assist both in the creation of a European single market by 1992 and in laying the foundations of a common European defence policy. Secondly, with the pressure of falling defence spending, national markets were recognised to be too small for efficient production. For example, a 1992 Commission Report estimated that up to 17% of EU countries' spending on weapons projects could be saved by more effective collaboration.[59] This seemed to offer the only way of keeping up with the US, particularly in high technology research.[60] Major defence companies across Europe had already arrived at the same conclusion and were amalgamating, sometimes on a trans-national basis, at a speed that governments found difficult to control.[61] This placed European companies in a stronger position to face their giant American counterparts.

Maastricht was viewed by France and Germany, amongst others, as an opportunity to advance the cause of weapons collaboration, linking the WEU with the European Union. In the Declaration on the WEU that accompanied the Treaty, it was declared that cooperation in the sphere of armaments would be increased 'with the aim of creating a European armaments agency' (Declaration on the WEU, Treaty on European Union, Section C). Such an agency had long been called for and was a key element in the recommendations of the 1975 Tindermans Report.[62] This led in December 1992 to the West European Armaments Group (WEAG) subsuming the functions and the membership (the ten WEU states plus Denmark, Turkey and Norway) of the IEPG. This was not a controversial development in the eyes of Alliance members because it had always been ensured that the IEPG was compatible with NATO. Although the WEAG was closely aligned to the WEU it still fell short of the model of a dedicated European armaments agency that had been envisaged in the TEU.

Although the environment for collaboration appeared to have become more conducive, significant obstacles remained. There were still tensions between achieving greater efficiency in arms production and the desire to protect national defence industries, due to employment and technological considerations.[63] Even when joint projects were created, they did not necessarily lead to the optimum use of resources. Instead, the principle of *juste retour* remained in which states were guaranteed specific proportions of work, regardless of cost effectiveness.[64] The Panavia Tornado consortium provided an historical example; it suffered from enormous cost escalation and time delays. Similar problems have been experienced in the Eurofighter project involving Britain, Germany, Italy and Spain. Compromises in operational requirements have occurred as states have wanted the aircraft to be capable of fulfilling different roles, thereby adding to the complexity of the project.

Countries also differed over their approaches to the arms collaboration issue. Britain was suspicious of using defence industrial policy as a vehicle for closer European integration and opposed Commission involvement. Yet Britain was at the forefront of those willing to open up their markets to foreign competition and it had encouraged its own defence companies to restructure and merge in the face of a more competitive environment.[65] France and Germany were sympathetic to the ultimate goal of bringing the arms issue within the EU. Yet France, with its emphasis on national autonomy, kept its own defence market closed until 1995 and heavily subsidised domestic manufacturers. The anomalies caused by this French policy meant that its nationalised defence companies did not have to compete on equal terms. These and other problems demonstrated that the WEAG approach was not going to succeed in stimulating further cooperation. Attempting to negotiate amongst 13 member governments produced only deadlock.[66]

In the light of this paralysis, the WEU chose at the Ostend meeting in November 1996 to create a Western European Armaments Organisation (WEAO) as an executive part of the WEAG.[67] This decision was designed to press forward with cooperation until a Europe-wide arms agency could be established. However, an alternative approach, that attempted to seize the agenda, was evident from France and Germany, who began a bilateral initiative within the Brussels Treaty framework, that was entitled the 'Joint Armaments Cooperation Structure' (JACS). These two countries committed themselves to a 'common industrial strategy'.[68] The JACS was made open to other states and was joined, in November 1996 by Britain and Italy, while the Netherlands and Belgium indicated their interest. This represented an attempt to achieve cooperation through more *ad hoc* mechanisms rather than waiting for all states to agree.

In the field of weapons collaboration as in others, the 1990s has witnessed a failure to fulfil the grand ambitions that were conceived at the outset. Admittedly, this sphere has presented difficulties because it touches upon important economic and social policy areas for governments. Nevertheless, the tortuous progress of establishing a European armaments agency has proved the enduring nature of specifically national priorities.

Conclusion

The EU–WEU nexus contributed to the prevention of a renationalisation of defence in Europe and assisted in the stabilisation of the continent. Yet there has been a failure to realise the goals that were embodied in the TEU. Efforts to build the WEU into a organisation that could be tasked by the EU to conduct independent military operations have made little progress. No common defence policy has been agreed and the forces available could conduct only limited missions. The decision not to duplicate the existing NATO military structure has left the WEU without an independent command capability and there has been only desultory progress in forging a European arms procurement system.

Furthermore, a disjunction emerged between the expectations of the WEU by some of its members and the reality of external events. The Bosnian crisis injected a heavy dose of realism into the situation and Europe's defence identity was judged by what it achieved, rather than what it represented.[69] Whereas earlier crises in the EPC era had tended to stimulate deeper cooperation, Bosnia highlighted the brittle nature of CFSP and the inadequate strength of the WEU. The CFSP was recognised to have papered over the differing perceptions of interest amongst its members. The WEU's involvement in the crisis was to carry out quasi-police roles which were far removed from the 'peacemaking' rhetoric of the Petersberg Declaration.

The reasons for the disappointing WEU–EU relationship lay in the complex interactions between the three main powers. The Franco–German partnership acted as the main motivating force towards a stronger ESDI and Paris was willing to generate extra defence to realise its objective. Yet these two countries were unable to achieve an ESDI alone and bilateral tensions constrained their effectiveness. Germany regarded closer European foreign and defence cooperation as a desirable complement to economic and political integration, but it was unwilling to pursue these goals at the cost of its US–NATO relationship. Britain frustrated the efforts of its two partners because of its attachment to sovereignty and its adherence to the Atlantic Alliance. In view of its importance as a military power and its ability to wield a veto within the WEU and the EU, British opposition placed a straight-jacket around institutional developments. Continental allies were right to point out that the UK approach condemned the WEU to a peripheral role in the continent's security.

References and Notes

1. A new directorate, DG1A, was set up inside the European Commission to oversee the CFSP.

2. Federal Trust, *Security of the Union: The Intergovernmental Conference of the European Union*, Federal Trust Papers 4, London, October 1995, p. 5.

3. Broek, H. van den, 'The Common Foreign and Security Policy in the context of the 1996 Intergovernmental Conference', *Studia Diplomatica*, Vol. XLVIII, No. 4, 1995, p. 31.

4. Jopp, M. *The Strategic Implications of European Integration*, Adelphi Paper 290, Brassey's for the IISS, London, July 1994, p. 62.

5. WEU Assembly Report, Rapporteur Mr Soell, 'A European Security Policy', Document 1439, 10 November 1994, p. 33.

6. WEU Assembly Proceedings, 38th ordinary Session (First Part) 'Minutes of Official Reports of Debates', June 1992, p. 61.

7. WEU Council of Ministers, Noordwijk Declaration, 14 November 1994.

8. Ibid, paragraph 5.

9. Cutileiro, J. 'WEU's operational development and its relationship to NATO', *NATO Review*, Vol. 43, No. 5, September 1995, p. 10.

10. Speech in Paris to the European Movement, quoted in WEU Assembly Report, Rapporteur Mr Baumel, 'The Evolution of NATO and its Consequences for WEU', Document 1410, 23 March 1994, p. 22.

11. Mitterand referred to the idea in January 1992 as noted by Boyer, Y. 'France and the new security order', in Schmidt, P. (ed) *In the Midst of Change: On the Development of West European Security and Defence Cooperation*, Nomos Verlagsgesellschaft, Baden-Baden, 1992, p. 28. Also, Chirac raised the issue in 1996. See Agence Europe, No. 6745, 10-11 June 1996, p. 4.

12. Croft, S. 'European integration, nuclear deterrence and Franco–British nuclear cooperation', *International Affairs*, Vol. 72, No. 4, October 1996, pp. 770-780.

13. See Yost, D. 'France's nuclear dilemmas', *Foreign Affairs*, Vol. 75, No. 1, January-February 1996.

14. This emerged as the 'Common Strategic Concept' of December 1996, cited in Agence Europe, No. 6990, 25 January 1997, p. 3.

15. Boniface, P. 'French nuclear strategy and European deterrence: 'Les rendez-vous manqués', *Contemporary Security Policy*, Vol. 17, No. 2, August 1996, p. 235.

16. Rees, G. W. 'Britain and the Western European Union', *European Security*, Vol. 5, No. 4, Winter 1996, p. 535.

17. See Rosengarten, B. 'The role of the Western European Union Planning Cell', in Deighton, A. (ed) *Western European Union 1954-1997: Defence, Security, Integration*, European Interdependence Research Unit, St Antony's College, Oxford, 1997.

18. This was described by a British Defence Ministry official as 'a clearing house (for) the streams of information that are needed for an operation' House of Commons, 'Western European Union', Defence Committee 4th Report, No. 105, HMSO, 8 May 1996, p. 11.

19. WEU Council of Ministers, Paris Declaration, 13 May 1997, paragraph 31 in Agence Europe, No. 2036, 17 May 1997, p. 5.

20. Statement on the Defence Estimates 1996, HMSO, p. 51. The defence budget experienced a 20% cut in the five years after 1990. Planned spending is anticipated to rise to only £22 624 million by 1998-99, despite the onset of expensive weapons programmes such as the European Fighter Aircraft and the Apache helicopter. See

Cowper-Coles, S. 'From defence to security: British policy in transition', *Survival*, Vol. 36, No. 1, Spring 1994.

21.   Chilton makes the interesting point that 'operational integration' has been going on alongside the debate about a common defence policy and has effectively eclipsed the latter. Chilton, P. 'A European security regime: Integration and cooperation in the search for common foreign and security policy', *Journal Of European Integration*, Vol. 19, Winter 1996, p. 222.

22.   Schlör, W. F. *German Security Policy*, Adelphi Paper 277, London, June 1993, pp. 39-43.

23.   Rühe, V. 'Shaping Euro–Atlantic policies: A grand strategy for a new era', *Survival*, Vol. 35, No. 2, Summer 1993 p. 132. However, its commander stated clearly in 1994 that it was 'not ... the nucleus of a European army', Willman, H. 'The European corps — political dimension and military aims', *The Royal United Services Institute Journal*, Vol. 139, No. 4, August 1994, p. 29.

24.   See Foster, E. 'The Franco–German Corps: A "theological" debate?' *The Royal United Services Institute Journal*, Vol. 137, No. 4, August 1992.

25.   Gordon, P. H. *France, Germany, and the Western Alliance*, Westview Press, Boulder, 1995, p. 42.

26.   Stein, G. 'The Euro-Corps and future European security architecture', *European Security*, Vol. 2, No. 2, Summer 1993, p. 200.

27.   Interviews conducted at the Institute for International Affairs, Rome, October 1996.

28.   Gordon, P. H. *Certain Idea of France: French Security Policy and the Gaullist Legacy*, Princeton University Press, 1993, p. 181.

29.   Lewis, J. 'France is determined to play a central role in Europe's defence', *Jane's Defence Weekly*, 12 February 1997.

30.   Agence Europe, No. 6905, 1 February 1997, p. 6.

31.   As well as the overseas interventionary capabilities of France, Italy and Spain have also established force projection capabilities over a period of time. Italy created the 'Forza di Intervento Rapido' (FIR) whilst Spain created the 'Fuerza Operativa de Intervención Rapida' (FOCIR).

32.   Gordon, P. 'The Franco–German security partnership', in McCarthy, P. (ed) *France-Germany 1983-1993. The Struggle to Cooperate*, Macmillan, Basingstoke, 1993, p. 155.

33.   Wyllie, J. *European Security in the New Political Environment*, Addison Wesley Longman, Essex, 1997, p. 43.

34.   To facilitate this, the Karlsrühe Federal Constitutional Court has ruled that Germany can participate in overseas military actions under a UN mandate if a simple majority of the Bundestag vote their support.

35.   Several European states have been involved in the development of a Future Large Aircraft to address their deficiencies in long-range aerial transportation.

36.   One report estimated that it might cost European states up to $40 billion to acquire a sizeable sea and air lift capability. *The Economist*, 'Survey: Defence in the 21st Century', 5 September 1992, p. 10.

37.   House of Commons, op. cit. p. 11.

38.   Petersberg Declaration, Council of Ministers, WEU, Bonn, 19 June 1992, Part II.

39. 'Italy plays host to first WEU exercise', *International Defence Review*, December 1993.

40. Cuteilero, J. op. cit. p. 8.

41. See Dobbie, C. 'A concept for post-Cold War peacekeeping', *Survival*, Vol. 36, No. 3, Autumn 1994.

42. Taylor, T. 'Challenges for Western European Union operations', in Deighton, A. (ed) op. cit. p. 148.

43. Agence Europe, No. 6723, 8 May 1996, p. 4.

44. For details of the conflict see Kelleher, C. *The Future of European Security: An Interim Assessment*, Brookings Occasional Papers, The Brookings Institution, Washington DC, 1995.

45. Forster, A. 'The United Kingdom' in Moens, A. and Anstis, C. (eds) *Disconcerted Europe: The Search for a New Security Architecture*, Westview Press, Boulder, 1994, p. 147.

46. Wood, P. C. (1994) 'France and the post Cold War order: The case of Yugoslavia', *European Security*, Vol. 3, No. 1, Spring 1994, p. 134.

47. Edwards, G. 'The potential limits of the CFSP: The Yugoslav example' in Regelsberger, E., de Schoutheete de Tervarent, P. and Wessels, W. (eds) *Foreign Policy of the European Union: From EPC to CFSP and Beyond*, Lynne Reiner, London, 1997, pp. 186-187.

48. The involvement of the WEU in planning for possible ground operations in former-Yugoslavia, such as the protection of convoys or the oversight of heavy weapons, did not cease after October but never resulted in actual deployments. For further details of WEU discussions see Vierucci, L. *WEU: A Regional Partner of the United Nations?*, Chaillot Paper 12, Institute for Security Studies Western European Union, Paris, December 1993, pp. 24-29.

49. Willem van Eekelen addressing the WEU Assembly on 1st June 1992 in WEU Assembly Proceedings, 38th ordinary Session, op. cit, p. 62.

50. Agreed at the Joint Session of the North Atlantic Council and the Council of Western European Union, Brussels, 8 June 1993.

51. WEU Assembly Report, Rapporteur Sir Russell Johnston, 'Parliamentary Cooperation with the Countries of the WEU Forum of Consultation', Document 1414, 4 May 1994.

52. Interviews conducted at the Italian Foreign Ministry, Rome, October 1996.

53. Willem van Eekelen did raise the possibility of the WEU or NATO guaranteeing the security of these states in relation to the embargo operation. Atlantic News, No. 2531, 4 June 1993, p. 2.

54. This was in spite the fact that it was convened at the instigation of the French, and that Prime Minister Balladur had declared his preference for his country's forces to be under WEU leadership. Transcript of speech given by Edouard Balladur to WEU Parliamentary Assembly, Paris, Courtesy French Embassy London, 30 November 1994.

55. Although Gnesotto makes the point that they kept a consistently united outward front. Gnesotto, N. *Lessons of Yugoslavia*, Chaillot Papers 14, Institute for Security Studies Western European Union, Paris, March 1994, p. 22.

56. Mathews, R. *European Armaments Collaboration*, Harwood Academic Publishers, Reading, 1992, p. 31.

57. Agence Europe, No. 6836, 19 October 1996, p. 6.

58. There was certainly an unequal pattern of trade in defence goods in the past. Hayward refers to trans-Atlantic trade as resembling a 'west-east one way highway'. Hayward, K. *Towards a European Weapons Procurement Process*, Chaillot Papers No. 27, Institute for Security Studies Western European Union, Paris, June 1997, p. 44.

59. Quoted in the House of Commons report, op. cit., p. xiv. The benefits of 'Single European Market' for defence products has been questioned by Uttley. For details see Uttley, M. 'The integration of west European defense procurement: Issues and prospects', *Defense Analysis*, Vol. 11, No. 3, 1995, pp. 284-289.

60. Dowdy, J. 'European defense industries face new threats', *The Wall Street Journal*, 3 February 1997.

61. Examples have included the creation of 'Eurocopter' from Aérospatiale of France and MBB of Germany and the joining of the missile divisions of British Aerospace and Matra of France.

62. Mathews, R., op. cit., p. 36.

63. Moravcsik refers to the arms market as 'a highly regulated oligopoly with ... inherent market imperfections'. Moravcsik, A., op. cit., p. 72.

64. Ibid, pp. 74-76.

65. See Walker, W. and Gummett, P. 'Britain and the European arms market', *International Affairs*, Vol. 65, 1989.

66. Interview conducted at the Institute for International Affairs, Rome, October 1996.

67. Agence Europe, No. 6856, 20 November 1996, pp. 3-4.

68. See Hayward, K. op. cit. pp. 34-46.

69. Rühle, M. 'NATO's evolving role in the new Europe', *European Security*, Vol. 1, No. 3, Autumn 1992, p. 263.

5

Relations Between the WEU and NATO

Introduction

In addition to serving as the defence identity of the European Union, the Maastricht agreement accorded the WEU the task of acting as NATO's European pillar. On one level, this was a more straight forward role as the WEU had long been acknowledged as representing a European interest group within the Alliance.[1] The WEU and NATO were both defence actors and had much in common. This was borne out by the rapidity of the linkages that were formed between them, a process that was achieved more smoothly than in the WEU–EU situation. The aim was to achieve transparency and to this end weekly meetings were inaugurated between NATO and WEU ambassadors and regular contacts were made between subordinate officials. The Secretary-General of the WEU was accorded the right to attend ministerial level meetings of the NAC, whilst the Secretary-General of NATO was invited to WEU meetings.[2]

On another level, however, there was likely to be considerable tension between the WEU and NATO because of the potential for institutional competition, particularly over out of area operations. France had made no secret of the fact that it envisaged the expansion of European defence responsibilities taking place at the expense of NATO. Although the WEU was the junior partner of the Atlantic Alliance, countries such as the UK were fearful that the uncertain nature of the American commitment to European security could facilitate the WEU's encroachment on NATO's functions. It was consequently the relationship between these two organisations that preoccupied much of the attention of security analysts in the early years of the 1990s.

NATO Transformation

To a large extent, as pointed out in Chapter Three, the future of the WEU depended on the extent of NATO's transformation to the post-Cold War security environment. The ability of the Alliance to reform its internal structures and assume new operational tasks would determine whether greater European responsibility for defence would be pursued through NATO, as the UK wanted, or outside, as the French desired. Because of its membership of the WEU, Britain possessed the means to slow down and frustrate the emergence of a European defence identity, thereby granting NATO the time to adapt itself. In contrast, France, because of its semi-detached status within NATO, was less influential in holding back the reform of the Alliance.

At the Copenhagen NATO Council in June 1991[3] and the subsequent Rome Summit in November, the Alliance was stated to be 'the essential forum for consultation among its members'.[4] At Rome, it was accepted that there was a role for an enlarged European defence identity and European forces were welcomed as contributors to the wider defence effort. NATO was signalling that it did not reject the development of a European defence identity but that it was concerned to preserve the primacy of its own position.

The British were pleased with the Rome text which formalised the military restructuring of the Alliance. The UK had earlier signalled their commitment to the transformation of NATO by supporting its move to a broader political role and a more relaxed military posture.[5] They had also taken a pivotal role by assuming the status of framework nation in the newly created Allied Rapid Reaction Corps (ARRC). The UK pledged two divisions to this force, one in the UK and one in Germany, and secured for itself both the role of commander and the provision of the bulk of its headquarters' staff.[6] They hoped that this formation would cool the ardour of states seeking alternative structures to NATO as it was a multinational force with a flexible interventionary capability. By comparison, the French government was highly critical of the Rome Summit. They were wary of involvement in multinational force structures and the creation of rapid reaction capabilities appeared to herald NATO's shift to new tasks, which the French wanted to develop in the context of the WEU–EU relationship.

A further complication in the situation was the uncertainty surrounding the future role of the US in NATO. Due to its long-standing position as *primus inter pares*, the part played by the US would be a vital factor in the Alliance transformation process. The US was itself undergoing a period of reassessment about its foreign policy priorities and was sending out mixed signals to its allies about its intentions.[7] The reduction in the size of its military forces based on the continent, from the 175 000 planned for under the Bush Administration to 100 000 under Clinton, seemed to presage a gradual American disengagement from the continent.[8] Such an interpretation was reinforced by the domestic debate in the United States over multilateralism and unilateralism which fuelled the impression that the US was intending to relinquish its leadership role. Washington wanted, henceforward, to be more discriminating about its overseas commitments and it appeared that Europe would be accorded a lower priority.[9]

In reality, although the US was re-thinking its role in the world, it was determined to retain the influence it had painstakingly built up in Europe through NATO.[10] It was suspicious about a European defence identity principally because it was being driven by the French government. Officials within the State Department and Pentagon were sceptical about the feasibility of an ESDI and regarded it as focused more on symbols than on substance. Nevertheless, symbols could develop a momentum and the US was also concerned that European views could come to represent an inflexible bloc within the NAC.[11] Had they been more introspective, they might have concluded that they were alarmed at the possibility of the Europeans encroaching on their leadership position.

The depth of US unease at European assertiveness could be measured by incidents such as the Bartholomew Letter of February 1991 and the speech of President Bush to the NATO Rome Summit.[12] The infamous letter, written by Reginald Bartholomew, Raymond Seitz and Timothy Dobbins in the State Department, was a reaction to the Franco–German initiative to subordinate the WEU to the European Council.[13] It questioned both the European capability to act without the US and their need for American assistance in times of crisis. For his part, President Bush challenged European leaders to say if they still wanted the US to play a major role on the continent. The two events were viewed as over-reactions in the capitals of Europe. The French argued that they each illustrated the high-handed American approach to Alliance affairs.[14] They did indeed show that the US was unsure about how best to oppose the ESDI concept but they also demonstrated the depth of American attachment to the status quo.

Amongst the European countries there was no consensus over what role they wanted the US to play. France and Spain were at one end of the spectrum of opinion whilst Britain and Holland were at the other, with Germany adopting a more middle course. No European state was calling for the rapid withdrawal of the US nor the dismantling of the Atlantic Alliance. NATO was accepted by all as a guarantor of territorial defence and as a hedge against a possible resurgent Russia or the vicissitudes of reform in central and eastern Europe. Nevertheless, those championing the cause of a stronger European defence identity envisaged a concomitant weakening of the Alliance's position.

The 'Europeanisation' of NATO

The failure of European states, as outlined in Chapter Four, to generate alternative capabilities to those of NATO undermined the ability of the WEU to develop into a competitor to the Alliance. US fears of exclusion proved to be unfounded in the absence of the political will in Europe to mount such a challenge. NATO, by contrast, had shown the capacity to change and modify its structures. Germany was unwilling to put at risk its traditional security relationship with the United States, whilst Britain had all along been committed to the primacy of NATO.[15] It was apparent that the WEU would remain an actor of subordinate importance to the Alliance and thus it became possible for the US to adopt a more benign attitude towards its role as the Alliance's European pillar.

The formal acknowledgement of this understanding occurred in the 1994 NATO Brussels Summit.[16] At the Summit, alongside important initiatives such as the Partnership for Peace, the Clinton Administration gave its 'full support to the development of a European Security and Defence Identity'.[17] A new equilibrium had been established in trans-Atlantic relations which allowed the US to regard greater European efforts in defence as reinforcing rather than undermining the Alliance. The US was now willing to embrace a division of labour with its allies as well as to search for ways to improve WEU–NATO cooperation.[18] This raised the potential for consultations to take place during a crisis and for the US to consider providing support to Europe-only operations, where American interests were not engaged.

The NAC agreed that as part of its Combined Joint Task Forces (CJTF) concept,[19] 'collective assets of the Alliance' could be made available for WEU operations.[20] Furthermore, joint Council meetings between the two organisations could take place. At the WEU's earlier Luxembourg meeting in November 1993, it had requested access to NATO resources and this was now sanctioned through the concept of 'separable but not separate capabilities'.[21] The WEU was offered access to detachable NATO assets, thereby increasing its credibility as a defence actor. This appeared to end the rivalry between the two organisations and reinforced the concept of overlapping institutions. Drawing on common NATO doctrines and experience of working together, the European countries were being offered the means to bridge the shortfalls in their operational capabilities without the need for heavy additional defence expenditures. The fact that the US was embracing a modest European defence identity succeeded in undermining the position of those that called for a replacement of the trans-Atlantic defence structure.[22]

The acceptance of the primacy of NATO was most difficult for France, due to its history of championing the ESDI concept. Yet even the French government had grown to accept that the enhancement of the WEU as the EU's defence arm had fallen short of its expectations and it had experienced frustration over the failure to build a common defence policy.[23] Its other European partners had not shared France's enthusiasm to create alternatives to NATO. France's calls for a more muscular role for the WEU in Bosnia had gone unheeded.[24] Meanwhile, it had witnessed NATO transforming itself without a French input into the process.[25] The country's ability to maximise its own interests by acting as a maverick was no longer serving its purpose. France was able to present its change in policy as the result of America's acceptance of a European defence identity.[26] In reality, however, self interest had dictated France's rapprochement with NATO.

France gradually harmonisd its relationship with NATO so as to advance its interests from inside, rather than outside, trans-Atlantic structures. Having already reconciled the EuroCorps to coming under SACEUR's command in an emergency,[27] France announced that its Defence Minister or Chief of Staff could attend NATO meetings when the subjects under discussion were pertinent to national interests. In May 1995 the process was advanced further when President Chirac replaced Mitterand. This culminated in a decision, at the end of 1995, that France would resume its seat in NATO's Military Committee, whilst remaining outside the Nuclear Planning Group and the Defence Planning Committee.[28] Like the 'Prodigal Son' of the New Testament, France returned to NATO, thereby facilitating its inclusion in the planning process on a range of issues.[29] The symbolic importance of this initiative was considerable as it underlined the fact that a shift in French thinking had occurred in relation to the WEU and NATO.

However, it would be a misunderstanding to think that France abandoned its ambition to cultivate a more capable European defence identity: rather, this was to be pursued from inside NATO. President Chirac wanted the balance in NATO to be readjusted to take account of a more cohesive European defence expression[30] and for greater American power sharing with their allies. France argued for traditional American command positions within the Alliance's military structure to be transferred to European officers and stimulated a debate about how best NATO could be 'Europeanised'.[31] Dissatisfaction with the readiness of the US to make changes was regularly voiced by Paris. Although the role of the Deputy-SACEUR was strengthened, making it possible for this officer to be placed in charge of a Europe-only operation, there was disagreement over the two European sub-commands, particularly the Southern Command at Naples.[32] The US refused French requests to relinquish this post and insisted that France rejoin NATO's existing structures.

Although France had compromised to the extent that it was working through NATO structures, an important objective of its policies was to make the WEU more capable of conducting operations with assets drawn from the Alliance's inventory. The core assumption in French thinking, that European and Atlantic interests would inevitably diverge over time, did not disappear. Thus, the longer term ambitions of the French government were consistent with those of the past, only the means had changed.[33] Evidence of this was demonstrated in a speech by the then French Foreign Minister Alain Juppe in March 1996. He called for the establishment of a European Army[34] which he foresaw as consisting of contributions of 50 000 troops from the major countries. Such a force was to be capable of acting autonomously overseas under a WEU mandate.[35] This served to illustrate that grand designs were still harboured in French minds.

NATO and the Use of Force

Just as the crisis in Bosnia exposed the limitations of the WEU's military capabilities and the divergent foreign policy interests of the European states (see Chapter Four); so it illuminated the continuing centrality of NATO in dealing with crises that demand the exercise of military power. Although the Alliance was slow to use its military strength against the Bosnian Serbs and was for a long time hamstrung by its dependency on UN authorisation; when force was employed, it was done so decisively. The role of the Alliance in Bosnia demonstrated its vitality in the face of complex and novel problems. It also showed its ability to unify European actions under the direction of the US and its ability to compel a determined protagonist to bend to its will. NATO demonstrated in Bosnia that it had adapted itself to the task of peacemaking, unlike any other security or defence organisation in Europe. It then showed it possessed the political will to deploy military forces to enforce a peace agreement.[36]

The Alliance's initiation into the Balkan conflict had started with the Oslo meeting in June 1992, where it was agreed that the organisation would 'support ... peace-keeping activities under the responsibility of the CSCE',[37] and later under the UN (December 1992). This signalled the willingness of NATO to broaden its agenda of responsibilities, as part of Article IV of the Washington Treaty, to respond to lesser crises that did not directly threaten the territories of its members. France vehemently opposed these efforts as it perceived correctly that if the Alliance adapted itself to such tasks, then it would rapidly eclipse the potential role of the WEU. This was borne out in Bosnia where it was to NATO, rather than the WEU, that European states turned for action. Initially, the humanitarian mission (UNPROFOR) was conducted by national contingents under the auspices of the UN, but the involvement of the Alliance gradually increased. In August 1992 a NATO headquarters was deployed to Croatia and by the middle of 1993, NATO had been mandated to protect the six UN-designated 'Safe Areas' in Bosnia-Hercegovina. NATO first used military power when its jets shot down Serb aircraft violating the 'No Fly Zone'[38] and in the summer of 1995, after much hesitation, the Alliance role escalated to the punitive use of force. Large-scale offensive action had illustrated the need for NATO's military prowess and for American leadership.

When the Dayton Peace Accord was finally hammered out between the warring parties, under US pressure, it was NATO that was given responsibility for enforcing the agreement. As part of 'Operation Joint Endeavour', NATO proceeded to provide the bulk of the 60 000 strong Implementation Force (IFOR). It also made available a framework, as part of its Partnership for Peace arrangement, by which a coalition of states outside of the Alliance could participate in IFOR.[39] In spite of the fact that two-thirds of the troop contribution within IFOR was derived from west European countries, the WEU was not involved and operations were strictly answerable through NATO's Southern Command.

Following on from the success of IFOR in 1996, a smaller Stabilisation Force (SFOR) was appointed as its successor, still under Alliance direction. It was indicative of the changed debate about the WEU and NATO that all European states deliberately avoided discussion of a Europe-led force taking over responsibility for Bosnia.[40] When European Commissioner Hans van den Broek had the temerity to make a private suggestion in Washington that the EU could take the lead in the post-IFOR mission, his remarks resulted in accusations of irresponsibility — ironic as this reprimand came from the French and German Foreign Ministers.[41] British Foreign Secretary Malcolm Rifkind dispelled any doubts about European attitudes to the future of Bosnia when he stated: 'let no-one expect our forces to stay in Bosnia when US forces leave ... we went in together ... we will leave together'.[42]

The Bosnian experience provided salutary lessons for France and Germany. To the Germans, it exposed their continuing sensitivity to military missions outside of their territory. During the conflict, Germany had been constrained from providing forces that could act directly in the conflict zone and the *Luftwaffe* even agonised about its personnel remaining in AWACS aircraft monitoring aerial activity over the region.[43] Although the *Bundeswehr* was able to provide a contingent of 4 000 personnel for IFOR,[44] these were principally in a logistical role. Once again, the inability of the largest European country to use force undermined the case for increased reliance on the WEU. France, having witnesssed the ineffectiveness of the WEU, was more respectful of the need for NATO assets and US power to be utilised. Its government had been willing to act alongside NATO in the enforcement of the No Fly Zone and had served under US leadership in Operation Deliberate Force.

The British felt that their approach had been confirmed by the experience of Bosnia. NATO, with the US in the vanguard, had proved to be the decisive defence actor in the crisis and European support had been mobilised effectively through Alliance channels. But the British were forced to learn an unpleasant lesson from the crisis: namely, that US-European divergences were not exclusively the result of pressures for an ESDI. The US decision to unilaterally withdraw from the conduct of the Adriatic embargo in November 1994 had shocked London because it showed that America could not always be counted upon to act in Europe's best interests.[45] Britain was left to digest the lesson that US leadership could not be taken for granted in all circumstances.

Conversely, there were important lessons for the American government.[46] From the outset, US reluctance to become embroiled in the conflict had been matched only by their unwillingness to follow the European lead. Washington was a consistent critic of European efforts in the Balkans. For example, they were critical of the failure to lift the arms embargo on the Bosnian Muslims and they were reluctant in their support for the Vance-Owen Peace Plan, on the grounds that it rewarded Serb aggression.[47] Yet at the same time the US was not oblivious to the damage that was being done to NATO by internal disagreements in the face of its first major post-Cold War crisis. Brenner refers to a 'storm' brewing in trans-Atlantic relations[48] and there was a real fear that 45 years of American investment in the Alliance could have been thrown away by the crisis. Therefore, when the US moved its military and diplomatic weight behind the effort to end to the conflict, this was motivated above all else by its determination to preserve the Alliance and its own central role therein.[49]

CJTF and an Emasculated European Capability?

The Bosnian experience had shown that in the absence of an all-encompassing post-Cold War threat, it could no longer be assumed that all western states would be involved in the resolution of future crises. It was more likely for 'arrangements of the willing'[50] to be organised amongst those states that perceived their interests to be involved. The CJTF concept was consistent with this thinking. It opened up greater flexibility for organisations such as NATO and the WEU: coalitions of countries and appropriate packages of forces could be assembled according to the requirements of the situation.

The WEU, recognising the potential of the NATO offer, contributed its own thinking to the debate. Its Planning Cell produced a set of interim thoughts in a paper entitled 'Criteria and modalities for effective use by the WEU of the CJTF'.[51] In April 1995 there were direct talks between the staffs of the two organisations. These were focused on how the CJTF concept could be implemented; whether dedicated headquarters would have to reside within the NATO structure, what types of missions were envisaged and the divisions of responsibility between the two organisations.[52] In the light of these discussions a new WEU paper was put forward in May 1995. The length of time that it was taking to reach an agreement between the WEU and NATO was illustrative of fundamental differences of approach. France and the United States disagreed over the practical implications of the CJTF idea and, such was the nature of the impasse, the whole initiative was in danger of being stillborn.

The US approach was to adapt the traditional NATO military structure to undertake out of area operations, such as peacekeeping and, potentially, peacemaking. The US wanted some of the Major NATO Commands (MNCs) to have the nucleus of a CJTF headquarters within them.[53] In the event of a crisis, this capability could then be detached, expanded and personnel added to the headquarters. This approach tied the CJTF concept to the existing NATO structure and ensured that the chain of command would continue to lead up to an American SACEUR.[54] The Americans justified their argument on two grounds. The right of SACEUR to oversee an operation was necessary because the bulk of the military equipment that would be made available through NATO would belong to the US and would require the approval of the President, and possibly the Congress, before it could be released.[55] Secondly, even if resources were released to a coalition in which the US was not involved, the possibility of escalation in a conflict meant that the US might be called upon to assist its allies at a later date. Thus, the US contended that it needed to have a voice in the conduct of an operation.

The French government took a diametrically opposite view, fearing that the US were seeking to undermine the potential role of the WEU. France argued that the CJTF should lie outside of the existing NATO structures and that no lines of command should apply. France envisaged the possibility of independent operations conducted by the WEU, which would draw on some of NATO's military capabilities, but would not fall under Alliance command. A vital pre-requisite for running a WEU mission would be access to a NATO headquarters, experienced in integrating the armed forces of several countries.[56] Yet the idea of a US officer having a veto over a military operation that would be predominantly European in nature, was a bone that stuck in French throats. They insisted that there should be an automatic right of access to NATO assets and that European military officers should be able to replace their American counterparts in a NATO headquarters. They raised the prospect of the US attempting to obstruct the provision of vital capabilities to its allies in an emergency, on the grounds that Washington might disagree with some of their objectives.

It was clear that the root of the French disagreement was political rather than technical; they did not believe that the US could be trusted.

The French were to be disappointed with the level of support that they received from the British and German governments over their disagreement with the US. The British were content to see some sort of face-saving formula agreed but they were suspicious of the French demands. As far as the UK was concerned, US- European interests were sufficiently harmonious to trust that American assets would be available for a WEU-led CJTF.[57] In a UK government Memorandum on the WEU that was written in March 1995, it was stated that there was confidence 'of the continued commitment of our North American Allies to act ... in the conduct of crisis management operations'.[58] The British were satisfied that their approach to an ESDI had come to be accepted by their allies and they pointed out that only the compatibility of the WEU with NATO had rendered the CJTF concept viable.

The German government had welcomed the French rapprochement with NATO. It had eased the tension for Germany between cooperating with the Alliance and maintaining good relations with France. Furthermore, it appreciated the benefits of what the US was offering through the CJTF mechanism, an opportunity to raise the credibility of WEU-led operations without additional spending on duplicate capabilities. It was apparent in Bonn that no European countries would find additional resources to devote to defence spending — in its own case, the political imperative of meeting the criteria for monetary union, would tie its hands.

At the NAC meeting in Berlin in June 1996, France accepted a compromise over the CJTF concept. NATO would remain 'one system capable of performing multiple functions',[59] thereby avoiding the creation of separate command arrangements for European-only operations. This was an endorsement of the American position as it assured NATO a *droit de regard* over all operations. The conduct of a WEU operation that drew upon the resources of the Alliance would necessitate NAC approval. This confirmed NATO as the main vehicle for crisis management beyond Europe. In deference to French pressure, it was agreed that there would be exercises to practice how WEU-led operations could be detached from NATO's structure.[60] Berlin appeared to resolve the impasse between the different approaches to the CJTF concept but it was difficult to avoid the conclusion that the likelihood of the WEU acting as the lead organisation in a future military operation had decreased. This viewpoint was based on three main arguments.

Firstly, it was made explicit at the Berlin meeting that NATO would have first choice over whether to become involved in a military operation. If NATO were to be involved then it would be the dominant framework for action under the leadership of the United States. It would be deemed preferable to operate through NATO in most instances, as this would be likely to offer the greatest chance of success. Therefore the role that emerged for the WEU was to be prepared to act in circumstances where NATO eschewed participation. Yet no demarcation in the types of tasks was agreed between the Alliance and the WEU. NATO Secretary-General Javier Solana was only able to refer to the possibility of 'times when a European-led force will be appropriate'.[61] Not only did NATO retain its traditional responsibility for collective defence — which was no longer considered a priority — it had also proven its capacity to adapt to lower intensity missions. As US Ambassador to NATO, Robert Hunter, commented in a speech in Washington, 'if there is any serious security venture in Europe, we [the US] will be there'.[62]

The second set of doubts concerned the willingness of the United States to delegate the leadership of a military operation to its European allies. As Cornish has pointed out, American refusal to lead in an operation would not automatically equate to a willingness to hand it over to the WEU.[63] Although, in the words of French Foreign Minister Hervè de Charette, the Berlin agreement had acknowledged that CJTFs could be 'under the strategic direction of the WEU',[64] there were likely to be practical problems with European countries being granted access to US military equipment. Much of the equipment would have to be operated by US nationals, which would raise the question of command as the US has always insisted that its personnel be under American officers. All of the NATO allies would have to agree to the use of Alliance assets by the WEU. Moreover, the possibility of escalation would lead to caution by the US in case it might be called upon to assist in extricating its allies from a deteriorating situation. If the US, as a NATO member, had decided not to become involved in a crisis, it would probably be because Washington disapproved of the situation and it was difficult to envisage an American President supporting European action in such circumstances. Accordingly, the CJTF concept could be interpreted as a way of keeping the WEU closely tied to NATO structures and preventing it from developing autonomous capabilities independent of the US.

US opposition would render it hard for the Europeans to proceed in a crisis. Without the US acting as the cement that binds them together, the Europeans have always struggled to find the unity of purpose to act. Under their Presidency of the WEU from January 1997, the French government attempted to alter this situation by emphasising the concept of a WEU 'lead nation' being made responsible for an operation. Yet with the need to draw on US equipment it was not apparent that the 'lead nation' concept would resolve all the problems. It might depend to a large extent where the operation was to take place: if it was a region where European states enjoyed a long history of influence and possessed important interests, then an operation was conceivable. But if the trouble spot was a long distance from Europe, or there was a serious possibility of escalation, then the Europeans would be unlikely to act without some US involvement.

Finally, the WEU has been rendered less important by the shift towards *ad hoc* coalitions of countries. European states have taken steps to increase the flexibility of their forces by agreeing to coordination mechanisms in advance of a crisis. For example, France and Britain created the European Air Group (FBEAG) as a coordination cell between their air forces for missions outside of Europe.[65] Such initiatives draw attention to the fact that the WEU can add little to a multilateral operation. Its involvement would make it necessary for all ten members to approve of an operation, even if only a smaller group actually deployed military forces. Its only contribution would be to add legitimacy to an operation by conducting it under the umbrella of a multilateral organisation, or by providing a coordination function. The emphasis upon flexible coalitions of states, assembled according to need, addresses the more selective interests of countries, but also calls into question the need to involve the WEU.[66] The Secretary-General of the WEU, José Cutileiro, has warned that *ad hoc* coalitions risk undermining the principle of solidarity in Europe.[67]

This has indeed proved to be the case in three recent crises. Despite the proclivity of some states to seek opportunities for the WEU, intervention by the organisation was either not considered or was rejected. In the face of the appalling genocide in Rwanda in 1994, France and Belgium initially evacuated their nationals by a national effort, on the grounds that speed was essential. France subsequently proposed to the WEU Permanent Council in June 1994 that an intervention force should be despatched in order to end the violence. Considerable argument raged within the WEU about the appropriateness of such a mission, particularly in view of the historical links of some European countries with Rwanda. The WEU expressed its willingness to support the efforts of its member states and coordinate their efforts through the Planning Cell but it failed to reach a unanimous decision to intervene. France became exasperated at the prevarication and chose to take action under a UN Security Council resolution (UNSCR 929) in 'Operation Turquoise'.[68]

In the subsequent crises, one concerning refugees in the Great Lakes region in 1996 and the other the breakdown of public order in Albania, the WEU only acted as a forum for debate. In the Great Lakes situation, the Ministerial Council in Ostend in November tasked the Planning Cell and the Political-Military Group to investigate the possibility of a European contribution to a multinational force being placed under the direction of the WEU.[69] This was consistent with earlier ideas that the WEU should prepare a force that could intervene with speed in an African emergency, before being replaced by an African-led force. It appeared to meet the criteria for a European-led CJTF as the US did not wish to be involved but was willing to lend its assets. However, members of the WEU failed to reach agreement on the subject and in the event, the return of the refugees from Zaire to Rwanda removed the need for military intervention.

In the case of Albania, the breakdown of civil order in the early part of 1997 raised the issue of outside intervention. The opposition of countries such as Germany and Britain made WEU involvement impossible, to the public chagrin of the French government and the WEU Assembly. It was eventually decided that an *ad hoc* force be assembled to ensure the distribution of humanitarian supplies. As part of 'Operation Alba', Italy took the lead in a 5 000 strong force that included contingents from France, Spain and Greece. Once again, the WEU had been left standing on the sidelines during an operation on Europe's doorstep.

Regardless of the grand sounding architectural language, the concept of a European pillar within NATO has been shown to enjoy little substance. Whilst France sought to create an independent capability for the WEU that drew on NATO resources, its attempts were eventually marginalised due to lack of support. By contrast, Germany and Britain were content to allow the CJTF mechanism to subordinate the WEU to NATO. As in the 1980s, the pillar of the Alliance concept was no more than a way of increasing the visibility of the European contribution to a trans-Atlantic framework.[70]

Conclusion

The years since the signing of the Maastricht Treaty have witnessed the resolution of the ambiguity in the relationship between the WEU and NATO. The Alliance has adapted, it has demonstrated its continuing purpose in reconciling the divergent security interests of its members and it has preserved the trans-Atlantic linkage. NATO remains the organisation with responsibility for the territorial defence of western Europe — something that was never seriously challenged by WEU. Yet it also stands as the organisation primarily responsible for out of area operations where it has the first choice of involvement. The Alliance no longer regards the WEU as a potential duplicator of its functions, rather, it views the WEU as a junior partner.[71]

The limited capabilities of the WEU and the diversity of interests amongst its members contributed to this outcome. As a result, the key military capabilities that the WEU would require to undertake an operation remain at the discretion of the Alliance. The WEU is now squeezed from both above and below. Above stands NATO, with an effective veto over WEU operations, whilst below are *ad hoc* groupings of European states.

Although the Brussels Summit in 1994 claimed to herald the re-invigoration of the WEU by granting it access to NATO assets, this has proved to be little more than a face-saving formula. It would be difficult to see what the WEU could do, that could not be achieved by NATO or by an *ad hoc* grouping of European states.[72] WEU Secretary-General Cutileiro demonstrated his consternation at the problem when he noted in relation to Operation Alba that, 'good will coalitions ... must not become the norm for military interventions'.[73]

Nor should the influence of external events be denied in the process. The conflict in Bosnia — representing, in the words of one commentator, a 'mixture of American detachment and European vacillation'[74] — placed enormous pressures upon the new-born ESDI and caused the Europeans to recognise their frailties. In turn, NATO was confronted with urgent challenges that forced it to reassess its *raison d'etre*. The US had to face the reality that unless it seized the opportunities to bring the war to an end, the vehicle by which it had exercised influence in Europe since 1949, risked being irreparably damaged.

To a large extent, the subordination of the WEU to NATO has accorded with British objectives. The British government was always determined to ensure that the WEU did not encroach upon the primacy of NATO. British membership of the WEU meant that it was able to block formal efforts to develop European structures that rivalled NATO. As for the German government, it was never supportive of European efforts that detracted from NATO and has been content to witness the successful adaptation of the Alliance to undertake new tasks such as peacekeeping.

The most significant change in position was made by France over its return to NATO. It had made no secret of its desire, at the beginning of the 1990s, to circumscribe the responsibilities of NATO whilst advancing the cause of the WEU. It had to accept that the political will did not exist in Europe to press forward towards a stronger defence capability. Therefore, the French isolation from the Alliance had become counter-productive. The French government skilfully reoriented its stance by drawing closer to NATO and advocating a stronger European identity within the context of the Alliance. This inevitably meant a loss of autonomy for France but it offered a more realistic mechanism for remedying Europe's military weaknesses in a longer term perspective. Yet France's return to NATO may be only an interim strategy until such a time as its ambitions for a European defence capacity can be realised.

References and Notes

1. 'The Platform on European Security Interests', The Hague, 27 October 1987, in Cahen, A. *The Western Union and NATO: Building a European Defence Identity*

Within the Context of Atlantic Solidarity, Brassey's Atlantic Commentaries No.2, London, 1989, pp. 91-96.

2. Steps were taken to make documents available from NATO to the WEU and in June 1996 agreement was reached on the sharing of material with a 'Secret' classification.

3. North Atlantic Council, Communique, Copenhagen, 6-7 June 1991.

4. 'Rome Declaration on Peace and Cooperation', North Atlantic Council of Heads of State and Government, Rome, 7-8 November 1991.

5. 'Declaration on a Transformed North Atlantic Alliance', North Atlantic Council, London, 5-6 July 1990.

6. Stein, G. 'The Euro-Corps and future European security architecture', *European Security*, Vol. 2, No. 2, Summer 1993, pp. 206-207.

7. Heisbourg, F. 'The European-US Alliance: Valedictory reflections on continental drift in the post-Cold War era', *International Affairs*, Vol. 68, No. 4, October 1992, pp. 669-673.

8. Snider, D. 'US military forces in Europe: how far can we go?' *Survival*, Vol. 34, No. 4, Winter 1992-93, p. 27.

9. It needs to be borne in mind that the stationing of US troops in Germany has wider benefits in American foreign policy as it provides a forward presence for US forces to act overseas.

10. See Gebhard, P. *The United States and European Security*, Adelphi Paper 286, Brassey's for the IISS, February 1994.

11. Murray, C.'View from the United States: Common Foreign and Security Policy as a centrepiece of US interest in European political union', in Rummel, R. (ed) *Toward Political Union*, Westview, Boulder, 1992, p. 213.

12. Myers, J. A. *The Western European Union: Pillar of Nato or Defence Arm of the EC?* London Defence Studies 16, Brassey's, London, May 1993, p. 38.

13. I am grateful to Alasdair Blair for material on this subject that he obtained through interviews with US officials.

14. Moens, A. 'The European security and defense identity and the non-concert of Europe', *European Security*, Vol. 2, No. 4, Winter 1993, p. 576.

15. Moens, A. 'Behind complementarity and transparency: The politics of the European security and defence identity', *Journal of European Integration*, Vol. 16, Pt 1, 1992, p. 38.

16. This summit built upon discussions that had been conducted in the previous October in Travemünde.

17. Declaration of Heads of State and Government, NATO Council, 10-11 January 1994.

18. See WEU Assembly Report, Rapporteur Mr Baumel, 'The Evolution of NATO and its Consequences for WEU', Document 1410, 23 March 1994.

19. The CJTF concept grew from the US national Joint Task Force Concept which emphasised the importance of bringing all three services together. In the Alliance context, this was broadened to include operations with allies and other interested countries.

20. Declaration of Heads of State and Government, 10-11 January 1994, op. cit.

21. Ibid.

22. Gordon, P. H. 'Recasting the Atlantic Alliance', *Survival*, Vol. 38, No. 1, Spring 1996.

23. Menon, A. 'Defence policy and integration in Western Europe', *Contemporary Security Policy*, Vol 17, No. 2, August 1996, p. 278.

24. See Lellouche, P. 'France in search of security', *Foreign Affairs*, Spring 1993.

25. Foreign Minister Juppe said in 1993 that NATO was adapting whilst France was relegated to the role of a 'mere spectator'. Quoted in Menon, A. 'From independence to cooperation: France, NATO and European Security', *International Affairs*, Vol. 71, No. 1, January 1995, p. 29.

26. Charette, H. de, 'France for a streamlined NATO: Setting the record straight', *The International Herald Tribune*, 10 December 1996.

27. This was based on three conditions: France and Germany had to agree, France had to approve the mission for its force and the EuroCorps had to act as a cohesive unit.

28. Millon, C. 'France and the renewal of the Atlantic Alliance', *NATO Review*, Vol. 44, No. 3, May 1996, pp. 13-15.

29. Cornish, P. 'European security: The end of architecture and the new NATO', *International Affairs*, Vol. 72, No. 4, October 1996, p. 757.

30. Chirac speech in February 1996, before a joint session of the US Congress.

31. Many ideas have been floated to Europeanise NATO. Mahncke has suggested a European SACEUR or a rotating post between the Europeans and the Americans, Mahncke, D. *Parameters of European Security*, Chaillot Papers 10, Institute for Security Studies of the Western European Union, Paris, September 1993, p. 34. Rühle and Williams have argued for a WEU representative to fill the post of a second Deputy Chairman of the Military Committee, Rühle, M. and Williams, N. 'Nato enlargement and the European Union', *The World Today*, Vol. 51, No. 5, May 1995, p. 87.

32. Charette, H. de, op. cit.

33. Wyllie makes a similar assessment of French policy. See Wyllie, J. *European Security in the New Political Environment*, Addison Wesley Longman, Essex, 1997, p. 100.

34. Agence Europe, No. 6688, 15 March 1996, p. 2.

35. This echoed an earlier call by the High Level Group for a European force projection capability to be assembled. See High Level Group of Experts on the CFSP, 'European Security Policy Towards 2000: Ways and Means to Establish Genuine Credibility', First Report, Chaired by J. Durieux, Brussels, 19 December 1994.

36. Based on the experience of the Balkans conflict, Kaiser noted that 'NATO has been transformed into an instrument of collective security', Kaiser, K. 'Reforming NATO', *Foreign Policy*, No 103, Summer 1996, p. 139.

37. Oslo Communique, North Atlantic Council, June 1992.

38. 'Operation Deny Flight', NATOData, NATO Information and Press Service, Brussels, 18 January 1995.

39. As the NATO Secretary-General stated 'the CJTF concept is having a trial run in Bosnia, driven partly by the requirements of assembling the IFOR from the Alliance and non-Alliance troop and asset contributions'. Solana, J. 'NATO's role in Bosnia: Charting a new course for the Alliance', NATO Review, Vol. 44, No. 2, March 1996, p. 5.

40. *The Economist*, 'Europe's foreign policy: The 15 at sixes and sevens', 18 May 1996, p. 42.

41. Agence Europe No. 6723, 8 May 1996, p. 4.

42. Transcript of speech by the British Foreign Secretary, Mr Malcolm Rifkind, at the Carnegie Endowment for International Peace, Washington, 10 March 1997, Foreign and Commonwealth Information Department.

43. Kamp, K-H. 'The future role of the German Bundeswehr in out-of-area operations', *European Security*, Vol. 2, No. 4, Winter 1993, p. 608.

44. These have included combat engineering, transport and hospital support services.

45. The US decision to withdraw from the embargo resulted from pressure on the Clinton Administration from a Republican dominated Congress. See Brenner, M. *The United States Policy in Yugoslavia*, Ridgway Papers No. 6, The Mathew B. Ridgway Center for International Security Studies, University of Pittsburgh, pp. 22-23.

46. See Haglund, D. 'Must NATO Fail? Theories, Myths and Policy Dilemmas' in Trifunovska, S, (ed) *The Transatlantic Alliance on the Eve of the New Millenium*, Kluwer Law International, The Hague, 1996.

47. Gebhard, P. op. cit. p. 27.

48. Brenner, M. op. cit. p. 19.

49. What made US intervention possible at this time was domestic support for the Bosnian Muslims and the fact that the military situation in Bosnia had changed due to the offensive by Croatian forces.

50. McCausland, J. 'European security with or without America?' in Trifunovska, S. (ed) op. cit. p. 112.

51. Cutileiro, J. 'WEU's operational development and its relationship to NATO', *NATO Review*, Vol. 43, No. 5, September 1995, p. 11.

52. Barry, C. 'NATO's Combined Joint Task Forces in theory and practice', *Survival*, Vol. 38, No. 1, Spring 1996, p. 92.

53. Ibid, p. 84.

54. The US Supreme Allied Commander also has the role of Commander of US forces in Europe.

55. Assets such C-5 Galaxy heavy lift aircraft and reconaissance satellites all belong in the US national inventory.

56. The only existing European headquarters belonged to the EuroCorps.

57. Italy expressed similar views on this subject. Interview conducted in the Italian Foreign Ministry, Rome, October 1996.

58. House of Commons Library, 'Memorandum on the United Kingdom's Approach to the Treatment of European Defence Issues at the 1996 Inter-governmental Conference', March 1995, paragraph 9.

59. Ministerial Meeting of the North Atlantic Council, Berlin, 3 June 1996.

60. Although the first WEU-led exercise was not scheduled until 1999.

61. Solana, J.'The new NATO and the European security architecture', speech to the Federation of Austrian Industries, Vienna, NATOData Service, Brussels, 16 January 1997.

62. Agence Europe, No. 6779, 27 July 1996, p. 5.

63. Cornish, P. op. cit. p. 761.

64. Agence Europe, No. 6740, 3-4 June 1996, p. 2.

65. This was agreed at the November 1994 Chartres Summit between Prime Ministers Balladur and Major and was to be located at High Wycombe, UK.

66. Nooy argues for cooperation amongst an inner core of west European states as the most effective model for a CJTF, see Nooy, G. C. de, *Towards a Military Core Group in Europe?*, Clingendael Paper, Netherlands Institute of International Relations Clingendael, The Hague, March 1995

67. Agence Europe, No. 6970, 8 May 1997, p. 2.

68. See Destexhe, A. 'The third genocide', *Foreign Policy*, No. 97, Winter 1994-95.

69. Agence Europe, No. 6854, 16 November 1996, p. 2-3.

70. See Gnesotto, N. 'Common European defence and transatlantic relations', *Survival*, Vol. 38, No. 1, Spring 1996.

71. Jopp, M. *The Strategic Implications of European Integration*, Adelphi Paper 290, Brassey's for the IISS, London, July 1994, p. 68.

72. As a NATO official remarked in 1995, if NATO had advanced the CJTF concept prior to the Brussels Summit, then the need for a revised role for the WEU might have been removed. Interview conducted at NATO Headquarters, Brussels, January 1995.

73. Agence Europe, No. 6987, 4 June 1997, p. 5.

74. Howe, G. 'Bearing more of the burden: In search of a European foreign and security policy', *The World Today*, Vol. 52, No 1, January 1996, p. 24.

6

The Enlargement of the WEU

Introduction

Throughout the 1990s, amidst the debate about institutional adaptation, the issue of the enlargement of western organisations was constantly under consideration. This issue was important for a number of reasons, not least the sort of Europe that would emerge from the Cold War. But for the institutions themselves, enlargement raised the question of the roles they would play in the security of the continent. According to official pronouncements, the major institutions such as NATO and the European Union were interlocking and mutually supportive. Yet in reality there was considerable competition between them as the organisation that enlarged most rapidly was likely to increase its influence. Although there was general agreement about the sorts of values that would be desirable to foster in the new Europe, there was no concerted strategy between the institutions regarding enlargement. Whether there would be parallel admissions to all three organisations or separate accessions, was allowed to emerge by default.[1]

The WEU was an attractive organisation as far as prospective new members were concerned.[2] It was a part of the organisational design of Europe and an actor that embodied binding defence guarantees. The WEU had the benefit over NATO that its involvement in a crisis did not carry the risk of confrontation between the United States and Russia.[3] Furthermore, the WEU's status as the defence arm of the EU was an incentive to new members. If a common defence policy were to emerge then this might offer attractive security guarantees to states in central and eastern Europe (CEE).

The WEU stood at the centre of the debate about institutional enlargement. It was in a complex position for two reasons. Firstly, following the TEU, the WEU was organically linked to the European Union and NATO and, as a result, its enlargement made little sense other than in relation to the two larger organisations. Furthermore, a former Secretary General, Alfred Cahen had laid down that membership of the EC and NATO would have to be obtained before admission into the WEU (the 'Cahen Doctrine'). Secondly, the collective defence guarantees within Article V of the modified Brussels Treaty had always been operationalised by NATO which gave the Alliance a unique influence over the WEU's activities. Hence the debate about WEU enlargement was to be pursued in the broader context of EU and NATO enlargement.

WEU Linkage to the European Union and NATO

The linkage of the WEU to the European Union and NATO held considerable potential for prospective members. The EU represented the concentration of the richest and most politically stable states in western Europe who were embarked on a programme of economic and political integration. For states outside of this elite club, admission offered the opportunity to participate in greater economic prosperity and external investment.[4] Aspirant states were also aware of the overlap in membership between the WEU and NATO. The Atlantic Alliance was regarded as the foremost defence organisation because it included the United States, who alone was judged to be capable of off-setting the power of Russia.

As a result, there was no shortage of candidates who saw the WEU as a precursor to entry into the key European and trans-Atlantic institutions. In the forefront were CEE states who were eager to establish new arrangements that would satisfy their defence requirements. Many of these states had emerged from the Warsaw Treaty Organisation (WTO) and the Council for Mutual Economic Assistance (CMEA) but now existed in a security vacuum. As western institutions alone had proved their ability to survive the Cold War, CEE countries saw their future in terms of gaining entry to these organisations. Admission would confirm their claim to be part of the European family of nations.[5] German Foreign Minister Klaus Kinkel echoed these sentiments when he declared that 'The heart of Europe beats in Budapest, Prague and Warsaw just as in Vienna, Berlin and Paris'.[6]

The desire of these states to be associated with European institutions was sharpened by the evidence of growing conflict in the eastern half of the continent. Although Russia was capable of exerting little more than residual pressure outside of its borders in the short term, its long term status was unclear. The internal stability of the country was thrown into doubt by the experience of the civil war in Chechnya in 1995. Other conflicts that emerged in areas contiguous to western Europe, such as former-Yugoslavia and North Africa, also tempered the early enthusiasm of those who predicted a peaceful path of development for the continent. In the face of these numerous threats it was possible to present a compelling argument to the WEU that newly democratised states should not be abandoned to a security limbo but should be assimilated quickly into the western family.

Central and east European countries believed that the experience of previous enlargements of the WEU encouraged them to feel optimistic about early membership. Spain and Portugal, for example, had been admitted to the WEU in November 1988 as a means of promoting their democratic orientations. Despite turbulent post-war histories, these states had been granted entry to NATO, the EC and the WEU in order to lock them into Europe's political mainstream. Such a rationale now seemed to be appropriate for the CEE states who had for so long languished on the periphery of western Europe. It seemed realistic to expect that they would be welcomed into the WEU as long as they were prepared to accept its central tenets: namely, the modified Brussels Treaty, the Rome Declaration and the Hague Platform.[7]

Furthermore, the Maastricht negotiations had demonstrated the apparent willingness of the WEU to modify itself in order to embrace the broadest cross-section of countries. The aim had been to reconcile the problem of uneven memberships between the WEU, EU and NATO, to prevent them from pursuing contradictory objectives. States that were already EU members were 'invited to accede to WEU'[8] as full members. Under this arrangement Greece was made the tenth member of the WEU in November 1992.[9] Denmark and the Republic of Ireland chose to decline the offer of membership and opted for the status of WEU Observers. This was because Denmark was unwilling to compromise its membership of NATO[10] and Ireland was wedded to its policy of neutrality. States that were part of NATO, but not the EU, were offered the category of WEU Associate membership. This was duly accepted by Turkey, Norway and Iceland and allowed these states to cooperate in the activities of the WEU.

This same principle was applied to the former European Free Trade Area (EFTA) states of Sweden, Finland, Norway and Austria who were seeking entry into the European Union. At the Edinburgh meeting of the European Council in December 1992 it was decided to begin the negotiating process that would allow these states to enter the EU. Norway eventually decided that it did not wish for membership but the other three successfully negotiated accession and were formally admitted in January 1995. These states were then granted Observer status in the WEU.

Thus a precedent had been established that the WEU would countenance different levels of membership with variable obligations and rights: something which has been avoided by the European Union and NATO. Secondly, the WEU had granted observer status to countries that continued to adhere to a policy of neutrality. This was again in contrast to the practice of NATO whose members were all signatories to the Article V collective defence guarantee of the Washington Treaty. This was inter-preted as a signal by the CEE states that the WEU was a more flexible organ-isation that might be willing to offer them membership in the short term.

However, it was naive of the CEE states to expect rapid entry, first into the WEU and then to either the European Union or NATO. It was funda-mentally misguided to draw direct parallels between earlier admissions and their own situations. With the end of the Cold War the circumstances were very different, there was no longer an external threat that provided a justification for the enlargement of western institutions. Instead, there was a broad array of states, of great diversity, all pressing for admission simultaneously. Their levels of economic development were generally poor after decades as planned economies and they threatened to be a drain on the resources of their new benefactors. In addition, their political stability was questionable.

None of the western organisations, including the WEU, had made explicit the criteria by which they would assess states for membership. It was unclear whether the focus of attention would relate to their democratic credentials or to each country's ability to contribute to security. Although there was an assumption that enlargement had to add to, rather than detract from, the existing security of members, the manner in which this was to be achieved was left vague.[11] They had also avoided spelling out a timescale for admitting new countries. Some aspirants were clearly more eligible for entry than others, if the objective was to enhance the security of all rather than just export stability to the east.

The WEU had to be aware of the ramifications of enlargement upon its own organisation. It needed to weigh carefully the impact of new members upon its structures for fear that its own character would be altered by the influx . Aspirant states could be expected to bring new types of concerns, that might dilute the WEU's homogeneity. The speed of decision making within the WEU could also be dramatically reduced as a result of enlargement. This raised the issue of whether it would be necessary to reform the mechanisms of the WEU before new members were admitted.

In practical terms it would be easier for states to join the WEU than it would be to join NATO. Unlike the Alliance, there was no Integrated Military Structure in the WEU and the financial demands were less burdensome. Yet the WEU was aware that its defence guarantees had always been carried out by NATO and it could not assume that if it admitted new members, the Alliance would assume the additional obligation. Indeed, the Alliance had expressed reservations that states might gain access to its Article V provisions by the 'backdoor' of entry into the WEU. It was considered unacceptable by the United States that undertakings could be made in this way. Nor could it be taken for granted that WEU membership would result in admission to the Alliance. It was quite conceivable that the US Senate would resist being cornered into extending NATO membership on the basis of decisions that had been made by America's European allies.[12] Therefore, it was acknowledged by the WEU that it would only be able to extend its security guarantees with the concurrence of NATO.

There was a corresponding lack of clarity regarding the process of EU enlargement and its relationship to the WEU. It was acknowledged that EU membership would have to precede entry into the WEU but it was uncertain whether the process would occur simultaneously or over a period of time. It was inherently complex because the relationship between the EU and the WEU was itself evolving. The picture was further clouded by the different priorities of the three governments of Britain, France and Germany towards the enlargement of the WEU, the EU and NATO.

From the outset, the French government had made clear its opposition to NATO enlargement as part of its attempt to circumscribe the Alliance's role. At the same time, the French were sceptical about the rapid enlargement of the European Union on the grounds that widening might slow down the progress of deepening integration. The French priority was to concentrate upon advancing western integration, including to foreign and defence matters, in order to tie down German power.[13] President Mitterand feared that Germany's influence could be increased by the addition of CEE states. The French pressed instead for the building up of the Conference on Security and Cooperation in Europe to act as a broad pan-European security framework. Meanwhile, the EU and the WEU would be able to advance the process of integration, whilst NATO would remain static. In conjunction with Vaclav Havel of Czechoslovakia, President Mitterand raised the possibility of a loose 'European Confederation' amongst eastern states that would act as an interim step towards EU membership.[14] The implicit message within the French proposal was that central European states first seek cooperation amongst themselves before attempting to enter western organisations.

Germany and the United Kingdom stood at the other end of the spectrum of this debate, albeit for different reasons. Germany was the most ardent advocate of EU and NATO enlargement for several reasons. Having engineered unification with the former German Democratic Republic, Germany felt obligated to offer the same sorts of opportunities to other central European states and particularly to Poland. Germany was eager to end its position as the front line of the west and to overcome its historically negative image in central and eastern Europe.[15] Yet the Kohl government appreciated that it had to be sensitive in its relations with the area. Germany was determined to avoid leaving any countries, including the territories of the former Soviet Union, feeling a sense of isolation.[16] Bonn did not perceive there to be a contradiction between the objective of deepening cooperation within the EU and simultaneously enlarging its membership. Neither was there felt to be a problem with taking new members into NATO.

Whilst Britain supported Germany's stance on the early enlargement of the EU, its rationale was quite different. The British government saw in the prospect of enlargement a mechanism to dilute and slow down Franco–German pressures for closer integration. The British shared the American emphasis on enlarging the EU rather than broadening its areas of responsibilities. As far as NATO was concerned, the British were cautious about its enlargement for fear of weakening its strength. This led them to oppose rapid WEU enlargement on two grounds. Firstly, they feared that WEU enlargement might increase its standing in European defence and promote it as a competitor to the Atlantic Alliance, particularly by associating central European states with the emerging defence aspirations of the EU. Secondly, they were concerned that the entry of a group of states with disparate defence interests would undermine the WEU's existing cohesion.[17] As a consequence, there was a tension in British policy between welcoming the rapid enlargement of the EU, whilst expressing opposition to the broadening of the membership of the WEU.

Many of the other states in the WEU shared some of these perceptions. A distinct view emanated from those countries, such as Spain, Portugal and Greece, that had close ties to the Mediterranean region. They expressed the fear that concentration on the eastern enlargement of the WEU might have the effect of detracting attention from the needs of southern states.[18] Although the Mediterranean states were not considered to be eligible for WEU membership in the foreseeable future, it was felt that their needs should not be ignored. The WEU's linkage to the economic and political power of the EU made it an appropriate instrument in reaching out to Mediterranean states whose problems were judged to be principally of a socio-economic rather than a military nature. The WEU had instituted a dialogue with countries such as Algeria, Morocco, Tunisia and Egypt. This was intensified following the Kirchberg meeting in 1994 but there was a limit to the practical policies that developed from these contacts.

Turkey, as a southern state within NATO, had first applied to join the WEU in 1987 and was aggrieved at its continuing exclusion. This was exacerbated by the fact that CEE states were being considered for membership. It expressed itself most forcefully on this issue when it threatened to disrupt or even block the progress of NATO expansion if its aspiration to join was not treated more seriously. Turkey felt that it had played an important role in NATO during the Cold War and that it should therefore be allowed to enter the WEU and the EU. It was also worried that Greek membership of these organisations could be prejudicial to its interests.

The Process of WEU Enlargement

At the Vianden meeting in June 1991, the WEU Council took its first steps towards a policy of deepening its relationship with CEE countries. This was founded upon the results of a fact-finding mission to the central European states that had been undertaken by the Secretary General, Willem van Eekelen.[19] The most pressing need at the time was to ascertain the perceptions of newly-liberated governments about the threats to their security and the level of contact that they desired with the west. The Vianden discussions led to the offer of meetings at ministerial level between the WEU Council and aspirant countries. In addition, the WEU set out to disseminate more information about its work through the activities of the Assembly and the Institute for Security Studies.

The WEU took its lead from the EC in determining with which states to develop contacts. The EC had chosen in December 1991 to establish 'Association' or 'Europe Agreements' with three countries in central Europe; the 'Visegrad' states of Poland, Hungary and Czechoslovakia.[20] These Association Agreements were designed to develop patterns of trade and financial assistance to these states, as a precursor to possible accession negotiations.[21] The EC had chosen to differentiate amongst the various CEE states rather than dealing with them all together, which avoided the problem of only being able to move at the speed of the slowest. The WEU co-opted this approach and by basing its own linkages on the Association Agreements, endorsed the relationship between the WEU and the newly-created European Union — rather than NATO.

The WEU chose the Visegrad states because they were regarded as the most economically and politically advanced in central Europe, with highly developed civil societies. They had been at the forefront of the peaceful revolutions in 1989 and could therefore claim preferential access to western organisations. The WEU was deliberately seeking to engender a particular vision of the future development of the continent. The WEU extended its invitation to dialogue to the states of Romania and Bulgaria. Although these countries were less advanced, in political and economic terms, than their Visegrad neighbours, their geographical position made it possible for their status to be enhanced.

The most controversial step taken by the WEU was its decision to accord a privileged relationship to the three Baltic states. Here the WEU was acting in advance of the EU, which did not offer Association Agreements to Latvia, Lithuania and Estonia until the European Council meeting at Essen in December 1994. Until then they had only obtained the concession of a free trade area.[22] The Baltic states were in a highly sensitive position because of their recent separation from and geographical proximity to Russia. NATO had adopted a low profile in relation to these countries as it was fearful of damaging its own relations with Moscow. However, the orientation of the Baltic states and their espousal of western political and economic values, made it important for the WEU to support them. This stance also enabled the WEU to assert its own unique identity in the enlargement debate.

The meeting of the Council in November 1991 laid the foundation for a new body, the 'Forum of Consultation', to be created between the WEU and its CEE neighbours. This was formalised at the subsequent Petersberg meeting in June 1992. The Forum inaugurated meetings of foreign and defence ministers and provided twice yearly contact between the WEU Permanent Council and the ambassadors of the CEE states. Its aim was to develop a mechanism for preventive diplomacy[23] and it offered a means by which aspirant states could learn about the EU's security priorities and, in particular, the CFSP. The Forum focused attention on arms control, the CSCE and issues concerning the stability of the continent — all of which lay within the CFSP's remit. At the Rome meeting of the Forum in May 1993 it was agreed to set up a special Counsellors Group of senior representatives from the various states that would meet more frequently and prepare the agenda for the full assembly.[24]

The creation of the Forum for Consultation was influenced by the parallel activities that were going on in NATO. US–German[25] diplomacy had resulted in NATO announcing a new organisation at its 1991 Rome Summit that was designed to conduct a dialogue with states to the east. This became the 'North Atlantic Cooperation Council' (NACC) which embraced over thirty states in central and eastern Europe, including members of the Commonwealth of Independent States (CIS). The NACC was foremost a consultative organisation and as such caused dissatisfaction amongst central European states. They were shrewd enough to perceive that the NACC was an attempt by NATO to defer the issue of enlargement.

NATO looked with a sense of mistrust on the WEU's new Forum, seeing in it an attempt to create a rival base for relations with central Europe. Yet there were important differences between the two bodies and WEU Secretary-General van Eekelen insisted that the Forum for Consultation was not intended to replicate the NACC.[26] The WEU had decided, by focusing on the nine states, to pursue a policy of differentiation, which mirrored the approach of the European Union. The NACC, by comparison, had thrown open its doors to all countries, including Russia. The fact that the Visegrad states and others were dissatisfied with the NATO attitude to deepening relations provided an opportunity that the WEU could exploit.

The Alliance had been careful to pursue policies that caused the minimum amount of friction with Russia. Russia remained concerned about NATO enlargement due to the Alliance's role in the Cold War and the presence of the United States. Russia had signalled that enlargement of the Alliance would be interpreted as a hostile act. In comparison, debate surrounding the expansion of the WEU had not been subjected to the same degree of criticism from the Kremlin, partly because the Russians knew little about the organisation and perceived it to be of only marginal importance. The Russians tended to view the WEU as part of the process of European integration. This benign attitude could have changed if the WEU had become a more powerful organisation, independent of NATO or if the accession of states into the WEU had acted as a stepping stone to entry into the Alliance.[27]

As far as the WEU states were concerned, there were a variety of issues to resolve with Forum members before they might be offered entry into the organisation. The first problem was to sort out any disputes that existed between CEE states to avoid them being imported into the WEU. Secondly, the west wanted to be sure that the new democracies had enshrined civilian rather than military control over their armed forces, in order to guarantee domestic stability. Finally, there was the need to make the militaries of these aspirant countries compatible with their western neighbours. This was important not just in the types of principal weapon systems but also in communications, logistical support and operating procedures. The WEU members had built their armed forces around the NATO model whereas the CEE states had been forced to model their armed forces upon the former Soviet Union.

The desire to improve the eligibility of CEE states was the motivation behind a European initiative by the Balladur government in France in 1993. Known as the 'Stability Pact', it was made a CFSP Joint Action and was designed to address residual border and national minority issues between states with Association Agreements.[28] It sought to use the influence that western organisations possessed over these states as a form of 'preventive diplomacy'[29] prior to entering the EU. Reform of each states' military arrangements was made a necessary but not a sufficient condition for entry into the EU. There was a recognition that once states were granted admission to western institutions, the ability to influence their behaviour would diminish. The formal document on the Stability Pact was agreed at Paris in March 1995 and then transferred to the OSCE for the process of implementation.

Nevertheless, although the west European states were developing a clearer vision of the criteria for WEU membership,[30] it was impossible to disguise the organisation's inability to offer material security benefits. This message was reinforced by the unequal security dialogue that was conducted within the Forum on Consultation. Whilst the nine CEE states were voicing their demand for security guarantees, the agenda of the WEU members was weighted towards other concerns. Based on its Petersberg meeting (Bonn, June 1992), the WEU was emphasising its capacity to undertake low-level military tasks. The WEU wished to draw Forum members into preparations for conflict-management and peacekeeping tasks, where their additional manpower might prove to be useful, but was unable to offer territorial guarantees in return. This difference of perspective was evident at the Rome meeting in May 1993, when the WEU members encouraged the central Europeans to concentrate upon contributions to the Petersberg tasks.[31]

The WEU responded to the growing dissatisfaction amongst states in the Forum by seeking to elevate their status, short of offering them full membership. Discussions took place in the context of the third annual meeting between Germany, France and Poland in Warsaw in November 1993 when the Polish Foreign Minister Andrj Olechowski pressed for closer ties with the WEU.[32] This was supported at the WEU Council meeting in Luxembourg in November 1993 and in the Kirchberg Declaration of the following year. The CEE states were formally upgraded from members of the Forum for Consultation to 'Associate Partner' status. Once again, the WEU chose to emphasise that the rationale for this initiative lay in drawing the WEU closer to the EU. The Kirchberg Declaration stated that the WEU was 'preparing these states for their integration and eventual accession to the European Union'.[33]

Associate Partner status was designed to reassure the nine states of their special place in the eyes of the WEU and enable them to take a greater part in its activities. Although it fell short of accession to the modified Brussels Treaty, their ability to cooperate with the WEU was increased to the same level as that of the Associate members Turkey, Iceland and Norway. Henceforth, in what was an important recognition of their European legitimacy, they were able to become involved in WEU working groups, maintain liaison arrangements with the Planning Cell and gain access to the WEU Council. They were also allowed to participate in Petersberg tasks and nominate forces to the FAWEU concept. The only limitation was that they could not veto decisions taken by the ten full members.[34] The central Europeans welcomed their enhanced status in the WEU but still expressed frustration that this fell short of full membership.

The WEU did not escape criticism for its creation of Associate Partnership status. From countries such as the United States, there were whispers that the WEU had been mistaken in sacrificing the coherence of its organisation in an attempt to broaden its appeal. The WEU now represented a total of 27 states with varying levels of obligation. There was an inherent danger that the WEU could become an unwieldy body, unable to reach decisions on security issues. Some contended that the WEU had undertaken this step rashly, in order to improve upon what was being offered by NATO in the NACC forum.

Criticism was also forthcoming from states in eastern Europe, such as the Ukraine and Russia. The Ukraine felt excluded by the WEU's concentration on central Europe and, in August 1996, made its own application for Associate Partner status.[35] Fears were expressed that the policy of differentiation pursued by the WEU could return Europe to a period of renewed divisions, rather than working towards the integration of the whole continent. It was argued that the WEU should seek to integrate as many countries as possible into west European organisations rather than choose only those countries with which it felt the closest affinity. Moscow made clear that it opposed enlarging any security organisations in which Russia was not a member.

A 'NATO First' Policy

It was evident that the conferment of Associate Partner status had taken the WEU as far as it could go alone in the enlargement process. The WEU's attractiveness was now diminished as it was unable to offer full membership until aspirant states were admitted to the EU and NATO. In addition, its linkage to the European Union was no longer the source of strength that it had once appeared. The limited progress that had been achieved in the development of the CFSP and the paralysis of west European states in the face of the carnage in Bosnia, placed a question mark over the WEU's capacity to act on behalf of the EU. The WEU had been hamstrung by the opposition within its membership to developing its mission as the expression of the European defence identity. Although the Associate Partners were granted the right to become involved in the WEU's 'Reflection' on a Common Defence Policy,[36] the fact that there had been no progress in the development of this policy since Maastricht gave the CEE states no cause for confidence.

Neither was it any clearer as to the timetable by which the European Union would admit new members.[37] It had always been recognised that the enlargement of the EU would involve substantial costs and complexities. The body of law, or *acquis*, would have to be absorbed by new members; programmes such as the Common Agricultural Policy and the Cohesion Funds would have to be extended and the EU would have to find a way to re-focus its support from states such as Greece, Ireland and Portugal to the CEE countries. The issue of EU enlargement was universally acknowledged to be highly technical due to the need to align the economies of potential new members with the existing structures of the organisation. Furthermore, the EU was consumed with its own internal debate about the process of integration. Unless the 1996 Inter-governmental Conference found ways to reform the EU's decision-making structures, there was a growing danger that the enlargement of the organisation could result in paralysis.[38]

Both the WEU and the EU were constrained by the attitudes of some of their member states. Britain remained wary about WEU enlargement in light of the ramifications for the centrality of NATO's position in European security. Meanwhile, Germany had grown to be more cautious about the enlargement of the EU, due to its own experience of the cost of assimilating East Germany and its fear of damaging the integration process within the EU. None of the key European states were in a position to take a leadership role in the enlargement question, which condemned the WEU and the EU to a policy of wait and see.

In contrast, at the very time when the WEU enlargement process had reached a hiatus, the prospect of NATO enlargement began to crystallise. NATO had previously been forced to tread slowly by the caution amongst its own members and by the vocal opposition of Russia. The Russian government hardened its stance in the latter half of 1993 towards the enlargement of the Alliance. It had long argued that a broader forum, such as the OSCE, should become the security framework for the continent and that organisations such as the NACC should be accorded a subordinate role. Russian membership of the OSCE made it favourably predisposed towards the organisation and its loosely knit structure served to increase Russia's influence. Russia also made periodic forays into trying to establish a Great Power 'Security Council' to manage defence issues on the continent. This would have accorded Russia a leading role, and predictably this was something that the US and the west Europeans were reluctant to countenance. It was apparent that Moscow wanted to be treated in a qualitatively different way to other CEE states and desired a veto power over the NATO enlargement process.

It had been envisaged that NATO and EU enlargement would occur in parallel.[39] Yet by the latter part of 1994, NATO was moving ahead of the EU and the WEU over the issue of enlargement. A number of factors conspired to change the Alliance's position. Firstly, the US attitude towards the issue hardened, partly as a result of pressure from within the Congress and partly due to evidence of growing political instability in Russia.[40] Secondly, frustration amongst the CEE states with the lack of progress in WEU–EU enlargement, coupled with fear of Russia, was driving these states to look for NATO defence guarantees. Thirdly, amongst the west European states there was a recognition that NATO offered the least costly enlargement and one that could be effected in the shortest possible time.[41]

A further factor — similar to its decision to engage in the Bosnian imbroglio — was NATO's realisation that the issue of enlargement was vital to its continuing credibility in Europe.[42] Whilst the establishment of the NACC had attempted to defer the problem, by 1994 it was apparent that a more constructive approach was necessary. NATO risked its own marginalisation the longer it stood apart from the enlargement issue and the Clinton Administration was determined to prevent America's position in Europe from being weakened. In turn, the west Europeans came to see enlargement as one amongst a range of measures by which the US could be locked into the continent's security arrangements.

The earliest evidence of NATO taking the lead in enlargement was manifested at the NATO Summit in January 1994 where the 'Partnership for Peace' (PfP) programme was launched.[43] It offered states who were members of the OSCE an opportunity to cooperate with NATO on all issues pertinent to their military security. This included matters relating to the national control over the armed services, finance, training and equipment. PfP provided interested states with a common 'Framework Document' on relations with NATO, as well as the opportunity to construct individual 'Work Programmes', which could be adapted to the priorities of each of the governments.

These individual work programmes reversed the traditional NATO approach because they allowed central and east European states to introduce self-differentiation. Rather than treating all the states similarly, or elevating a particular group as the WEU had done; NATO was granting potential members the means to influence their own speed of accession. Those such as the Visegrad states, who were seen as being in the front rank of the accession process, could mould themselves into the image of the Alliance by taking steps to standardise their forces and alter their military doctrine. The onus was thrown back upon the aspirant states to bring themselves up to a level that would make them worthy of membership. For its part, the Russian government made it clear that it was opposed to PfP becoming a pathway to NATO membership but, after much hesitation, it signed the Framework Document in May 1995.

Although PfP was conceived of as a way to defer enlargement, its effect was to place NATO at the centre of the debate and to begin a process in which the momentum would drive the Alliance to admit new members. In December 1994, NATO Foreign Ministers commissioned a report to investigate the principles on which enlargement should take place,[44] followed by a subsequent study[45] which sought to determine who, and according to what time scales, should be admitted. The effect of this NATO activity was to relegate the importance of the WEU. With the US under-writing both NATO's conventional and nuclear guarantees, there was little for aspirant states to gain by admission into the WEU, once they had been granted entry into the Alliance. The WEU could play no more than a secondary role in the enlargement process and remained dependent on the progress of the European Union.

This secondary role was highlighted in the steps taken by the Alliance in drawing PfP signatories into peacekeeping and humanitarian operations. This had been the focus of WEU's outreach programme to the Associate Partner states. Subsequently, PfP members were invited to participate in both the Implementation and Stabilisation Force missions in Bosnia under the Dayton Accords. This reinforced the key role that was being played by NATO in the continent's security and contrasted with the role of the WEU. The lesson for the aspiring CEE states was that only NATO possessed the power to manage conflicts.

After lengthy negotiations with Russia, NATO announced in May 1997 that an agreement had been reached on the enlargement of the Alliance. In the 'Founding Act on Mutual Relations, Cooperation and Security', NATO and Russia established a Permanent Joint Council which was to ensure Russia was given an influential voice in security decisions, but not a veto. The culmination of this process was an announcement at the NATO Madrid Summit in July 1997 that three states; Poland, Hungary and the Czech Republic were to join the Alliance by 1999.[46] It was emphasised that these were only the first wave of new members and that others would follow.[47] Yet it has raised concerns that concentric circles of unequal security might emerge in Europe after the first wave of NATO enlargement. It was possible that the window of opportunity would close after the accession of the first three states, rendering it difficult to absorb others at a later date.

There was a desire to find compensation for those states not in the first wave of enlargement. NATO sought to upgrade its Partnership for Peace arrangements to make them more attractive and there was some discussion about the possible role that the WEU could play. At no time was it seriously considered that entry into the WEU could be extended as an alternative to NATO membership. After all, enlarging the WEU to include new members such as the Baltic states would count for little unless defence guarantees were underwritten by NATO. However, it was suggested that a useful role could be played by the WEU in enhancing contact with those countries, such as the Ukraine and Belarus, who were unlikely to be able to join the Alliance in the future. The geostrategic sensitivity of these countries in relation to Russia accords the WEU the opportunity to enable such countries to feel involved in the European security system.

Conclusion

Through the 1990s, the major European institutions jockeyed for position in the enlargement debate. The WEU found itself constrained and frustrated amidst this process because its own enlargement was dependent on NATO and the EU. As a result the organisation was not the master of its own destiny. This was compounded by the attitude of the three major European countries who all held different priorities in relation to the issue of enlargement. None of the three possessed the power (and some might argue, the vision) to carry a policy forward, in the same way that the US came to dominate the NATO enlargement debate after 1994. This left the WEU in a policy vacuum over enlargement.

Beyond Associate Partnership, the WEU found that it had little to offer aspirant states, particularly in defence terms, as its territorial defence guarantees remained the responsibility of NATO. It could not promise assistance against aggression to countries in central and eastern Europe who were interested in joining the WEU. Hence, the Forum of Consultation was concerned with the promotion of a security dialogue with aspirant countries, whilst the Associate Partner arrangements facilitated CEE cooperation with the WEU's Petersberg tasks. The attraction of the WEU was always secondary to that of NATO and once the Alliance resolved its own internal debate about enlargement, the WEU was rapidly eclipsed. In the longer term perspective, it remains unclear what would happen if NATO chooses not to enlarge to all of the 10 states that enjoy WEU Associate Partner status. Whether the WEU would refuse them entry into its organisation and thereby grant the Alliance the power of veto over its own enlargement, is a question that still has to be faced.

The linkage of the WEU to the European Union was both a source of strength and of weakness. It was a source of strength in the sense that access to the WEU conferred a sense of a European identity and closer contact with the economic strength of the EU. The ten states that were made Associate Partners were the same states that had entered into Association Agreements with the EU and were regarded as the most eligible for EU membership. Yet the inherent complexity of EU enlargement and the tension within the parallel integration process made the WEU vulnerable to delay. The EU eventually decided that negotiations with prospective entrants would not begin until six months after the Inter-governmental Conference and no timescale was agreed for the actual admission of new members. It was evident that the complementary enlargement of the WEU would have to wait until after that time.

References and Notes

1. WEU Assembly Report, Rapporteur Mr Soell, 'A European Security Policy', Document 1439, 10 November 1994, p. 23.

2. States were entitled to apply for membership of the WEU through Article XI of the modified Brussels Treaty.

3. Rogov notes that 'in Russia, the WEU is not perceived as a threatening military bloc'. Rogov, S. 'Russia, NATO and the Western European Union', in

Deighton, A. (ed) *Western European Union 1954-1997: Defence, Security, Integration,* European Interdependence Research Unit, St Antony's College, Oxford, 1997, p.89.

4. In 1991 it had been agreed in the EC that the issue of membership would have to be addressed before the organisation could move forward. Moens, A. 'Behind complementarity and transparency: The politics of the European security and defence identity', *Journal of European Integration,* Vol. 16, Pt 1, 1992, p.40.

5. Podraza talks of the revolutions in the east as being part of a process of 'returning to Europe'. Podraza, A. *The Western European Union and Central Europe: A New Relationship,* Royal Institute of International Affairs Discussion Papers No.41, London, 1992, p.4.

6. Quoted by Jakobson, M. 'NATO: The coming "Charter" with Russia will have a price', *The International Herald Tribune,* 9 October 1996.

7. In the case of the Hague Platform the admission of Spain had been controversial because of its ambivalent attitude towards nuclear weapons. Rodrigo, F.'The end of the reluctant partner: Spain and western security in the 1990s', in Aliboni, R. (ed) *Southern European Security in the 1990s,* Pinter, London, 1992, p.109.

8. Declaration on the WEU, Treaty on European Union.

9. The accession of Greece brought its age-old tension with Turkey into the WEU. An understanding was reached by which Greece could not evoke the collective defence guarantees of the modified Brussels Treaty in furtherance of this dispute. Nevertheless, tensions between the two countries have continued and at the Ostend meeting of the WEU in November 1996, Greece threatened to veto Turkish participation in a WEU-led military operation, whilst Turkey retaliated by threatening to veto the use of NATO assets by the WEU. Agence Europe, No. 6857, 21 November 1996, p.4.

10. Danish Commission on Security and Disarmament, *Danish and European Security,* Copenhagen, 1995.

11. Mahncke, D. *Parameters of European Security,* Chaillot Papers 10, Institute for Security Studies of the Western European Union, Paris, September 1993, p.7.

12. I am indebted to Stuart Croft for this point.

13. Janning, J. 'A German Europe — a European Germany? On the debate over Germany's foreign policy', *International Affairs,* Vol. 72, No. 1, January 1996, p.39.

14. For a more detailed explanation of this idea see Duke, S. *The New European Security Disorder,* Macmillan, London, 1994, pp.106-108.

15. Interviews conducted at the German Foreign and Defence Ministries, Bonn, November 1995.

16. See Dabrowa, S. 'Security problems facing central and eastern Europe after German unification', in Stares, P. (ed) *The New Germany and the New Europe,* The Brookings Institution, Washington, 1992.

17. The fact that states with historical policies of neutrality were subsequently admitted to the EU and gained Observer status in the WEU brought this question into sharper focus. Much depends upon the assumptions that are made about the relevance of neutrality in post-Cold War Europe. For example, Finnish President Martti Ahtisaari stated before the WEU Assembly in June 97 that his country would consider sending troops to carry out Peterberg tasks. Agence Europe, No. 6988, 5 June 1997, p.2.

18. Aliboni, R. 'Southern European security: perceptions and problems', in Aliboni, R. (ed) op. cit. pp.11-12.

19. See Eekelen, W. van, 'WEU's post-Maastricht agenda', _NATO Review_, Vol. 40, No. 2, April 1992.

20. The name Visegrad derived from the place of their meeting in February 1991. These three states expanded to four with the separation of the Czech and Slovak Republics in January 1993.

21. See, for example, Ham, P. van, _The EC, Eastern Europe and European Unity: Discord, Collaboration and Integration Since 1947_, Pinter, London, 1993.

22. WEU Assembly Report, Rapporteur Sir Russell Johnston, 'Parliamentary Cooperation with the Countries of the WEU Forum of Consultation', Document 1414, 4 May 1994, p.8.

23. Jacomet, A. 'The Role of the Western European Union', in Goldstein, W. (ed) _Security in Europe: The Role of NATO after the Cold War_, Brassey's, London, 1994, p.32.

24. WEU Assembly Report, Rapporteur Mr Wintgrens, 'WEU's Relationship with Central and Eastern European Countries', Document 1387, 8 November 1993, p.5.

25. Rummel, R. 'Germany's role in the CFSP', in Hill (ed) _The Actors in Europe's Foreign Policy_, Routledge, London, 1996, p.49.

26. Sauerwein, B. 'WEU closing in on NATO: Room for two?' _International Defence Digest_, March 1993, p.187.

27. Danilov, D. 'Development of Russian-Western European Union relations analyzed', _Nezavisimaya Gazeta_ (translation) Moscow, 27 December, 1995.

28. For details of the Stability Pact see Ueta, T. 'The Stability Pact: from the Balladur initiative to the EU joint action', in Holland, M. (ed) _Common Foreign and Security Policy: The Record and Reforms_, Pinter, London, 1997.

29. Jopp, M. _The Strategic Implications of European Integration_, Adelphi Paper 290, Brassey's for the IISS, London, July 1994, p.52.

30. The Copenhagen Summit in mid-1993 had spelt out the EU's criteria for admitting new members and was used as a model by the WEU.

31. See WEU Assembly Report, Document 1414, op. cit.

32. Atlantic News, No. 2571, 16 November 1993.

33. WEU Council of Ministers, Kirchberg, Luxembourg, 9 May 1994.

34. In June 1996, Slovenia became the tenth WEU Associate Partner state.

35. See WEU Assembly Report, Rapporteur Mr Antretter, 'The Eastern Dimension of European Security, Document 1542, 4 November 1996.

36. WEU Council of Ministers, Noordwijk, Netherlands, 14 November 1994.

37. Hughes, K. 'The 1990s Intergovernmental Conference and EU enlargement', _International Affairs_, Vol. 72, No 1, January 1996, p.4.

38. The European Council in Corfu acknowledged the linkage between the reform of the EU and its enlargement to the east. Presidency Conclusions, European Council, Corfu, 24-25 June 1994.

39. Rühle, M. & Williams, N. 'NATO enlargement and the European Union', _The World Today_, Vol. 51, No. 5, May 1995, p.84.

40. For example, President Yeltsin's dissolution of Parliament in 1993 and the movement of Russian military forces into Chechnya at the end of 1994.

41. Zelikow makes the controversial point that NATO enlargement has been seen by some as a largely symbolic offering to the east in lieu of the more substantial offer of EU membership. Zelikow, P. 'The masque of institutions', _Survival_, Vol. 38, No. 1, Spring 1996, p.15.

42. See Haglund, D., Macfarlane, N. and Sokolsky, J. *NATO's Eastern Dilemmas*, Westview Press, Boulder, 1994.

43. For details of PfP see Moltke, G. von, 'Building a Partnership for Peace', *NATO Review*, Vol. 42, No. 3, 1994 and Borawski, J. 'Partnership for Peace and beyond', *International Affairs*, Vol. 71, No. 2, April 1995.

44. This was presented in September 1995 as the 'Study on NATO Enlargement'.

45. Moltke, G. von, 'NATO moves toward enlargement', *NATO Review*, Vol. 44, No. 1, January 1996, p.6.

46. Agence Europe, No. 7013, 10 July 1997, p. 2.

47. In the meantime, the NACC was enhanced into a 'Euro–Atlantic Partnership Council'.

7

The Inter-governmental Conference and the WEU

Introduction

The prolonged period of time taken to achieve the ratification of the Maastricht Treaty rendered the 1996–97 Intergovernmental Conference of the European Union premature.[1] Nevertheless, Article J.4.6 of the TEU had set out the aim of reassessing the CFSP and the role of the WEU in 1996 in an attempt to remedy any weaknesses that had been found to be present. Many of the most sensitive issues at Maastricht had been left open in the expectation that they would evolve in the lead up to the 1996 IGC. Although NATO had asserted its primacy in European defence, the IGC offered the chance to redress the institutional balance by reinforcing the WEU–EU relationship.

The turbulence of the period since Maastricht had slowed down the integration process. This was a cause of concern to some states and a source of satisfaction to others. In the approach to the 1996 IGC, states such as Germany, the Netherlands, Italy, Belgium and Luxembourg were eager to press forward towards political union. Amidst the myriad number of issues under discussion within the IGC, they were determined to achieve major strides in the advancement of a European security and defence identity. Yet countries such as Britain supported only incremental changes and wanted to preserve a cautious, intergovernmental approach in the IGC. Britain insisted that the foreign and defence policies of the EU members states would have to align themselves more closely together before common policies and a single institutional framework could emerge.

Contrasting National Perspectives

The IGC opened at Turin in March 1996, under the auspices of the Italian Presidency. The Westendorp Report had been presented in the previous December as the considered reflection of the EU members on the issues to be negotiated.[2] A complementary report was delivered on behalf of the WEU at its Madrid meeting.[3] Neither reports could agree upon a definitive set of recommendations to the IGC and they chose instead to present a series of options. The inability to agree an agenda of reform reflected the diversity of views amongst the members across the entire spectrum of issues.

As in the earlier IGC, Franco–German efforts were the motivating force behind attempts at closer cooperation. The Germans were aware that their objectives for the EU could only be secured with French support; whilst Paris was keen to ensure German endorsement for its participation in monetary union. However, France and Germany were not completely at ease with each other due to their differences over the level of integration that they wished to achieve. Chancellor Kohl was vocal about the sort of Europe that he wanted to create; fully integrated, peaceful and open to the east. The fact that Germany had not obtained its sovereignty fully until 1990, made it less reluctant about relinquishing it within an EU framework. Germany was willing therefore to accord a much stronger role to supranational structures of the European Commission and the European Parliament.

The French attitude was highly complex and, due to the reassessment of policy under the new Chirac administration, it took a long time for its position on the IGC to be finalised.[4] On the one hand, there was a strong desire to partner Germany and at a summit meeting at Baden it was agreed that the two governments would make a joint approach in the negotiations. But on the other, increasingly supranational solutions to EU problems was causing France to confront its traditional ambivalence to integration. France wanted a strong Europe but with weak institutions and it continued to be wedded to the centrality of the nation-state. Paris was wary of transferring too much power to Brussels, particularly in matters concerning foreign policy and the exercise of military power where France still foresaw a central role for the state.

Consistent with its status in the earlier IGC, Britain was again the country most opposed to closer integration. The stance adopted by John Major's Conservative government was strongly influenced by domestic party considerations. Elements within the party were vehemently opposed to deeper integration and enjoyed disproportionate influence due to the government's narrow Parliamentary majority. Since Maastricht, the British had lost important allies in their opposition to defence integration, such as the Dutch, who were now inclining towards a more German vision of Europe's future.[5] Neither was it likely that there would be a repeat of the Anglo–Italian paper of October 1991, as Rome could find little in common with the position of London. At a summit between Italy and the UK in December 1995, a 'Joint Declaration' was issued, but this served only to restate the contrasting positions of the two countries and Britain found itself increasingly isolated.[6] Some countries made no secret of the fact that they hoped for a change of government to occur in Britain before the end of the IGC process. Yet it was far from certain that the British Labour Party would differ substantially from the government's position, particularly in the sensitive areas of foreign and defence policy.

Proposals for Reforming the CFSP

There was widespread disillusionment with the ineffectiveness of the CFSP and its reluctance to task the WEU (See Chapter Four). However, there was a limited amount that could be done to encourage states to use the instruments at their disposal and so the IGC had to focus upon improving the institutional mechanisms. A range of proposals were canvassed: the most ambitious being to transcend the intergovernmental approach to foreign policy by merging the second pillar into the first. This was quickly dismissed as unrealistic. The next most significant proposal was to alter the decision-making process and abandon the principle of unanimity. This had ramifications both for the effectiveness of the Union and the EU–WEU relationship. If the principle of unanimity in decision-making could be tempered, then it might have been possible to prevent a single state from vetoing an action of its allies. Along with lesser issues, such as the appointment of a representative to increase the EU's stature abroad and the creation of a planning section, this proved to be the focus of the debate in the IGC.

Germany possessed a clear vision for the CFSP; it wanted the Union to be capable of thinking and acting as a coherent whole in advance of potential crises. Werner Hoyer, Minister of State in the German Foreign Ministry, called for the CFSP to be freed from the 'straight-jacket' of the unanimity requirement.[7] Germany wanted the European Council to continue to be responsible for laying down policy guidelines by unanimity, but argued that decision-making through Joint Actions and Common Positions should occur by majority voting.[8] This aimed to overturn the system bequeathed by the Maastricht Treaty which gave states a double veto on Joint Actions.[9] In order to cater for states that might not wish to participate in a foreign policy action, a variety of permutations were put forward. 'Constructive Abstention' was suggested as a mechanism by which the decision not to participate by one state in a Joint Action would not constrain its allies from going ahead.[10] Another option that was canvassed was to allow voting by qualified majorities, yet enable a dissenting state to ask for a matter to be taken to the Council, where unanimity would be required.[11]

Initially, France was reluctant to support the German position as it deemed it necessary to be able to oppose a decision when its vital interests were at stake. However, after their Foreign Ministers' meeting in Freiburg in February 1996, France agreed to Germany's view[12] and the following month a joint proposal supporting 'Constructive Abstention' was launched. France was guided by the need to arrive at a pragmatic agreement with Bonn and appeared to have been reassured that its allies would not disregard its interests. The new proposal made it possible to 'opt out' of an operation but it demanded that non-participants demonstrate financial solidarity. France and Germany went on to argue for new weightings in Qualified Majority Voting (QMV) to better reflect population size and to prevent the risk of small countries outvoting large ones.[13]

The British emphasis upon evolutionary changes to the CFSP stood in marked contrast to that of Germany. In the UK White Paper on the IGC, published in March 1996,[14] it was argued that the EU's second pillar had to remain inter-governmental and that only the aim of increasing its efficiency should be pursued. The Foreign Office pointed out that European states continued to be far apart on many foreign policy issues. A commonly cited example was the intransigence of the Greek government over the recognition of Macedonia during the Balkans conflict, when Athens disregarded the common EU position. Based upon such experiences, the British argued that what was required was a pause for reflection, rather than attempts to generate an artificial consensus.

Britain rejected the extension of majority voting into foreign policy and was supported by Portugal, Greece and Denmark. A former Foreign Secretary, Lord Howe warned that the interests of the major countries had to be protected if cooperation was to succeed.[15] Like France, Britain was worried that the powers of the Commission and the European Parliament would be increased at the expense of national legislatures.[16] Other countries, such as Italy, did not share these Anglo–French fears and the smaller countries, in particular, tended to be sympathetic to the role of the Commission, seeing it as the guarantor of the interests of all the members.

In areas other than decision-making, France favoured the appointment of a High Representative for CFSP who would embody the Union's interests in the world.[17] France wanted the appointee to be a political figure who would enjoy a considerable period of time in office and would play a major coordinating role in the CFSP.[18] Its view was that a prestigious statesperson was required to project the identity of the Union in foreign affairs and to advance the cause of a common defence policy. France was supported by the Italians during their Presidency[19] who envisaged the High Representative being responsible for chairing the Political Committee and being a member of the Troika.[20]

In contrast, the Germans preferred a bureaucratic rather than a political figure. They were concerned that a political figure could trespass on the work of the European Commission and they were determined to prevent the widening of the division between the Union's first and second pillars.[21] On this subject, Germany and Britain were in harmony, albeit for different reasons. Britain was willing to endorse the appointment of a High Representative to assist on those occasions when small states with limited resources were occupying the Presidency. But Britain opposed giving such a figure independent powers of initiative as they feared that the position could come to resemble an EU Foreign Minister.[22] They wanted a figure who would do no more than represent the views of the Fifteen in international fora.

The Reflection Group and the High Level Group had also recommended the creation of a central analysis body for the CFSP.[23] Whilst an analysis body would have represented a step forward, France and Germany supported a more ambitious proposal for a planning body to be located either in the Council Secretariat or within the Commission. A planning body would have reduced the EU's dependency on national capitals, strengthened the linkage with the military planning capacity of the WEU and assisted in the process of defining common European interests. Predictably, the UK favoured only the more modest proposals as they saw foreign policy as essentially a reactive activity and wanted the focus of effort to remain in national foreign ministries. They were willing to improve the EU's analytical capacity but suggested that this should be achieved by strengthening the Council Secretariat to prepare more options for the Political Committee.[24]

Tasking the WEU by the European Council

Whilst the most significant question concerning CFSP was the reform of decision-making, the key defence question in the IGC was the relationship between the European Council and the WEU. This would determine the future of the WEU as it impacted on its autonomy. At the Madrid summit in November 1995, the WEU's 'Reflection Group' had laid out three options for the IGC. One of these, 'Option C', envisaged collapsing the WEU, over a period of time, into the EU so as to create a 'single institutional framework for European security and defence'.[25] The modified Brussels Treaty would be incorporated into the EU and a military instrument would be placed at the disposal of the CFSP. In the view of the integrationist states, such an action was consistent with the TEU which had initiated a process involving successive stages.[26]

Germany was once more in the vanguard of those states calling for WEU integration into the EU. As early as June 1995, Foreign Minister Klaus Kinkel had stated this to be his government's long term objective.[27] In March 1997, prior to the Amsterdam Summit, Germany, France, Italy, Belgium, Spain and Luxembourg submitted a paper to the Dutch Presidency calling for the absorption of the WEU in a three stage process.[28] Firstly, a White Paper would be drawn up incorporating agreement on a common defence policy. Secondly, the Secretariats of the organisations would be merged and EU Council decisions over the WEU would be made binding. Finally, the two Councils and their respective legislatures would be merged, with the European Commission being given the same rights of initiative in defence as they already enjoyed in CFSP.

These proposals did not specify the precise arrangements by which the EU would operationalise defence guarantees. Whilst it was relatively uncontroversial to include the Petersberg tasks within the pre-existing pillar structure, the inclusion of territorial defence commitments were likely to prove more problematic. One possibility was to bring defence within Title J of the CFSP and grant states the choice of opting out. This would have the benefit of representing a tight commitment amongst the participants. Alternatively, a separate protocol on defence could have been drafted and then attached to the Treaty. The present WEU members would have adopted this protocol and other states could have been offered the opportunity to opt in, thereby generating a looser commitment. This latter approach was designed to reassure the Observer states in the WEU that their membership of the EU would not compel them to participate in collective defence arrangements.

It was a popular misconception at the time that countries would be forced to commit troops to EU-inspired military operations. Of the nine states who supported the WEU's integration into the EU, all agreed that it would be unacceptable for a state to be compelled against their will to commit troops to combat. Such a decision would still require national approval. Indeed, Germany's particular sensitivity to the use of force would have rendered it the least likely state to allow its military forces to be subject to automatic involvement in an extra-territorial operation.

The British government rejected the proposal to absorb the WEU into the EU, irrespective of the time scale. It was sceptical that a more integrated institutional architecture could result in European states cooperating more effectively in defence. They argued that the EU was better off dealing with economic and environmental problems rather than becoming involved in defence.[29] The British feared that the unique strengths of the WEU might be jeopardised, especially its ability to act independently of the EU. Several

EU states were not members of NATO, yet the proposals to merge the WEU with the EU raised the prospect that they might effectively obtain NATO guarantees. This might cause NATO to reappraise its commitment to carry out the WEU's Article V mandate. Furthermore, a Minister of State at the Foreign Office warned against ignoring the variable geometry of obligations within the WEU: 'The time is not yet ripe to try to squeeze these different interests into a single straight-jacket. This would ... weak[en] the nature of the mutual defence commitment which lies at the heart of WEU'.[30]

The UK was fearful that the homogeneity evident in the WEU would be dissipated within a broader EU framework. In particular, there were EU states such as Denmark, Ireland, Sweden, Austria and Finland, that were willing to contribute to *ad hoc* humanitarian operations, but were ambivalent about participating in a European defence policy. The latter three states had deliberately chosen Observer status within the WEU, yet merging the organisations would grant them a veto power over the military actions of WEU members. The British were willing to accord Observers the right to opt in to appropriate operations but not to prevent tasks from taking place. In the future, optional involvement in military interventions would be likely to make it difficult enough to obtain agreement amongst a group of states to act together. Adding in states that did not share the defence priorities of the WEU members would, in British eyes, be to aggravate the problem further, particularly if the EU was enlarged.[31] UK Ambassador Goulden, declared that his country's emphasis was upon meeting real security challenges, rather than attempting to cater for 'institutional tidiness'.[32]

Critics of the UK suspected that its stance owed more to its desire to constrain the EU, than its fears for the undermining of European defence. In their view it was possible to engineer a formula by which the neutral states could be prevented from paralysing the capacity of EU states to undertake military operations. One suggestion, for example, was for the rules to be adapted to allow WEU states, or sub-groupings, to decide upon an operation within the European Council, without the non-members having the right to block their actions.[33] Even if the WEU was merged with the EU, coalitions of states would remain the mechanism for military actions. Countries such as France and Germany argued that the past ineffectiveness of the WEU highlighted the need for radical reform.

An intermediate, less ambitious proposal ('Option B' at the Madrid Summit) was to enhance the powers of the European Council over the WEU. Here, the aim was to narrow the autonomy of the WEU from the EU. A range of possible measures were debated. One possibility was to enable the European Council to lay down guidelines for the WEU, thereby replacing the 'request' for WEU action that had been embodied in the Maastricht text (Article J.2, TEU) An alternative was a legally binding link in which the WEU would be mandated to serve the EU. All of these arrangements had the benefit of preserving the separate identity of the WEU as well as its intergovernmental nature of decision-making, whilst simultaneously increasing the effectiveness of the EU and moving it towards a competence in defence. Unanimity would still be required in the European Council to task the WEU but there would no longer be a need for an additional vote in the WEU Council. As German Defence Minister Volker Rühe stated: 'Decisions should be with the EU, implementation with the WEU'.[34]

The French viewed this as a valuable compromise between the maximalist German position on the one hand, and the minimalist British position on the other. France was uneasy with the German emphasis on supranational structures such as the Commission and the European Parliament. Ever since the preparations for the Maastricht negotiations, Paris had called for the European Council to be accorded the power to determine guidelines for the WEU. In the lead up to the Amsterdam Summit, France argued for the European Council to be given the power to 'instruct' the WEU. This did not go far enough for the Germans but might have been acceptable as an interim measure, if it led to a convergence of the two organisations over the longer term.

Yet the British government refused to accept the European Council having any increased powers over the WEU.[35] The British government had spelt out its position on the future of the WEU in a Memorandum submitted to Parliament in March 1995.[36] The only innovation that the UK offered was the creation of a new body, at Heads of State level, that would meet back-to-back with European Council meetings to expedite defence decisions.[37] This was unlikely to appeal to other European allies as it duplicated the role they wanted to allocate to the European Council and it excluded the neutral states within the EU from defence issues. The subsequent UK White Paper on the IGC[38] offered only the rhetoric of a 'Reinforced Partnership' with the EU.[39] Britain focused upon improving practical cooperation between the two institutions such as the coordination of the EU Foreign Affairs Council meetings with the WEU Ministerial Council and cooperation between the Political Committee and the Permanent Council of the WEU.

The Concept of Flexibility

If compromises could not be found in the IGC process then it appeared inevitable that the Union would be condemned to advance at the pace dictated by its slowest member. This raised two sorts of dangers: firstly, that insufficient reform would have been achieved before the onset of enlargement and secondly, that those states frustrated by the lack of progress would pursue cooperation outside the boundaries of the EU. The example of the Contact Group, set up to deal with the crisis in Bosnia, demonstrated that the major powers could create *ad hoc* structures if they perceived that their interests could be better served outside of established frameworks.

'Variable geometry' or 'flexibility' appeared to offer a way out of this impasse. According to this idea, groups of interested states could be allowed to press forward with closer integration, bypassing obstacles, whilst allowing other states to remain uninvolved.[40] The model had been established in the Schengen Agreement as well as in the opt outs on monetary union and social policy in the Maastricht Treaty.[41] French Foreign Minister Hervé de Charette emphasised the need for key countries to be able to sustain the momentum of integration[42] and flexibility seemed to offer a way forward as progress in the IGC became more laboured.

Germany was prepared to accept that countries could move forward within the integration process at different speeds but was wary about creating an *a la carte* Europe as this might threaten to unravel the progress already achieved.[43] On behalf of the Christian Democrat group in the Bundestag, the Schäuble–Lamers paper,[44] had suggested a core of states pressing ahead in integration across a range of issues. An alternative approach would be to facilitate the development of different cores of countries on specific issues, such as CFSP and defence.[45] The ultimate aim would still be to merge the different 'cores' into a united grouping.

Germany was in favour of an automatic right to flexibility amongst those states that were interested and suggested that the concept could be applied to defence. In a joint letter to the IGC in October 1996, France and Germany proposed that 'enhanced cooperation' could occur in the creation of a common defence policy and in the area of armaments cooperation.[46] Britain, however, was uncomfortable with flexibility being applied to defence. It contended that the WEU was already a *de facto* core group on defence and that it could be undermined if a cabal of states advanced alone. As a result, the British accepted the principle of flexibility but with distinct qualifications.[47] They dismissed the creation of a 'fast-track' group of nations within the EU and insisted upon a unanimous vote before flexibility could be triggered.[48]

In the event, the debate proved to be academic because the Amsterdam negotiations excluded foreign policy and defence from the remit of flexibility.[49] Denmark and Sweden were known to be opposed to the concept and the requirement for all states to agree made it a subject that was jettisoned in the final text. Whether it would have worked, is hard to assess. It would have provided a mechanism by which the most ambitious states could have circumvented the most cautious, but there would inevitably have been costs associated with its usage. It risked exacerbating centrifugal forces within the Union and it could have enabled hostile states to exploit disagreements in policy positions amongst the EU members during a time of crisis.

The Treaty of Amsterdam

As the IGC progressed, it had become increasingly clear which issues could be resolved and which were stalemated. The British General Election in May 1997 brought the Labour Party into power but the change did not extend much beyond style and the reversal of the opt outs negotiated at Maastricht. The new Prime Minister, Tony Blair, was averse to conducting any significant change of policy towards foreign and defence issues which could have given his Conservative opponents a stick with which to beat his Party on subsequent occasions. As for the other European leaders, there was a recognition that there was little to be gained by pushing differences with Britain to a breaking point in the IGC, when the prospect of extracting further concessions was poor.

In respect to majority voting in CFSP, the Amsterdam European Council[50] heralded no significant progress. In Article 23 it was agreed that a state could abstain from a foreign policy decision whilst not preventing the measure from proceeding. Yet safeguards were added so that countries could issue a formal declaration which would exempt them from Common Positions and Joint Actions. Furthermore, if one third of the states abstained in this manner then no decision could be adopted. This served to weaken the sense of solidarity amongst the EU members by making it possible to opt out of foreign policy decisions. This raised the threat that the majority of states might dilute their proposals on CFSP in order to minimise the risk of a state disassociating itself from a decision.

By the time of the Irish draft treaty in December 1996, a compromise had been agreed over the appointment of a figure to represent the CFSP. In Article 18 the post of 'High Representative for the CFSP' was given to the Secretary-General of the Council of Ministers who was accorded the right to attend meetings of the General Affairs Council and COREPER. This represented a setback for the French and European Parlia- ment's support for a senior political appointee. Yet there were doubts about the potential effectiveness of this office as the Secretary-General was already overburdened with work and would find it difficult to assume an additional role. It was also unclear from the Treaty both what role this office would fulfil and how it would interact with the Commission and the Council Presidency.

A 'Policy Planning and Early Warning Unit' (PPEWU) was established in the General Secretariat of the Council, and was placed at the disposal of the new High Representative. Like its master, this body has the potential to make a significant contribution to the process of decision-making, being capable of drawing the member states and the agencies of the EU together.[51] It can also play a part in determining which areas of the world will be the focus of EU attention. Nevertheless, its effectiveness will depend to a large extent on the influence of the High Representative and the attitude and cooperation of the member states. If the member states choose to disregard the outputs of the PPEWU, and concentrate on national planning, then its activities may be marginalised.

The Treaty granted the European Council the right to set only 'general' guidelines for CFSP and for 'matters with defence implications' (Article 13). In CFSP, the European Council was accorded the power to decide on 'common strategies' which would help to determine the objectives, duration and instruments to be used by EU states in a policy area. This placed the emphasis on a top-down approach, which is likely to lead to slower decision-making in practice due to the infrequency of European Council meetings. As for defence, the Treaty rejected the British idea for a separate Heads of State forum but denied extra powers for the European Council over the WEU. The replacement of the word 'request' by 'avail' (Article 17) illustrated both the modesty of the accomplishments in the Treaty and the continuing fragility of the EU–WEU relationship.

Britain and the neutral countries were successful in countering pressure to collapse the WEU into the EU. At the Noordwijk meeting[52] in May 1997, the Dutch Presidency draft called for 'the objective of gradual integration of the WEU into the Union'.[53] Even during the Summit itself, the Dutch attempted to attach a Protocol to the Treaty which would have laid out a timetable for WEU integration.[54] But all efforts were frustrated by the obduracy of the British position. In Article 17 it was agreed only that the EU and the WEU would 'foster closer ... relations' and that there was a 'possibility of integration' if the European Council were to decide. The acknowledgement of such a possibility will be interpreted by some as an important marker for the future. But such a development would still necessitate the unanimous approval of all the member states and therefore the British would still be in a position to wield their veto.

In Article 17[55] the word 'progressive' replaced 'eventual' in relation to the 'framing of a common defence policy'. This could be interpreted as a stronger commitment to further action, but once again, this had been qualified by British insistence that the conditional phrase 'might lead to a common defence', remain in the Treaty. Similarly, it was reasserted that the European Council would have to sanction such a development. Maintenance of the separation between the EU and the WEU made it difficult to foresee substantive progress in a CEDP. In addition, the Treaty did not announce any further progress in the cause of developing a common armaments policy in the EU.

It was noted in the Irish draft treaty that a statement outlining the commitment to defend the territorial integrity of the EU was being considered by some of the member states. This represented an attempt to move beyond the general principles of protecting the common values and interests of the EU states, to a firmer defence commitment. This would have been considered attractive by those countries that were seeking entry into the EU. However, the Irish Presidency decided not to include this provision and it did not appear in the subsequent Amsterdam text. What was present in the Treaty (Article 11) was a commitment to 'safeguard ... the integrity of the Union', which was firmer language than that which had appeared in the Maastricht Treaty.

At the first WEU meeting attended by the new British Labour government, in Paris in May 1997, Foreign Secretary Robin Cook indicated that the UK would be willing to see the Petersberg missions included within the EU.[56] The Treaty duly included the Petersberg tasks into Article 17 and enabled the neutral states to be fully associated in planning and executing low intensity missions. Although relatively uncontroversial, this was an important concession by the UK as it established a precedent for the future. It granted states that were not signatories of the defence commitments of the modified Brussels Treaty a right of co-decision in operations that could involve the use of force. The inclusion of these tasks made more explicit the sort of missions that the EU–WEU envisaged they would be capable of performing in the appropriate circumstances.

Although the Amsterdam European Council was presented in the best possible light, there was no disguising the feeling of disappointment that so little had been achieved after two years of negotiation. Marginal improvements had been made in the areas of decision-making and the visible representation of the CFSP, but no progress had been achieved in defence, other than the inclusion of the Petersberg tasks. The warning that President Santer had made in November 1995 had been borne out in reality: the EU was left with 'feet of clay' to face future crises.[57]

Conclusion

The Amsterdam European Council illustrated once again that the foreign and defence interests of the leading west European states were divergent. At one end of the spectrum was the German approach which looked towards a fully integrated union with a communitarian foreign and defence policy. This view had gradually been winning more adherents and a majority of states in the IGC had called for the eventual integration of the WEU into the EU. At the other end of the spectrum was the British approach which called for a loose, inter-governmental union in which defence issues remained in the hands of an autonomous WEU. Britain had felt that the whole of the IGC negotiations had been overly focused on institutional questions. In the face of such contrasting approaches, the outcome was a Treaty that delivered only minimal changes.

However, the limited achievements of the Amsterdam European Council in foreign and defence policy had been easy to predict because the momentum had slipped from the EU some time before. The dominance of NATO in defence issues, symbolised by the Berlin agreement, had cast a shadow over the EU. The perceived failures of the EU to act more decisively in CFSP matters and its lack of progress in orchestrating a common defence policy, had also undermined its cause prior to Amsterdam. In the IGC itself, it had only been possible for the member states to address the symptoms of their problems, whilst the core issue of political will remained untouched.

Following on from the Amsterdam European Council, it is difficult to discern how the WEU will develop in relation to the European Union. Some have argued that the failure to bring it within the ambit of the EU will lead to the two organisations moving in opposite directions.[58] New states could join the EU without becoming members of the WEU and might gain voting rights in CFSP without obligations in the WEU. Yet such an estrangement appears unlikely as the member states would actively resist such a trend. The fact that the Petersberg tasks have been included in the Treaty draw the two organisations into focusing on the same types of missions. What is perhaps more likely is that the relationship will be susceptible to stagnation in the absence of the necessary political will to develop it further.

References and Notes

1. The ratification process of the TEU went on until November 1993 and in that time referendums in countries such as Denmark and France showed the fragile basis of support for what the governments had laboured so hard to negotiate. See Duff, A. 'Ratification' in Duff, A., Pinder, J. & Pryce, R. (eds) *Maastricht and Beyond: Building the European Union*, For the Federal Trust, Routledge, London, 1994.

2. Reflection Group's Report, Brussels, 5 December 1995.

3. WEU Council of Ministers, 'WEU Contribution to the EU Intergovernmental Conference of 1996', Madrid, 14 November 1995.

4. See Sutton, M. 'Chirac's foreign policy: Continuity with adjustment', *The World Today*, Vol. 51, No. 7, July 1995.

5. Interviews conducted at the Dutch Ministry of Foreign Affairs, The Hague, August 1995.

6. Italian Ministry of Foreign Affairs, 'Joint Declaration on the WEU in the context of European security', Italy-UK Summit, 6 December 1995.

7. Speech in February 1997, quoted in WEU Assembly Report, Rapporteur Mr Antretter, 'Maastricht II: The WEU Assembly Proposals for European Cooperation on Security and Defence', Document 1564, 9 May 1997.

8. It has been questioned whether majority voting would really improve the effectiveness of the CFSP. One argument is that orientations should be decided by unanimity whilst Joint Actions could be taken by majority vote. Federal Trust, *Security of the Union: The Intergovernmental Conference of the European Union*, Federal Trust Papers 4, London, October 1995, p. 11-12.

9. This double veto took the form of a vote on the nature of the action and then another vote on whether it could be implemented by qualified majority voting.

10. This had been advanced by the Dorr group of Foreign Ministers' representatives in the IGC.

11. Agence Europe, No. 6829, 10 October 1996, p. 3-5.

12. Agence Europe, No. 6677, 29 February 1996, p. 2.

13. Several small states were critical of this Franco–German initiative. The Belgium Foreign Minister warned against what he saw as a trend towards a 'European Security Council' in which the major countries took all of the important decisions. Agence Europe, No. 6746, 12 June 1996, p. 4.

14. 'A Partnership of Nations: The British Approach to the European Union Intergovernmental Conference 1996', Command 3181, Foreign and Commonwealth Office, March 1996.

15. Howe, G. 'Bearing more of the burden: In search of a European foreign and security policy', *The World Today*, Vol. 52, No 1, January 1996, p. 24.

16. *Economist, The* 'A convoy in distress', 16th March 1996, p. 38.

17. This was often referred to as a 'Monsieur' or 'Madame PESC'.The idea had found favour in the recommendations of the Reflection Group.

18. There were a variety of permutations around this idea. For instance, one suggested a formal linkage between the offices of the High Representative and the Secretary-General of the WEU, whilst another advocated the WEU Secretary-General also holding the position of an EU Commissioner for CFSP. See Menon, A. 'Defence policy and integration in Western Europe', *Contemporary Security Policy*, Vol. 17, No. 2, August 1996, p. 27.

19. Interviews conducted at the Italian Foreign Ministry, Rome, October 1996

20. The Troika consisted of the countries holding the past, present and future Presidencies of the EU.

21. Germany may also have feared that a political personality divorced from the institutions of the Union would be ineffective. Federal Trust, op. cit. p. 18.

22. Dejevsky, M. 'Rifkind warns EU on foreign policy role', *The Independent*, 6 March 1996, p. 7.

23. See High-level group of Experts on the CFSP, 'European Security Policy Towards 2000: Ways and Means to Establish Genuine Credibility', First Report, Chaired by J. Durieux, Brussels, 19 December 1994.

24. Agence Europe, No. 6786, 7 August 1996, p. 3.

25. WEU Council of Ministers, Madrid, 1995, op. cit. paragraph 76.

26. See, for example, Dutch Foreign Ministry Document for Parliament, 'European Foreign, Security and Defence Policy: Towards Stronger External Action by the European Union', 30 March 1995, pp.3-4.

27. WEU Assembly Proceedings, 40th Ordinary Session (Third Part) 'Minutes and Official Reports of Debates', Paris, June 1995, p. 81.

28. Agence Europe, No. 6941, 24-25 March 1997, p. 4-5.

29. Goulden, J. 'The WEU's role in the new strategic environment', *NATO Review*, Vol. 44, No. 3, May 1996, p. 22.

30. Heathcoat-Amory, D. 'The next steps fot Western European Union', *The World Today*, Vol. 50, No. 7, July 1994, p. 135.

31. Bailes, A. 'European defence and security: The role of NATO, WEU and EU', *Security Dialogue*, Vol. 27, No. 1, March 1996, p. 58.

32. Goulden, J. op. cit. p. 21.

33. Silvestri, S., Gnessotto, N. and Vasconcelos, A. 'Decision-making and institutions', in Martin, L. and Roper, J. (eds) *Towards a Common Defence Policy*, Institute for Security Studies of the Western European Union, Paris, 1995, p. 63.

34. Transcript of speech by Volker Rühe, 'Perspectives for European security in the context of trans-Atlantic partnership: A preview to the IGC 1996', to the Defence Planning Committee, German Embassy, London, 7 June 1995.

35. The British position enjoyed some support from within the WEU Secretariat which had a vested interest in preserving the autonomy of their institution from the EU. Interviews conducted at the WEU Assembly Secretariat, Paris, January 1996.

36. House of Commons Library, 'Memorandum on the United Kingdom's Approach to the Treatment of European Defence Issues at the 1996 Inter-governmental Conference', March 1995.

37. This had been called for by France and Germany in the period leading up to the Maastricht Treaty.

38. 'A Partnership of Nations: The British Approach to the European Union Intergovernmental Conference 1996', March 1996, op. cit.

39. The US supported British demands for no more than a 'Reinforced Partnership' to be built between the WEU and the EU. See Peterson, J. *Europe and America: The Prospects for Partnership*, (Second edition), Routledge, London, 1996, p. 165.

40. Rummel, R. 'The Intergovernmental Conference 1996: How to reform CFSP?' in Regelsberger, E., de Schoutheete de Tervarent, P. and Wessels, W. (eds) *Foreign Policy of the European Union: From EPC to CFSP and Beyond*, Lynne Reiner, London, 1997, p. 364.

41. *Economist, The* 'A flexible Europe', 18 January 1997, p. 18.

42. Agence Europe, No. 6761, 1-2 July 1996, p. 5.

43. German Foreign Minister Klaus Kinkel endorsed the idea in a document setting out Bonn's priorities for the IGC. Agence Europe, No. 6697, 28 March 1996, p. 4.

44. CDU/CSU Bundestag Paper, 'Reflections on European Policy', Bonn, 1 September 1994.

45. Silvestri, S., Gnessotto, N. and Vasconcelos, A. 'Decision-making and institutions', in Martin, L. and Roper, J. (eds) op. cit. p. 60.

46. Agence Europe, No. 6836, 19 October 1996, p. 2-3.

47. 'A Partnership of Nations: The British Approach to the European Union Intergovernmental Conference 1996', March 1996, op. cit.

48. The British Labour Party echoed this position whilst in opposition. Peston, R. and Stephens, P. 'Blair opposes a "high table" of EU members', *The Financial Times*, 16 January 1997.

49. Provisions for flexibility were written in to Pillars 1 and 3.

50. The Amsterdam European Council met on 16–17 June 1997 and marked the culmination of the Inter-governmental Conference. The Treaty of Amsterdam, agreed at this Council meeting, is framed as a series of amendements to earlier treaties. Owing to the large number of amendments, the Maastricht Treaty and the Treaty of Rome have had their articles renumbered, pursuant to Article 12 of the Amsterdam Treaty. References in the rest of this chapter are to the new article numbers in the amended Treaty on European Union (Maastricht Treaty).

51. The PPEWU will draw for its personnel on the General Secretariat, the member states, the Commission and representatives from the WEU.

52. The meeting at Noordwijk, on 26 May, was intended to iron out the substantive differences between the participants prior to the Amsterdam Summit.

53. Conference of the Representatives of the Governments of the Member States, 'Compilation of Texts Under Discussion', Section III, Brussels, 14 May 1997.

54. Helm, S. 'Blair steers steady course over treaty', *The Independent*, 18 June 1997.

55. This was formerly Article J.4 in the Treaty on European Union.

56. Lichfield, J. 'Cook says EU may have a defence role', *The Independent*, 14 May 1997.

57. Santer, J. 'The European Union's security and defence policy. How to avoid missing the 1996 rendez-vous', *NATO Review*, Vol. 43, No. 6, November 1995, p. 9.

58. Silvestri, S., Gnessotto, N. and Vasconcelos, A. 'Decision-making and institutions', in Martin, L. and Roper, J. (eds) op. cit. p. 52.

8

Conclusion

Throughout its long life, the WEU has suffered from being an actor caught in the ebb and flow of a debate between two larger organisations, NATO and the European Community/European Union. NATO represented the trans-Atlantic approach to the security problems of the continent; one that focused on the immediacy of the military threat and sought to ensure stability through the American presence in Europe. The WEU, although explicitly a defence organisation, delegated its core functions to the Alliance. It served as a forum for the expression of European views on defence and was intimately concerned with keeping the US engaged in continental security.

The other debate centred upon the long term objective of European integration. The Brussels Treaty Organisation and then the WEU represented a European identity in defence which was seen by many as a necessary part of the integration process. It was at first unclear whether defence would act as a stimulus or as a brake on integration. After the failure of the EDC the question was answered and security and defence issues were kept outside the framework of integration. There was a perception that defence would be left until the last stage in the construction of Europe. In the meantime it was accepted that Europe should contribute more to its own security in order to be seen to share the burden with the United States. The WEU acted as a useful symbol of that contribution on such occasions as the 1987 Gulf naval operation. Although the greater part of the European effort was channelled through NATO, the WEU served as a forum to galvanise European states when the US needed a demonstration that their allies were pulling their weight in protecting western interests.

The WEU was always regarded as an actor of secondary importance, possessing a 'reserve function' that was operationalised when other organisations were found to be inadequate.[1] Its development can only be understood in relation to periods of either progress or turbulence in trans-Atlantic relations and European integration. In 1954, the WEU provided a solution to a time urgent problem by enabling Germany to enter the Atlantic Alliance. In the 1980s, fears about the reliability of the US guarantee and pressures for closer European cooperation resulted in the revitalisation of the WEU as a venue where views on defence matters could be discussed. The WEU, therefore, performed different functions according to the demands of the time. It was a barometer of the state of US–European relations as well as the depth of integration on the continent.

In 1990, the WEU was brought to a crossroads. Hitherto, the trans-Atlantic link had always been accorded primacy due to the overarching nature of the military threat and the need to manage intra-European rivalries. But the end of the Cold War forced a fundamental reassessment of priorities and there was now pressure for integration to take precedence over trans-Atlanticism. It was no longer apparent that the US was required to underwrite European security, nor could it be assumed that the US would be willing to carry out such a role. In contrast, the rationale for European integration appeared to have 'come of age': it provided both a mechanism to tie down Germany's new found power and it offered a means to assert a clearer European identity on the world stage. It was assumed that such an identity would include a defence dimension and the WEU would act as a stepping stone to a full ESDI to be embodied in the European Community.

France and Germany were the driving force behind this initiative. Through the creation of a Common Foreign and Security Policy and the subordination of the WEU to the European Council, they sought the eventual collapse of the WEU into the EU. For the avowedly political motive of granting the EU competence over all policy areas, they attempted to build a common defence policy that would result in a common European defence. Despite achieving only a limited part of their objectives in the Treaty on European Union, the two states advanced their agenda in the subsequent period as well as in the 1996–97 Intergovernmental Conference. Yet their aspirations were undermined by events that followed the signing of the TEU, such as the Yugoslav crisis, as well as the gradual adaptation of the Atlantic Alliance to the new environment.

Germany had always insisted on constructing a defence identity that was compatible with NATO, because it believed in the need for multiple, interlocking institutions. The government in Bonn was unwilling to sabotage the Alliance after it had proved to be such a reliable guarantor of German security during the Cold War. France, however, suffered a setback because its goal of a European defence was not realised. It had been prepared to see a European defence identity that diminished the stature of NATO but was forced to accept failure and closer accommodation with the

Alliance. France's signal of its reconciliation with NATO defence structures in December 1995 marked the end of the grandiose pretensions for the WEU.

An additional factor that constrained the development of an ESDI was the realisation that it could not be built upon Franco–German foundations alone. Firstly, residual tensions existed in the relationship that made it difficult for each of the partners to trust becoming reliant upon the other. Secondly, the two countries lacked the resources and the political will to generate a European defence arrangement that could both defend their territorial integrity and project military power overseas. This was particularly marked in the case of Germany, with historical limitations upon exercising force outside its boundaries. But it was also true of France due to its relative neglect of its conventional forces during the latter stages of the Cold War. Finally, the interests of the two states were not entirely coterminous: Germany's focus was upon northern Europe and the issue of enlargement to central and eastern Europe, whilst France possessed a growing interest in the Mediterranean region.

The country that was needed to underpin the Franco–German tandem, if the ESDI was to succeed, was Britain due to its military prowess and its considerable influence in defence matters. Yet Britain did not share the goals of its two continental allies. It was hostile to deeper European integration and to the development of the EC into a meaningful defence actor. It saw in the WEU a means to limit the integration process in both of the Intergovernmental Conferences on Political Union. At Maastricht, through its power of veto, the British were able to insist upon the WEU remaining equi-distant from the European Union and NATO; whilst at Amsterdam, the UK blocked the process of integrating the WEU into the EU, in spite of pressure from the nine other members. The British rejected the broader political agenda for the WEU that governed the approach of its allies towards the organisation. It was prepared to see the WEU rendered more operationally capable but only in ways that avoided duplication with NATO.

It had become apparent that despite the intense theoretical arguments about European integration, there was insufficient support to build a defence identity outside of NATO. After a period of hesitation, the US had reasserted its leadership position within Europe. Through the experiences of Bosnia and the debate over enlargement, NATO had proved itself to be the pivotal organisation in European security and particularly in issues involving the use of force. In relation both to territorial guarantees and to new tasks, such as peacekeeping, the WEU's Madrid document acknowledged that the 'Alliance [would] remain the essential forum for consultation among its members'.[2] It was ironic that due to the stalemate in the IGC, the role of the WEU as the bridge to NATO witnessed greater progress than its other role as the defence arm of the EU. Rather than a competitor, the WEU had emerged as the junior partner of the Alliance.

The relative smoothness in relations between the WEU and NATO owed a great deal to the continuing modesty of the EU's capabilities in security and defence. If the EU had fulfilled the ambitions of its more ambitious aspirants, then the role of the WEU as the European pillar of the Alliance would have become infinitely more complicated. Although the WEU's relationship with the EU had faced a steep learning curve, nevertheless, it was undeniable that progress had been disappointing. This culminated in the Treaty of Amsterdam which illustrated the legalistic approach that paralysed the relationship between the European Council and the WEU.

The Combined Joint Task Forces concept marked the acknowledgement of NATO primacy over the ESDI, long before the Treaty of Amsterdam. As extra-territorial operations had been seen as the area of potential opportunity for WEU, the Berlin agreement of June 1996 signalled the WEU's subordination to NATO. The Alliance retained the right to choose whether to lead in a crisis and the Europeans acknowledged their dependency on the North Atlantic Council for the release of assets. With the IFOR and SFOR operations, NATO proved itself to be the most likely mechanism for the coordination of coalitions. In contrast, recent experience had shown the aversion amongst EU members to tasking the Western European Union; the quasi-military operation in Mostar had been the only example. The operational development of the WEU had been concentrated in capabilities at the lower end of the conflict spectrum, to deal with humanitarian crises. This has made it difficult to conceive of operations where the WEU would be accorded the leadership function. If the US was not be involved in an operation then the Europeans would be likely to either eschew action, or to mobilise an *ad hoc* coalition.

Thus, it is possible to see how one of the major post-Cold War questions in European security has been resolved. As the embodiment of the ESDI, the WEU has not arisen to challenge the primacy of NATO. Instead the Alliance has adapted to the new challenges and continues to occupy the centre ground in the defence debate. The likelihood that it could have been supplanted was never strong considering the modest capabilities possessed by the WEU and the opposition of one of its three most important European states, Britain. In the words of one commentator, 'the politics of ESDI [were] far ahead of its capabilities'.[3] Only if the United States had sought to withdraw from the continent might it have been possible for a fully capable ESDI to have emerged, and only then if the Europeans had invested resources over a sustained period of time. Once the US had reasserted its intention to lead and demonstrated its commitment through the crisis in former-Yugoslavia, any institutional competition that might have existed was at an end.

The only remaining question is what role the WEU will fulfil in the future? The year 1998 presents an appropriate moment to assess the future of the WEU because it is the organisation's fiftieth anniversary and because it was the period of time stipulated in the Brussels Treaty.[4] There is no particular requirement for the Treaty to be renegotiated and states have always possessed the right to announce their withdrawal from the Treaty's provisions. Thus far, no constituency has appeared that advocates the abolition of the WEU. Rather, the organisation has every prospect of continuing, but the precise role that it will fulfil is uncertain.

The WEU states face a future in which there will be no easily definable threat to bind them together. Recent crises on the periphery of Europe have illustrated the problem of organising cooperation amongst the WEU members when their interests have been affected to varying extents. They have also shown the unpredictability of conflict and the different sorts of capabilities that are needed to mount an effective response. Meanwhile, European states appear likely to be constrained by static or shrinking defence budgets. Much depends on the progress of European integration and whether the momentum from the inauguration of a single currency will generate additional pressure for foreign and defence cooperation.[5] If European defence efforts are not to stagnate then steps must be taken by the WEU members to define the interests that they share and to formulate a common defence policy. Some argue that the process is already underway but that it will take decades rather than years to complete. Others contend that European perspectives on foreign and defence policy remain far apart and are likely to diverge further.[6]

Differences continue to exist between France, Germany and Britain over their visions for ESDI. Even the concept of the WEU as the 'European pillar' of the Alliance' differs in the various national capitals. Britain has expressed satisfaction that the ESDI will be no more than the channelling of European views into the Alliance. Britain wishes to avoid further tension with the United States and is willing to see the ESDI concept subordinated to the goal of a strong trans-Atlantic relationship. In contrast, France envisages the ESDI as an equal pillar within the Alliance, capable of acting independently. It has accepted the need to build a European pillar in NATO before attempting to create a fully capable defence arm within the EU. At the Paris meeting of the WEU Council in May 1996 French Defence Minister Millon stated that, 'To deny WEU any real capability for military action, is also to give up on any real affirmation of a European security and defence identity'.[7] France's continued emphasis on separate European military capabilities and its declared dissatisfaction with the process of 'Europeanising' NATO, exemplifies its thinking.

A minimalist vision for the WEU would see it continuing as a forum for consultation between its members, thereby ensuring that European views are represented in all NATO's decisions. This would fail to satisfy the ambitious aspirations of some of its supporters but it would allow the organisation to continue to function as a European sounding board. In the words of one analyst, it would enable the WEU to serve as the 'lubric[ant] in the relationship between NATO and the EU, for as long as these institutions differ in their membership'.[8] In addition, it might strengthen its role in promoting defence procurement cooperation amongst its members so that a stronger European defence industrial base could stand alongside the United States.[9]

Operationally, the WEU is likely to be only capable, for some time, of carrying out military operations of modest size and intensity. It has, therefore, become hard to determine what role the WEU can fulfil at present, beyond that of coordinating the military contributions of European states in a crisis. The experience of recent conflicts has engendered the feeling that the WEU has been searching for a role. Its use for policing functions in Mostar and its subsequent advisory role in Albania, added to an impression of aimlessness. This has led to the most extreme suggestion that the WEU should be phased out and its functions taken over by other more capable organisations.[10] As the Article V responsibility has always been carried out by NATO, and the Treaty of Amsterdam subsumed the Petersberg tasks within the CFSP, a case can be made that the WEU has lost all its utility.

A more favourable vision of the WEU's future emphasises the hybrid nature of the organisation and its inherent flexibility to meet the evolving needs of its members. Due to its position at the interface between NATO and the EU, the WEU possesses the ability to expand its responsibilities according to the demands of a situation. Undeniably, the WEU will not deal with the breadth of security and defence issues that lie within the Alliance's purview, but it will have a sectoral role to play. In the political sphere, the WEU will be able to contribute to the goal of projecting stability into the eastern and southern parts of the continent. Although the rapid enlargement of the WEU is unlikely, due to its dependency on the Alliance and the EU, it may nevertheless sustain an important dialogue with those states not included in the first tranche of NATO enlargement. It may also offer such states practical assistance, such as in the training of personnel for low-intensity conflicts, which will demonstrate their participation in the European security system. Such roles will not be high profile in nature but they will serve useful functions and complement the work of both the Alliance and the EU.

As for its operational role, this is likely to remain modest but should not be discounted altogether. In crises, the WEU will be able to consult closely with NATO so as to determine which organisations should have the lead role in conflict management. Whilst there is likely to be caution about tasking the WEU so soon after its relationship to the Alliance has been resolved, there will be missions where the WEU will be the more appropriate actor.[11] These will focus upon low and quasi-security issues that derive from its linkage to the EU.[12] The WEU may take the lead in low-intensity operations such as the evacuation of nationals, humanitarian relief and the de-mining of former conflict zones.[13] There is every reason to believe that the US will not wish to be involved in some situations for the simple reason that it will not perceive its interests to be at stake. Although the US came to act decisively in Bosnia in 1995, it should not be forgotten that for the previous four years it was willing to watch its European allies manage the situation.

What becomes apparent from this analysis is that the future development of the ESDI will depend to a large extent upon the dynamics of the relationship between the US and Europe. Since the ending of the Cold War, much has changed in US–European relations. Most notably, the end of the Soviet threat has removed the keel of the trans-Atlantic boat, making it liable to blown more easily by the prevailing winds. As a consequence, the future course of the relationship is harder to predict than ever before with the US acting as a more discriminating ally, selective about the types of crises in which it becomes involved.[14] Yet in another sense, little can be said to have changed in the sorts of issues that will pre-occupy and cause tension in trans-Atlantic relations. The US is still a global power, treating Europe as one of a series of theatres in which it has vital interests, whereas Europe is unsure about the sort of actor that it wants to become.[15]

The principal issue on the trans-Atlantic agenda is likely to remain the debate over burden-sharing. Former British Foreign Secretary Howe has argued that 'Europe is going to have to bear more of the burden and pay more of the price for defending the values we hold dear',[16] whilst Haglund has warned that Europe's preoccupation with its own narrow security concerns may result in the US 'simply los[ing] interest'.[17] Europe will have to be willing to assist the US in other parts of the world if it wishes to preserve a strong American role on the continent and to influence its policies. The US will measure the value of its allies by their commitment to extra-European activities. According to some analysts, the Europeans must resist the temptation to join with the US only on certain operations when their interests are involved, for fear of creating division in the relationship.[18] The emphasis must lie on fostering solidarity and a confidence that burdens are shared equally within the Alliance.

The difficulty for the US is that there is no immediate prospect of it enjoying a European partner with whom it can share responsibilities. Although the US feared the emergence of European independence during the ESDI debate of the early 1990s, its problem in the future may be excessive European dependence. The Europeans feel reassured when the

US is exercising its leadership functions as this psychology was built up over many decades. The US will find it difficult to encourage their allies to do more for themselves and to assume a larger share of the tasks. The European predilection for reducing defence spending, their absence of force projection capabilities and their inability to construct adequate decision-making mechanisms for foreign and defence policy, will render them weak partners of the United States. It remains to be seen whether the US will be willing sustain its leadership role if its allies are unable to contribute more.

The most immediate test of the US–European relationship is represented by the situation in Bosnia and the debate about a successor mission for the Stabilisation Force. The post-SFOR mission is likely to present a major challenge to the existing structures as the US has made clear its determination to withdraw its forces in June 1998 and the Europeans appear unwilling to contemplate staying on without an American presence.[19] Yet to leave Bosnia without achieving more substantial progress in reconciliation and reconstruction would be to risk allowing the Dayton process to unravel and the region to degenerate back into chaos. Such an outcome could have the affect of throwing into question the equilibrium of the European security architecture and reopening tensions in trans-Atlantic relations.

Therefore, the future of the ESDI is uncertain and will be vulnerable to the vagaries of US–European relations. Although the WEU has failed to fulfil the expectations that were invested in it during the early post-Cold War, it would be premature to conclude that the organisation has no role of significance to play.

References and Notes

1. Schmidt, P. 'The WEU — A Union without a perspective?' *Aussenpolitik*, Vol.6, 1986, p.390.

2. WEU Council of Ministers, 'WEU Contribution to the EU Intergovernmental Conference of 1996', Madrid, 14 November 1995, paragraph 98.

3. Moens, A. 'The European security and defense identity and the non-concert of Europe', *European Security*, Vol. 2, No. 4, Winter 1993, p.568.

4. There has been disagreement over when the WEU Treaty should be re-assessed: some calibrate its fifty year duration from the signing of the modified Brussels Treaty in 1954, thereby giving a date of 2005. However, the majority accept that the fifty year period should be counted from the signing of the Brussels Treaty in 1948.

5. In the view of Mahncke, as long as true political union in Europe is unrealised, 'the usefulness of WEU will remain limited'. Mahncke, D. *Parameters of European Security*, Chaillot Papers 10, Institute for Security Studies of the Western European Union, Paris, September 1993, p.36.

6. Van Ham argues that without the Cold War the interests of the major states will move further apart. van Ham, P., 'The Prospects for a European Security and Defence Identity', *European Security*, Vol. 4, No. 4, Winter 1995, p.537.

7. Agence Europe, No.6973, 14 May 1997, p.2-3.

8. Cornish, P. 'European security: The end of architecture and the new NATO', *International Affairs*, Vol. 72, No. 4, October 1996, p.768. Five states in the EU are not full members of the WEU and four of them are not members of NATO.

9. Chilton has argued that this may prove to be the only worthwhile role for the WEU to fulfil in the future. Chilton, P. 'A European security regime: Integration and cooperation in the search for common foreign and security policy', *Journal Of European Integration*, Vol 19, Winter 1996, p.232.

10. I am indebted to John Roper for this point.

11. This was reaffirmed at the extraordinary meeting of the WEU Council of Ministers to approve the annex on the WEU to the Treaty of Amsterdam It was declared that: 'WEU will develop its role as the European politico-military body for crisis management, contribute to the progressive framing of a common defence policy and carry forward its concrete implementation through the further development of its own operational role'. Agence Europe, No. 7021, 22-23 July 1997, p.4.

12. Bailes, A. 'European defence and security: The role of NATO, WEU and EU', *Security Dialogue*, Vol. 27, No. 1, March 1996, p.58.

13. WEU Secretary-General José Cutileiro stated at the beginning of January 1997 that the organisation was concentrating on preparing for small operations. Agence Europe, No. 6890, 11 January 1997, p.2bis.

14. Heisbourg noted in 1992 that future US policy is likely to be 'more inward-looking ... with a set of priorities driven largely internally'. Heisbourg, F. 'The future of the Atlantic Alliance: Whither NATO, whether NATO?' *The Washington Quarterly*, Spring 1992, p.128.

15. Ham, P. van, op. cit. pp.527-528.

16. Howe, G. 'Bearing more of the burden: In search of a European foreign and security policy', *The World Today*, Vol. 52, No 1, January 1996, p.24.

17. Haglund, D. (ed) *From Euphoria to Hysteria: Western European Security After the Cold War*, Westview Press, Boulder, 1993, p.5.

18. Asmus, R. Blackwill, R. and Larrabee, S. 'Can NATO survive?' *The Washington Quarterly*, Vol. 19, No. 2, Spring 1996, p.95.

19. President Clinton's National Security Adviser, Samuel Berger, hinted at the possibility of the US staying on longer in Bosnia during a speech at Georgetown University in September 1997. Rhodes, T. 'Clinton aide says US must extend stay in Bosnia', *The Times*, 25 September 1997.

Bibliography

Books

Alford, J. & Hunt, K. (eds) *Europe in the Western Alliance: Towards a European Defence Entity?* Macmillan, Basingstoke, 1988.

Allen, D., Rummel, R. & Wessels, W. (eds) *European Political Cooperation: Towards a Foreign Policy*, Butterworth Scientific, London, 1992.

Aliboni, R. (ed) *Southern European Security in the 1990s*, Pinter, London, 1992.

Aliboni, R., Joffé, G, & Niblock, T. (eds) *Security Challenges in the Mediterranean Region*, Frank Cass, London, 1996.

Anstis, C. & Moens, A. (eds) *Disconcerted Europe: The Search for a New Security Architecture*, Westview, Boulder, 1994.

Anthony, I. Allebeck, A. & Wulf, H. *West European Arms Production*, Stockholm International Peace Research Institute Report, Sweden, October 1990.

Barker, E. *The British Between the Superpowers, 1945-50*, Macmillan, London, 1983.

Baylis, J. *Anglo-American Defence Relations 1939-1984*, Macmillan, London, 1984.

Baylis, J. *The Diplomacy of Pragmatism: Britain and the Formation of NATO, 1942-1949*, Kent State University Press, Ohio, 1993.

Beveren, R. van, *Military Cooperation: What Structure for the Future?* Chaillot Paper 6, Institute for Security Studies Western European Union, Paris January 1993.

Bloed, A. & Wessel, R. A. (eds) *The Changing Functions of the Western European Union: Introduction and Basic Documents*, Matinus Nijhoff Publishers, Dordrecht, 1994.

Bos, B. van den, *Can Atlanticism Survive? The Netherlands and the New Role of Security Institutions*, Netherlands Institute of International Relations Clingendael, The Hague, July, 1992.

Brenner, M. *The United States Policy in Yugoslavia*, Ridgway Papers No. 6, The Mathew B. Ridgway Center for International Security Studies, University of Pittsburgh.

Buzan, B., Kelstrup, M., Lemaitre, P., Tromer, E. & Wæver, O. *The European Security Order Recast. Scenarios for the Post-Cold War Era*, Pinter, London, 1990.

Cafruny, A. & Rosenthal, G. (eds) *The State of the European Community, Volume 2: The Maastricht Debates and Beyond*, Longman, London, 1992.

Cahen, A. *The Western Union and NATO: Building a European Defence Identity Within the Context of Atlantic Solidarity*, Brassey's Atlantic Commentaries No.2, London, 1989.

Calleo, D. *Beyond American Hegemony. The Future of the Western Alliance*, Basic Books, New York, 1987.

Carlsnaes, W. & Smith, S. (eds) *European Foreign Policy: The EC and Changing Perspectives in Europe*, Sage, London, 1994.

Coker, C. (ed) *Drifting Apart? The Superpowers and their European Allies*, Brassey's, London, 1989.

Cuthbertson, I. (ed) *Redefining the CSCE: Challenges and Opportunities in the New Europe*, Westview Press, Boulder, 1992.

Clarke, I. *Nuclear Diplomacy and the Special Relationship: Britain's Deterrent and America, 1957-1962*, Clarendon Press, Oxford, 1994.

Clarke, M. & Hague, R. (ed) *European Defence Cooperation: America, Britain and NATO*, Manchester University Press, 1990.

Croft, S. & Williams, P. (eds) *European Security Without the Soviet Union*, Frank Cass, London, 1992.

Cromwell, W. C. *The United States and the European Pillar: The Strained Alliance*, Macmillan Press, London 1992.

Danish Commission on Security and Disarmament, *Danish and European Security*, Copenhagen, 1995.

Davy, R. (ed) *European Detente: A Reappraisal*, Royal Institute for International Affairs, London, 1992.

Deighton, A. *The Impossible Peace. Britain, the Division of Germany and the Origins of the Cold War*, Clarendon Press, Oxford, 1993.

Deighton, A. (ed) *Western European Union 1954-1997: Defence, Security, Integration*, European Interdependence Research Unit, St Antony's College, Oxford, 1997.

DePorte, A. W. *Europe Between the Superpowers: The Enduring Balance*, Yale University Press, New Haven, 1979.

Deutsch, K. (et al) *Political Community and the North Atlantic Area: International Organisation in the Light of Historical Experience*, Princeton University Press, New Jersey, 1957.

Dockrill, S. *Britain's Policy for West German Rearmament 1950-1955*, Cambridge University Press, 1991.

Dodd, T. *Towards the IGC: Developing a Common Defence Policy*, Research Paper 95/45, House of Commons Library, London, April 1995.

Duff, A., Pinder, J. & Pryce, R. (eds) *Maastricht and Beyond: Building the European Union*, For the Federal Trust, Routledge, London, 1994.

Duke, S. *The New European Security Disorder*, Macmillan, London, 1994.

Eden, A. *Full Circle*, Cassell, London, 1960.

Featherstone, K. & Ginsberg, R. *The United States and the European Union in the 1990s: Partners in Transition*, (second edition) Macmillan Press, Basingstoke, 1996.

Federal Trust, *Security of the Union: The Intergovernmental Conference of the European Union*, Federal Trust Papers 4, London, October 1995.

Feld, W. J. *The Future of European Security and Defence Policy*, Lynne Rienner Publishers, Boulder 1993.

Hiro, D. *Desert Shield to Desert Storm: The Second Gulf War*, Paladin, London, 1992.

Fursdon, E. *The European Defence Community: A History*, Macmillan, Basingstoke, 1980.

Gaddis, J. L. *The Long Peace: Inquiries into the History of the Cold War*, Oxford University Press, 1987.

Gambles, I. *European Security Integration in the 1990s*, Chaillot Papers No. 3, Institute for Security Studies of the Western European Union, Paris, 1991.

Gambles, I. *Prospects for West European Security Co-operation*, Adelphi Paper 244, Brassey's for the IISS, August 1989.

Gambles, I. (ed) *A Lasting Peace in Central Europe?*, Chaillot Papers No. 20, Institute for Security Studies of the Western European Union, Paris, October 1995.

Gebhard, P. *The United States and European Security*, Adelphi Paper 286, Brassey's for the IISS, February 1994.

Gnesotto, N. & Roper, J. (eds) *Western Europe and the Gulf*, Institute for Security Studies of the Western European Union, Paris, 1992.

Gnesotto, N. *Lessons of Yugoslavia*, Chaillot Papers 14, Institute for Security Studies of the Western European Union, Paris, March 1994.

Goldstein, W. (ed) *Reagan's Leadership and the Atlantic Alliance: Views from Europe and America*, Pergamon-Brassey's, London, 1986.

Goldstein, W. (ed) *Security in Europe: The Role of NATO after the Cold War*, Brassey's, London, 1994.

Gordon, P. H. *A Certain Idea of France: French Security Policy and the Gaullist Legacy*, Princeton University Press, 1993.

Gordon, P. H. *France, Germany, and the Western Alliance*, Westview Press, Boulder, 1995.

Greenwood, S. *The Alternative Alliance: Anglo-French Relations Before the Coming of NATO, 1944-48*, Minerva Press, Montreux, 1996.

Gutjahr, L. *German Foreign and Defence Policy After Unification*, Pinter, London, 1994.

Haas, E. *The Uniting of Europe: Political, Social and Economic Forces 1950-57*, Stanford University Press, Stanford, 1958.

Haglund, D. *Alliance Within the Alliance? Franco-German Military Cooperation and the European Pillar of Defense*, Westview Press, Boulder, 1991.

Haglund, D. (ed) *From Euphoria to Hysteria: Western European Security After the Cold War*, Westview Press, Boulder, 1993.

Haglund, D., Macfarlane, N. & Sokolsky, J. *NATO's Eastern Dilemmas*, Westview Press, Boulder, 1994.

Halliday, F. *The Making of the Second Cold War*, Verso, London, 1983.

Ham, P. van, *The EC, Eastern Europe and European Unity: Discord, Collaboration and Integration Since 1947*, Pinter, London, 1993.

Hayward, K. *Towards a European Weapons Procurement Process*, Chaillot Papers No. 27, Institute for Security Studies of the Western European Union, Paris, June 1997.

Henderson, N. *The Birth of NATO*, Weidenfeld & Nicholson, London, 1982.

Heuser, B. & O'Neill, R. (eds) *Securing Peace in Europe 1945-62: Thoughts for the Post-Cold War Era*, Macmillan in association with St Anthony's College Oxford, Basingstoke, 1992.

Hill, C. (ed) *National Foreign Policies and European Political Cooperation*, Royal Institute for International Affairs by Allen and Unwin, London, 1983.

Hill, C. (ed) *The Actors in Europe's Foreign Policy*, Routledge, London, 1996.

Holland, M. (ed) *Common Foreign and Security Policy: The Record and Reforms*, Pinter, London, 1997.

Howe, G. *Conflict of Loyalty*, Macmillan, London, 1994.

Hyde-Price, A. *European Security Beyond the Cold War: Four Scenarios for the Year 2010*, Sage, London, 1991.

Jopp, M., Rummel, R. & Schmidt, P. (eds) *Integration and Security in Western Europe: Inside the European Pillar*, Westview Press, Boulder, 1991.

Jopp, M. *The Strategic Implications of European Integration*, Adelphi Paper 290, Brassey's for the IISS, London, July 1994.

Jopp, M. (ed) *The Implications of the Yugoslav Crisis for Western Europe's Foreign Relations*, Chaillot Papers 17, Institute for Security Studies of the Western European Union, Paris, October 1994.

Kaiser, K. and Roper, J. *British-German Defence Co-operation*, The Royal Institute of International Affairs, London, 1988.

Kelleher, C. *The Future of European Security: An Interim Assessment*, Brookings Occasional Papers, The Brookings Institution, Washington DC, 1995.

Kühne, W., Lenzi, G. & Vasconcelos, A. *WEU's Role in Crisis Management and Conflict Resolution in Sub-Saharan Africa*, Chaillot Papers 22, Institute for Security Studies of the Western European Union, Paris, December 1995.

Laird, R. *The Europeanization of the Alliance*, Westview Press, Boulder, 1991.

Laurent, P-H. (ed) *The European Community: To Maastricht and Beyond*, The Annals of the American Academy of Political and Social Science, No.531, January 1994, Special Edition.

Laursen, F. & Vanhoonacker, S. (eds) *The Intergovernmental Conference on Political Union: Institutional Reforms, New Policies and International Identity of the European Community*, European Institute of Public Administration, Martin Nijhoff Publishers, Maastricht, 1992.

Mahncke, D. *Parameters of European Security*, Chaillot Papers 10, Institute for Security Studies of the Western European Union, Paris, September 1993.

Martin, L. & Roper, J. (eds) *Towards a Common Defence Policy*, Institute for Security Studies of the Western European Union, Paris, 1995.

Mastny, V. *The Helsinki Process and the Redefining of Europe 1986-1991: Analysis and Documentation*, Pinter, London, 1992.

Mathews, K. *The Gulf Conflict and International Relations*, Routledge, London, 1993.

Mathews, R. *European Armaments Collaboration: Policy, Problems and Prospects*, Harwood Academic Publishers, Reading, 1992.

Maxwell. K. (ed) *Spanish Foreign and Defense Policy*, Westview Press, Boulder, 1991.

McCarthy, P. (ed) *France-Germany 1983-1993. The Struggle to Cooperate*, Macmillan, Basingstoke, 1993.

McInnes, C. *The British Army and NATO's Rapid Reaction Corps*, Centre for Defence Studies Pamphlets, No. 15, Brassey's, London, March 1993.

Miall, H. (ed) *Redefining Europe: New Patterns of Conflict and Cooperation*, Pinter, London, 1994.

Moens, A. & Anstis, C. (eds) *Disconcerted Europe: The Search for a New Security Architecture*, Westview Press, Boulder, 1994.

Morgan, R. & Bray, C. (eds) *Partners and Rivals in Western Europe: Britain, France and Germany*, Policy Studies Institute, Gower, London, 1986.

Moreton, E. (ed) *Germany Between East and West*, Cambridge University Press, 1987.

Myers, J. A. *The Western European Union: Pillar of Nato or Defence Arm of the EC?* London Defence Studies.16, Brassey's, London, May 1993.

Navias, M. *Nuclear Weapons and British Strategic Planning 1955-1958*, Clarendon Press, Oxford, 1991.

Newhouse, J. *The Nuclear Age: From Hiroshima to Star Wars*, Michael Joseph, London, 1989.

Nooy, G. C. de *Towards a Military Core Group in Europe?*, Clingendael Paper, Netherlands Institute of International Relations Clingendael, The Hague, March 1995.

Nuttall, S. *European Political Cooperation*, Clarendon Press, Oxford, 1992.

Osgood, R. *NATO: The Entangling Alliance*, University of Chicago Press, 1962.

Palmer, D. R. *French Strategic Options in the 1990s*, Adelphi Paper 260, Brassey's for the IISS, Summer 1991.

Peterson, J. *Europe and America: The Prospects for Partnership*, (second edition), Routledge, London, 1996.

Podraza, A. *The Western European Union and Central Europe: A New Relationship*, Royal Institute of International Affairs Discussion Papers No. 41, London, 1992.

Regelsberger, E., de Schoutheete de Tervarent, P. & Wessels, W. (eds) *Foreign Policy of the European Union: From EPC to CFSP and Beyond*, Lynne Reiner, London, 1997.

Roberts, F. *Dealing with Dictators. The Destruction and Revival of Europe 1930-70*, Weidenfeld and Nicholson, London, 1991.

Rummel, R. (ed) *Toward Political Union*, Westview, Boulder, 1992.

Schlör, W. F. *German Security Policy*, Adelphi Paper 277, London, June 1993.

Schmidt, P. (ed) *In the Midst of Change: On the Development of West European Security and Defence Cooperation*, Nomos Verlagsgesellschaft, Baden-Baden, 1992.

Schmidt, P. *The Special Franco-German Security Relationship in the 1990s*, Chaillot Paper 8, Institute for Security Studies of the Western European Union, Paris, June 1992.

Smith, M., Smith, S. & White, B. (eds) *British Foreign Policy: Tradition, Change and Transformation*, Unwin Hyman, London, 1988.

Smyser, W. *Germany and America: New Identities, Fateful Rift?*, Westview Press, Boulder, 1993.

Stares, P. (ed) *The New Germany and the New Europe*, The Brookings Institution, Washington DC, 1992.

Stockholm Internationational Peace Research Institute, *SIPRI Yearbook 1995: World Armaments and Disarmament*, New York, Oxford University Press, 1995.

Taylor, T. *European Defence Cooperation*, Chatham House Papers 24, The Royal Institute of International Affairs, Routledge and Kegan Paul, London, 1984.

Trifunovska, S, (ed) *The Transatlantic Alliance on the Eve of the New Millenium*, Kluwer Law International, The Hague, 1996.

Ullman, R. *Securing Europe*, Adamantine Press Limited, Twickenham, 1991.

Vestel, P. de, *Defence Markets and Industries in Europe: Time for Political Decisions?*, Chaillot Papers 21, Institute for Security Studies of the Western European Union, Paris, November 1995.

Vierucci, L. *WEU: A Regional Partner of the United Nations?*, Chaillot Paper 12, Institute for Security Studies of the Western European Union, Paris December 1993.

Wæver, O., Buzan, B., Kelstrup, M. and Lemaitre, P. *Identity, Migration and the New Security Agenda in Europe*, Pinter, London, 1993.

Walt, S. *The Origins of Alliances*, Cornell University Press, Ithaca, 1987.

Weger, M. *The Evolution of NATO: The Brussels Summit and beyond*, Centre for Defence Studies Pamphlets, No. 28, Brassey's, London, September 1995.

Weinberger, C. *Fighting for Peace*, Michael Joseph, London, 1990.

Weiner, J. (ed) *The Transatlantic Relationship*, Macmillan, London, 1996.

Winand, P. *Eisenhower, Kennedy and the United States of Europe*, St Martin's Press, New York, 1993.

Wyllie, J. *European Security in the New Political Environment*, Addison Wesley Longman, Essex, 1997.

Young, J. (ed) *The Foreign Policy of Churchill's Peacetime Administration 1951-1955*, Leicester University Press, 1988.

Articles

Anderson, S. 'EU, NATO, and CSCE responses to the Yugoslav crisis: Testing Europe's new security architecture', *European Security*, Vol. 4, No. 2, Summer 1995, pp. 328-353.

Asmus, R. Blackwill, R. & Larrabee, S. 'Can NATO survive?' *The Washington Quarterly*, Vol. 19, No. 2, Spring 1996, pp. 79-101.

Barry, C. 'NATO's Combined Joint Task Forces in theory and practice', *Survival*, Vol. 38, No. 1, Spring 1996, pp. 81-97.

Bailes, A. 'European defence and security: The role of NATO, WEU and EU', *Security Dialogue*, Vol. 27, No. 1, March 1996, pp. 55-64.

Bailes, A. 'NATO: Towards a new synthesis', *Survival*, Vol. 38, No. 3, Autumn 1996, pp. 27-40.

Bellamy, C. 'Soldier of fortune: Britain's new military role', *International Affairs*, Vol. 68, No. 3, July 1992, pp. 443-456.

Bertram, C. 'NATO on track for the 21st century?' *Security Dialogue*, Vol. 26, No. 1, 1995, pp. 65-71.

Blunden, M. 'Insecurity on Europe's southern flank', *Survival*, Vol. 36, No. 2, Summer 1994, pp. 134-147.

Boniface, P. 'French nuclear strategy and European deterrence: 'Les rendez-vous manqués', *Contemporary Security Policy*, Vol. 17, No. 2, August 1996, pp. 227-238.

Borawski, J. 'Partnership for Peace and beyond', *International Affairs*, Vol. 71, No. 2, April 1995, pp. 233-246.

Brenner, M. 'Multilateralism and European security', *Survival*, Vol. 35, No. 2, Summer 1993, pp. 138-155.

Broek, H. van den, 'The Common Foreign and Security Policy in the context of the 1996 Intergovernmental Conference', *Studia Diplomatica*, Vol. XLVIII, No. 4, 1995, pp. 186-204.

Brown, H. 'Transatlantic Security', *The Washington Quarterly*, Vol. 18, No. 4, Autumn 1995, pp. 77-86.

Cahen, A. 'Relaunching the Western European Union. Implications for the Atlantic Alliance', *NATO Review*, Vol. 34, No. 4, August 1986, pp. 6-12.

Cahen, A. 'Western European Union: Birth, development and reactivation', *The Army Quarterly And Defence Journal*, October 1987, pp. 391-399.

Chilton, P. 'A European security regime: Integration and cooperation in the search for common foreign and security policy', *Journal of European Integration*, Vol. 19, Winter 1996, pp. 221-246.

Clarke, J. 'Replacing NATO', *Foreign Policy*, No. 93, Winter 1993-94, pp. 22-40.

Coëme, G. 'The role of the IEPG', *NATO Review*, Vol. 39, No. 4, August 1991, pp. 15-20.

Coker, C. 'Britain's defence options', *The World Today*, Vol. 48, No. 4, April 1992, pp. 72-75.

Corbett, R. 'The Intergovernmental Conference on Political Union', *Journal of Common Market Studies*, Vol. 30, No. 3, September 1992, pp. 271-298.

Cordesman, A. 'The Reagan Administration: Its past, and future impact on the Western Alliance', *Royal United Services Institute Journal*, Vol. 31, No. 1, 1986, pp. 36-44.

Cordoue, B. de, 'Reshaping Europe's defence industries', *European Brief*, February 1995, pp. 55-56.

Cornish, P. 'European security: The end of architecture and the new NATO', *International Affairs*, Vol. 72, No. 4, October 1996, pp. 751-769.

Cowper-Coles, S. 'From defence to security: British policy in transition', *Survival*, Vol. 36, No. 1, Spring 1994, pp. 142-161.

Croft, S. 'European integration, nuclear deterrence and Franco-British nuclear cooperation', *International Affairs*, Vol. 72, No. 4, October 1996, pp. 771-787.

Cutileiro, J. 'WEU's operational development and its relationship to NATO', *NATO Review*, Vol. 43, No. 5, September 1995, pp. 8-11.

Debouzy, O. 'the case for a European nuclear deterrent', *European Brief*, November 1994, pp. 16-23.

Delors, J. 'European integration and security, *Survival*, Vol. 22, No. 2, March-April 1992, pp. 99-109.

Delors, J. 'European unification and European security', in 'European Security after the Cold War', Part 1, *Adelphi Paper* 284, January 1994, Papers from the 35th Annual Conference of the IISS, Brussels, 9-12 September 1993, Brassey's.

Destexhe, A. 'The third genocide', *Foreign Policy*, No. 97, Winter 1994-95, pp. 3-17.

Dezcallar, R. 'On West European defense cooperation: A Spanish view', *The Washington Quarterly*, Winter 1987, pp. 153-169.

Dobbie, C. 'A concept for post-Cold War peacekeeping', *Survival*, Vol. 36, No. 3, Autumn 1994, pp. 93-120.

Eekelen, W. van, 'Building a new European security order: WEU's contribution', *NATO Review*, Vol. 38, No. 4, August 1990, pp. 18-23.

Eekelen, W. van, 'WEU and the Gulf Crisis', *Survival*, Vol. 32, No. 6, November-December 1990, pp. 519-532.

Eekelen, W. van, 'WEU's post-Maastricht agenda', *NATO Review*, Vol. 40, No. 2, April 1992, pp. 13-17.

Eekelen, W. van, 'WEU prepares the way for new missions', *NATO Review*, Vol. 41, No. 5, October 1993, pp. 19-24.

Feld, W. J. 'Franco-German military cooperation and European unification', *Journal of European Integration*, Vol. 12, No. 2-3, 1989, pp. 151-164.

Fischmann, B. & Ruiz Palmer, D. 'NATO, making sense of the arms business', *European Brief*, February 1995, pp. 53-54.

Flockhart, T. 'The dynamics of expansion: NATO, WEU and EU', *European Security*, Vol. 5, No. 2, Summer 1996, pp. 196-218.

Foster, E. 'The Franco-German Corps: A "theological" debate?' *The Royal United Services Institute Journal*, Vol. 137, No. 4, August 1992, pp. 63-68.

Freedman, L. 'The case of Westland and the bias to Europe', *International Affairs*, Vol. 63, No. 1, Winter 1986-87, pp. 1-20.

Gnesotto, N. 'European Union after Minsk and Maastricht', *International Affairs*, Vol. 68, No. 2, April 1992, pp. 223-232.

Gnesotto, N. 'Common European defence and transatlantic relations', *Survival*, Vol. 38, No. 1, Spring 1996, pp. 19-31.

Gordon, C. 'The WEU and European defense cooperation', *Orbis*, Vol.17, No. 1, Spring 1973, pp. 247-257.

Gordon, P. H. 'Recasting the Atlantic Alliance', *Survival*, Vol. 38, No. 1, Spring 1996, pp. 32-57.

Goulden, J. 'The WEU's role in the new strategic environment', *NATO Review*, Vol. 44, No. 3, May 1996, pp. 21-24.

Gow, J. & Dandeker, C. 'Peace-support operations: the problem of legitimation' *The World Today*, Vol. 51, Nos. 8-9, August September 1995, pp. 171-174.

Grant, R. 'France's new relationship with NATO', *SurvivaL*, Vol. 38, No 1, Spring 1996, pp. 58-80.

Gray, C. 'NATO: In trouble at the crossroads again', *Strategic Review*, No. 4, Summer 1995, p. 7-15.

Guéhenno, J-M. 'France and the WEU', *NATO Review*, Vol. 42, No. 5, October 1994, pp. 10-12.

Haglund, D. 'Who's afraid of Franco-German military cooperation?' *European Security*, Vol. 2, No. 4, Winter 1993, pp. 612-630.

Halstead, J. G. 'The security aspects of European integration', *Journal of Economic Integration*, Vol. 9, No. 2-3, Winter/Spring 1986, pp. 177-192.

Ham, P. van, 'The prospects for a European security and defence identity', *European Security*, Vol. 4, No. 4, Winter 1995, pp. 524-545.

Heathcoat-Amory, D. 'The next steps for Western European Union', *The World Today*, Vol. 50, No. 7, July 1994, pp. 133-136.

Heisbourg, F. 'The future of the Atlantic Alliance: Whither NATO, whether NATO?' *The Washington Quarterly*, Spring 1992, pp. 127-139.

Heisbourg, F. 'The European-US Alliance: Valedictory reflections on continental drift in the post-Cold War era', *International Affairs*, Vol. 68, No. 4, October 1992, pp. 665-678.

Hibbert, R. 'The war in Bosnia: can the Balkans be saved from Balkanisation?', *The World Today*, Vol. 51, Nos. 8-9, August/September 1995.

Hintermann, E. 'European defence: A role for the Western European Union', *European Affairs*, Vol. 2, No. 3, Autumn 1988, pp. 31-38.

Holbrooke, R. 'America, a European power', *Foreign Affairs*, March/April 1995, p.38-52.

Howe, G. 'The WEU: the way ahead', *NATO Review*, June 1989, pp. 13-15.

Howe, G. 'Bearing more of the burden: In search of a European foreign and security policy', *The World Today*, Vol. 52, No 1, January 1996, pp. 23-27.

Hughes, K. 'The 1990s Intergovernmental Conference and EU enlargement', *International Affairs*, Vol. 72, No 1, January 1996, pp. 1-8.

Hurd, D. 'Developing the Common Foreign and Security Policy', *International Affairs*, Vol. 70, No. 3, July 1994, pp. 421-428.

Ifestos, P. 'European political cooperation (EPC): Its evolution from 1970 to 1986, and the Single European Act', *Journal of European Integration*, Vol. 11, No. 1, Fall 1987, pp. 47-62.

Janning, J. 'A German Europe — a European Germany? On the debate over Germany's foreign policy', *International Affairs*, Vol. 72, No. 1, January 1996, pp. 33-42.

Johnsen, W. & Young, T.-D. 'France's evolving policy toward NATO', *Strategic Review*, Vol. 23, No. 4, Fall 1995, pp. 16-25.

Jones, E. 'After the Summit: Military realities', *Royal United Services Institute Journal*, Vol. 139, Part 1, February 1994, pp. 1-5.

Kaiser, K. 'Reforming NATO', *Foreign Policy*, No. 103, Summer 1996, pp. 128-143.

Kamp, K-H. 'The future role of the German Bundeswehr in out-of-area operations', *European Security*, Vol. 2, No. 4, Winter 1993, pp. 603-611.

Kirchner, E. 'Has the Single European Act opened the door for a European security policy?' *Journal of European Integration*, Vol. 13, No. 1, 1989, pp. 1-14.

Klaiber, K. P. 'The essential European security triangle - A German view', *Royal United Services Institute Journal*, Vol. 139, Part 1, February 1994, pp. 36-38.

Krautscheid, A. 'Contemporary German security policy a view from Bonn' *Paper given at the conference organised by the Institute for German Studies*, University of Birmingham, 18 October 1995.

Laird, R. 'West Europeans and peacekeeping', *European Security*, Vol. 3, No. 1, Spring 1994, pp. 95-118.

Lansford, T. 'The question of France: French security choices at century's end', *European Security*, Vol. 5, No. 1, Spring 1996, pp. 44-65.

Lellouche, P. 'Does NATO have a future? A European view', *The Washington Quarterly*, Vol. 5, No. 3, Summer 1982, pp. 40-53.

Lellouche, P. 'France in search of security', *Foreign Affairs*, Spring 1993, pp. 122-132.

Mearsheimer, J. 'Back to the future: Instability in Europe after the Cold War', *International Security*, Vol. 15, No. 1, Summer 1990, pp. 5-56.

Meimeth, M. 'France gets closer to NATO', *The World Today*, Vol. 50, No. 5, May 1994, pp. 84-86.

Menon, A., Forster, A. & Wallace, W. 'A common European defence?' *Survival*, Vol. 34, No. 3, Autumn 1992, pp. 98-118.

Menon, A. 'From independence to cooperation: France, NATO and European Security', *International Affairs*, Vol. 71, No. 1, January 1995, pp. 19-34.

Menon, A. 'Defence policy and integration in Western Europe', *Contemporary Security Policy*, Vol. 17, No. 2, August 1996, pp. 264-284.

Millon, C. 'France and the renewal of the Atlantic Alliance', *NATO Review*, Vol. 44, No. 3, May 1996, pp. 13-16.

Moens, A. 'Behind complementarity and transparency: The politics of the European security and defence identity', *Journal of European Integration*, Vol. 16, Pt 1, 1992, pp. 29-48.

Moens, A. 'The European security and defense identity and the non-concert of Europe', *European Security*, Vol. 2, No. 4, Winter 1993, pp. 567-584.

Moltke, G. von, 'Building a Partnership for Peace', *NATO Review*, Vol. 42, No. 3, 1994, pp. 3-7.

Moltke, G. von, 'NATO moves toward enlargement', *NATO Review*, Vol. 44, No. 1, January 1996, pp. 3-6.

Moravcsik, A. 'The European armaments industry at the crossroads', *Survival*, January/February 1990, pp. 65-85.

Neville-Jones, P. 'The Genscher-Colombo proposals on European union', *Common Market Law Review*, Vol. 20, 1983, pp. 657-699.

Nunn, S. 'NATO: Saving the Alliance', *The Washington Quarterly*, Vol. 5, No. 3, Summer 1982, pp. 19-31.

Perle, R. 'Reykjavik as a watershed in US-Soviet arms control', *International Security*, Summer 1987, Vol. 12, No. 1, pp. 175-178.

Pond, E. 'Germany in the New Europe', *Foreign Affairs*, Vol. 71, No. 2, Spring 1992, pp. 114-130.

Poos, J. 'Prospects for the WEU', *NATO Review*, Vol. 35, No. 4, August 1987, pp. 16-19.

Rees, G. W. 'Britain and the Western European Union', *European Security*, Vol. 5, No. 4, Winter 1996, pp. 529-542.

Rees, G. W. 'Constructing a European defence identity: The perspectives of Britain, France and Germany', *European Foreign Affairs Review*, Vol. 1, No. 2, November 1996, pp. 231-247.

Regelsberger, E. & Wessels, W. 'The CFSP institutions and procedures: A third way for the Second Pillar', *European Foreign Affairs Review*, Vol. 1, No. 1, 1996, pp. 29-54.

Ruggie, J. 'Consolidating the European pillar: The key to NATO's future', *The Washington Quarterly*, Vol. 20, No. 1, Winter 1997, pp. 109-124.

Rühe, V. 'Shaping Euro-Atlantic policies: A grand strategy for a new era', *Survival*, Vol. 35, No. 2, Summer 1993, pp. 129-137.

Rühle, M. 'NATO's evolving role in the new Europe', *European Security*, Vol. 1, No. 3, Autumn 1992, pp. 262-272.

Rühle, M. & Williams, N. 'NATO enlargement and the European Union', *The World Today*, Vol. 51, No. 5, May 1995, pp. 84-89.

Sabin, P. 'British defence choices beyond Options for Change', *International Affairs*, Vol. 69, No. 2, April 1993, pp. 267-288.

Salmon, T. 'Testing times for European political cooperation: The Gulf and Yugoslavia, 1990-1992', *International Affairs*, Vol. 68, No. 2, April 1992, pp. 233-253.

Santer, J. 'The European Union's security and defence policy. How to avoid missing the 1996 rendez-vous', *NATO Review*, Vol. 43, No. 6, November 1995, pp. 3-9.

Schmidt, P. 'The WEU - A Union without a perspective?' *Aussenpolitik*, Vol. 6, 1986, pp. 388-399.

Serfaty, S. 'Atlantic fantasies', *The Washington Quarterly*, Vol. 5, No. 3, Summer 1982, pp. 74-82.

Serfaty, S. 'Half before Europe, half past NATO', *The Washington Quarterly*, Vol. 18, No. 2, Spring 1995, pp. 49-58.

Sloan, S. 'NATO's future in a new Europe', *International Affairs*, Vol. 66, No. 3, July 1990, pp. 495-512.

Sloan, S. 'US perspectives on NATO's future', *International Affairs*, Vol. 71, No. 2, April 1995, pp. 217-232.

Snider, D. 'US military forces in Europe: how far can we go?' *Survival*, Vol. 34, No. 4, Winter 1992-93, pp. 24-39.

Solana, J. 'NATO's role in Bosnia: Charting a new course for the Alliance', *NATO Review*, Vol. 44, No. 2, March 1996, pp. 3-6.

Stein, G. 'The Euro-Corps and future European security architecture', *European Security*, Vol. 2, No. 2, Summer 1993, pp. 200-226.

Stoltenberg, G. 'Managing change: Challenges and tasks for the Eurogroup in a changing political environment', *NATO Review*, Vol. 38 No. 4, August 1990, pp. 15-23.

Sutton, M. 'France and the Maastricht design', *The World Today*, Vol. 49, No 1, January 1993, pp. 4-8.

Sutton, M. 'Chirac's foreign policy: Continuity with adjustment', *The World Today*, Vol. 51, No. 7, July 1995, pp. 135-139.

Taylor, T. 'West European security and defence cooperation: Maastricht and beyond', *International Affairs*, Vol. 70, No. 1, January 1994, pp. 1-16.

Thies, J. 'Germany: Europe's reluctant Great Power', *The World Today*, Vol. 51, No. 10, October 1995, pp. 186-191.

Tod, J. R. 'UK perspectives of current security arrangements', *Royal United Services Institute Journal*, Vol. 139, Part 1, February 1994, pp. 31-35.

Uttley, M. 'The integration of west European defense procurement: Issues and prospects', *Defense Analysis*, Vol. 11, No. 3, 1995, pp. 279-291.

Yost, D, 'France, West Germany and European security cooperation', *International Affairs*, Vol. 64, No. 1, 1988, pp. 97-100.

Yost, D. 'France and West European defence identity', *Survival*, Vol. 33, No. 4, July/August 1991, pp. 327-351.

Yost, D. 'France's nuclear dilemmas', *Foreign Affairs*, Vol. 75, No. 1, January-February 1996, pp. 108-119.

Walker, W. & Gummett, P. 'Britain and the European arms market', *International Affairs*, Vol. 65, 1989. pp. 419-442.

Walker, W. & Willett, S. 'Restructuring the European defence industrial base', *Defence Economics*, Vol. 4, 1993, pp.141-160.

Wallace, W. 'European defence cooperation: The reopening debate', *Survival*, Vol. 26, No. 6, November/December 1984, pp. 251-261.

Willman, H. 'The European corps - political dimension and military aims', *The Royal United Services Institute Journal*, Vol. 139, No. 4, August 1994, pp. 28-33.

Wood, P. C. 'France and Yugoslavia', *European Security*, Vol. 3, No. 1, Spring 1994, pp. 129-153.

Zeeman, B. 'Britain and the Cold War: An alternative approach. The Treaty of Dunkirk example', *European History Quarterly*, Vol. 16, No. 3, July 1986, pp. 344-367.

Zelikow, P. 'The masque of institutions', *Survival*, Vol. 38, No. 1, Spring 1996, pp. 1-22.

Official Publications (listed chronologically)

WEU Assembly

WEU Assembly Proceedings, 38th ordinary Session (First Part) 'Minutes and Official Reports of Debates', June 1992.

WEU Assembly Report, Rapporteur Mr Moya, 'Turkey', Document 1341, 6 November 1992.

WEU Assembly Report, Rapporteur Mr Goerens, 'European Security Policy', Document 1342, 6 November 1992.

WEU Assembly Report, Rapporteurs Mr Henares and Mr Tummers, WEU Information Report, Parts 1-3, February 1993.

WEU Assembly Report, Rapporteur Mr Ward, 'The Enlargement of WEU', Document 1360, 19 April 1993.

WEU Assembly Report, Rapporteur Mr Goerens, 'Interpretation of Article XII of the Brussels Treaty', Document 1369, 24 May 1993.

WEU Assembly Report, Rapporteur Mr Wintgrens, 'WEU's Relationship with Central and Eastern European Countries', Document 1387, 8 November 1993.

WEU Assembly Report, Rapporteur Mr Baumel, 'The Evolution of NATO and its Consequences for WEU', Document 1410, 23 March 1994.

WEU Assembly Report, Rapporteur Sir Russell Johnston, 'Parliamentary Cooperation with the Countries of the WEU Forum of Consultation', Document 1414, 4 May 1994.

WEU Assembly Report, Rapporteur Sir Keith Speed, 'An Operational Organisation for WEU: Naval and Maritime Co-operation', Document 1415, 10 May 1994.

WEU Assembly Report, Rapporteur Mr Ferrari, 'WEU in the Process of European Union: Reply to the Thirty-ninth Annual Report of the Council', Document 1417, 10 May 1994.

WEU Assembly Report, Rapporteur Mr Borderas, 'The European Armaments Agency Reply to the Thirty-ninth Annual Report of the Council', Document 1419, 19 May 1994.

WEU Assembly Report, Rapporteur Mr Decker, 'The Role and Future of NATO Weapons', Document 1420, 19 May 1994.

WEU Assembly Report, Rapporteur Mrs Baarveld-Schlaman, 'The WEU Planning Cell', Document 1421, 19 May 1994.

WEU Assembly Report, Rapporteur Mr Roseta, 'Security in the Mediterranean', Document 1371, 24 May 1994.

WEU Assembly Report, Rapporteur Mr Hardy, 'The Readiness and Capabilities of Airferres in the WEU Member State', Document 1444, 17 October 1994.

WEU Assembly Report, Rapporteur Mr Baumel, 'A European Defence Policy', Document 1445, 17 October 1994.

WEU Assembly Report, Rapporteur Mr Atkinston, 'Transatlantic Co-operation on European Anti-missile Defence', Document 1435, 9 November 1994.

WEU Assembly Report, Rapporteur Mr Soell, 'A European Security Policy', Document 1439, 10 November 1994.

WEU Assembly Report, Rapporteur Mr Baumel, 'WEU Relations with Russia', Document 1440, 10 November 1994.

WEU Assembly Report, Rapporteur Mr Hunt, 'National Parliaments, European Security and Defence and the Road to the 1996 Intergovernmental Conference', Document 1459, 22 May 1995.

WEU Assembly Proceedings, 40th Ordinary Session (Third Part) 'Minutes and Official Reports of Debates', Paris, June 1995.

WEU Assembly Report, Rapporteur Mr R Estrella, 'European Security and Defence Identity and Combined Joint Task Forces', October 1995.

WEU Assembly Report, Rapporteurs Mrs Guirado and Lord Dundee, 'WEAG: The Course to be Followed', Document 1483, 6 November 1995.

WEU Assembly Report, Rapporteur Mr Baumel on behalf of the Defence Committee, 'Organising Security in Europe: Defence Aspects', Document 1510, 8 February 1996.

WEU Assembly Report, Rapporteur Mr Antretter, 'The Eastern Dimension of European Security, Document 1542, 4 November 1996.

WEU Assembly Report, Rapporteur Mr Antretter, 'Maastricht II: The WEU Assembly Proposals for European Cooperation on Security and Defence', Document 1564, 9 May 1997.

Speeches

Transcript of speech by M. Cheysson, Foreign Policy Debate in the French National Assembly, 3 May 1984.

Transcript of speech by Hans Dietrich Genscher, 'Strengthening WEU', Press Department, Embassy of the Federal Republic of Germany, London, 12 September 1984.

Transcript of speech given by Mr Richard Luce at the WEU Assembly in Paris, 4 December 1984.

Transcript of speech of French Foreign Minister Claude Cheysson at the WEU Assembly Meeting, 3 January 1985.

Transcript of speech by M. Roland Dumas, Minister for External Relations, WEU Ministerial Meeting in Bonn, 23 April 1985.

Transcript of speech by Lady Young at the WEU Assembly, 'European Defence and Security Cooperation', 3 June 1986.

Transcript of speech of M. François Mitterand, President of the Republic, at the Royal Institute of International Affairs, London, 15 January 1987.

Transcript of speech given by Sir Geoffrey Howe at WEU Assembly in Paris, 7 December 1988.

Transcript of speech by General Klaus Naumann, 'German Security Policy and Future Tasks of the Bundeswehr', Royal United Services Institute for Defence Studies, 21 October 1994.

Transcript of speech given by Prime Minister Edouard Balladur to WEU Parliamentary Assembly, Paris, Courtesy French Embassy London, 30 November 1994.

Transcript of speech by Volker Rühe, 'Perspectives for European security in the context of trans-Atlantic partnership: A preview to the IGC 1996', to the Defence Planning Committee, German Embassy, London, 7 June 1995.

Transcript of speech by Javier Solana, 'The new NATO and the European security architecture', to the Federation of Austrian Industries, Vienna, NATO Data Service, Brussels, 16 January 1997.

Transcript of speech by the British Foreign Secretary, Mr Malcolm Rifkind, at the Carnegie Endowment for International Peace, Washington, Foreign and Commonwealth Information Department, 10 March 1997.

Communiqués

Treaty of Economic, Social and Cultural Collaboration and Collective Self-Defence, Brussels, 17 March 1948 and amended by the Protocol Modifying and Completing the Brussels Treaty, Paris, 23 October 1954.

WEU Ministerial Council Meeting, 'Patform on European Security Interests', The Hague, 27 October 1987.

North Atlantic Council, 'Declaration on a Transformed North Atlantic Alliance', London, 5-6 July 1990

North Atlantic Council, Communiqué, Copenhagen, 6-7 June 1991.

North Atlantic Council, 'Declaration on Peace and Cooperation', Rome, 7-8 November 1991.

Treaty on European Union, Maastricht, 7 February 1992.

WEU Ministerial Council Meeting, 'Petersberg Declaration', Bonn, 19 June 1992.

WEU Ministerial Council Meeting, Communiqué, Rome, 20 November 1992.

North Atlantic Council, 'Declaration of the Heads of State and Government', NATO Headquarters, Brussels, 10-11 January 1994.

WEU Ministerial Council Meeting, 'Kirchberg Declaration', Luxembourg, 9 May 1994.

European Council, Presidency Conclusions, Corfu, 24-25 June 1994.

WEU Ministerial Council Meeting, 'Noordwijk Declaration', 14 November 1994.

WEU Council of Ministers, 'WEU Contribution to the EU Intergovernmental Conference of 1996', Madrid, 14 November 1995.

'Declaration of Western European Union on the Role of Western European Union and its Relations with the European Union and with the Atlantic Alliance, attached to the Treaty of Amsterdam, 22 July 1997.

European and National Documentation

CDU/CSU Bundestag Paper, 'Reflections on European Policy', Bonn, 1 September 1994.

High-level group of Experts on the CFSP, 'European Security Policy Towards 2000: Ways and Means to Establish Genuine Credibility', First Report, Chaired by J Durieux, Brussels, 19 December 1994.

House of Commons Library, 'Memorandum on the United Kingdom's Approach to the Treatment of European Defence Issues at the 1996 Inter-governmental Conference', London, March 1995.

Dutch Foreign Ministry Document for Parliament, 'European Foreign, Security and Defence Policy: Towards Stronger External Action by the European Union', 30 March 1995.

House of Commons, 'The Future of NATO: The 1994 Summit and its Consequences', Defence Committee 10th Report, No. 747, HMSO, London, 19 July 1995.

Report of the Reflection Group, Brussels, 5 December 1995.

Italian Ministry of Foreign Affairs, 'Joint Declaration on the WEU in the context of European security', Italy-UK Summit, 6 December 1995.

House of Commons, 'Western European Union', Defence Committee 4th Report, No. 105, HMSO, London, 8 May 1996.

'A Partnership of Nations: The British Approach to the European Union Inter-governmental Conference 1996', Command 3181, Foreign and Commonwealth Office, London, March 1996.

Department of Foreign Affairs, ' Challenges and Opportunities Abroad', White Paper on Foreign Policy, Dublin, 1996.

Public Records Office Documents, London (listed chronologically)

DG 1/5/29, Record of Conference of the Five Defence Ministers and Chiefs of Staff of the Brussels Treaty Powers, London, 30/4/1948.

DG 1/1, Records of Sessions of the Consultative Council, 2nd Meeting, The Hague, 20/7/1948.

DG 1/3/13, M Bidault Speech at Second Session of the Consultative Council, 'Federation of Europe', The Hague, 20/7/1948.

Records of the WEU, DG 1/6/36, Minutes of Meetings of Chiefs of Staff Committee of the Five Powers - FP (48) 32, 26/8/1948.

DG 1/6/37, Military Committee of the Five Powers - WMC (48) Thirty Second Meeting, 23/9/1948.

DG 1/5/30, Meeting of Ministers of Defence at the Ministry of War, Paris, 27-28/9/1948.

DG 1/6/36, Western Union Chiefs of Staff Committee - FC (48) Second Meeting, 'Western Union Defence Policy', 8/10/1948.

Records of Third Meeting of the Consultative Council, Paris, 25-26/10/1948.

DG 1/5/31, FC (48) 30 (Final) Western Union Chiefs of Staff Committee, 'Organisation and Structure of National Forces in the Western Union', 4/1/1949.

Records of Fourth Meeting of the Consultative Council, London, 27-28/1/1949.

Records of Fifth Meeting of the Consultative Council, London, 14-15/3/1949.

DG 1/5/32, MD (49) 7, 28/3/1949.

DG 1/4/16, 'Relations with West Germany', Memorandum by the Netherlands Government, 16/6/1949.

DG 1/5/34, MD (49) Fifth Meeting, 'Western Union Defence Committee', 23/11/1949.

DG 1/7/40, Western Union Defence Organisation Military Committee - MC (49) Forty Seventh Meeting, 'Relations Between the Brussels Treaty and the Atlantic Pact', 28/10/1949.

DG 1/11/56, Western Union Defence Organisation Military Committee - MD (50) 12, 'Measures to Improve Our Defence Preparedness', 5/7/1950.

DEFE4/96 JP (57) 28 (Final), Brief for Chairman, Chiefs of Staff Committee, 22/3/1957.

Newspapers (listed alphabetically)

Agence Europe, No. 6688, 15/1/1996.
Agence Europe, No. 6677, 29/2/1996.
Agence Europe, No. 6697, 28/3/1996.
Agence Europe, No. 6723, 8/5/1996.
Agence Europe, No. 6740, 3-4/6/1996.
Agence Europe, No. 6745, 10-11/6/1996.
Agence Europe, No. 6746, 12/6/1996.
Agence Europe, No. 6761, 1-2/7/1996.
Agence Europe, No. 6779, 27/7/1996.
Agence Europe, No. 6786, 7/8/1996.
Agence Europe, No. 6829, 10/10/1996.
Agence Europe, No. 6836, 19/10/1996.
Agence Europe, No. 6854, 16/11/1996.
Agence Europe, No. 6856, 20/11/1996.
Agence Europe, No. 6857, 21/11/1996.
Agence Europe, No. 6890, 11/1/1997.
Agence Europe, No. 6990, 25/1/1997.

Agence Europe, No. 6905, 1/2/1997.
Agence Europe, No. 6941, 24-25/3/1997.
Agence Europe, No. 6970, 8/5/1997.
Agence Europe, No.6973, 14/5/1997.
Agence Europe, No. 2036, 17/5/1997.
Agence Europe, No. 6987, 4/6/1997.
Agence Europe, No. 6988, 5/6/1997.
Agence Europe, No. 7013, 10/7/1997.
Agence Europe, No. 7021, 22-23/7/1997.
Atlantic News, No. 2531, 4/6/1993.
Atlantic News, No. 2571, 16/7/1993.
Bloom, B. 'Europe may breathe new life into WEU', *The Financial Times*, 12/6/1984.
Charette, H. de, 'France for a streamlined NATO: Setting the record straight', *The International Herald Tribune*, 10/12/1996.
Danilov, D. 'Development of Russian-Western European Union relations analyzed', *Nezavisimaya Gazeta*, (translation) Moscow, 27/12/1995.
Davidson, I. '1954 comes around again', *The Financial Times*, 16/4/1984.
Dejevsky, M. 'Rifkind warns EU on foreign policy role', *The Independent*, 6/3/1996.
Dowdy, J. 'European defense industries face new threats', *The Wall Street Journal*, 3/2/1997.
Economist, The 'Survey: Defence in the 21st century', 5/9/1992, pp.10-14.
Economist, The 'A convoy in distress', 16/3/1996, p.38.
Economist, The 'Europe's foreign policy: The 15 at sixes and sevens', 18/5/1996, pp. 42-47.
Economist, The 'The future of NATO: A new kind of alliance?', 1/6/1996, pp. 23-24.
Economist, The 'A flexible Europe', 18/1/1997, pp. 18-20.
Helm, S. 'Blair steers steady course over treaty', *The Independent*, 18/6/1997.
International Defence Review, 'Italy plays host to first WEU exercise', 12/1993.
Jakobson, M. 'NATO: The coming "Charter" with Russia will have a price', *The International Herald Tribune*, 9 /10/1996.
Lewis, J. 'France is determined to play a central role in Europe's defence', *Jane's Defence Weekly*, 12/2/1997.
Lichfield, J. 'Cook says EU may have a defence role', *The Independent*, 14/5/1997.
Mauthner, R. 'Star Wars to dominate Bonn talks', *The Financial Times*, 22/4/1985.
Morrison, J. 'Chirac calls for Western Europe to draw up its own security charter', *The International Herald Tribune*, 3/12/1986.
Peston, R. and Stephens, P. 'Blair opposes a "high table" of EU members', *The Financial Times*, 16/1/1997.
Reuters, 'WEU lifts Bonn arms ban', *The Financial Times*, 28/6/1984.
Rhodes, T. 'Clinton aide says US must extend stay in Bosnia', *The Times*, 25/9/1997.
Sauerwein, B. 'WEU closing in on NATO: Room for two?' *International Defence Digest*, 3/1993.
Schwarz, W. 'Genscher calls for the revival of WEU', *The Guardian*, 21/6/1984.
Wyles, J. 'European Foreign Ministers will discuss closer defence cooperation', *The Financial Times*, 9/4/1984.

British Newspaper Library, Colindale, London.

Aron, R. 'The European Army I: Divided French opinion', *Manchester Guardian*, Box 427, 13/4/1954.
'Enlarging the Brussels Treaty', *The Times*, Box 538, 19/10/1954.
'Brussels Pact changes', *The Times*, Box 538, 25/10/1954.
'Super states', *The Manchester Guardian*, Box 537, 9/10/1954.

Interviews

Interviews, on a non-attributable basis, were conducted at the following institutions:
NATO Headquarters, Brussels, January 1995
WEU Headquarters, Brussels, January 1995
Foreign and Commonwealth Office, London, April 1995
Ministry of Defence, London, July 1995
Dutch Ministry of Foreign Affairs, The Hague, August 1995
Dutch Defence Ministry, The Hague, August 1995
'Clingendael' Institute of International Relations, The Hague, August 1995
German Foreign Ministry, Bonn, November 1995
German Defence Ministry, Bonn, November 1995
French Institute for International Affairs, Paris, January 1996
WEU Institute for Security Studies, Paris, January 1996
WEU Assembly Secretariat, Paris, January 1996
Institute for International Affairs, Rome, October 1996
Italian Foreign Ministry, Rome, October 1996

Index